Flora B Nelson, Fannie Birdsall, Thomas Hiram Nelson

Garden of Spices

a choice collection for revival meetings, missionary meetings, rescue work, church and Sunday schools

Flora B Nelson, Fannie Birdsall, Thomas Hiram Nelson

Garden of Spices
a choice collection for revival meetings, missionary meetings, rescue work, church and Sunday schools

ISBN/EAN: 9783337090692

Printed in Europe, USA, Canada, Australia, Japan

Cover: Foto ©Andreas Hilbeck / pixelio.de

More available books at **www.hansebooks.com**

GARDEN OF SPICES

A CHOICE COLLECTION
FOR

Revival Meetings, Missionary Meetings, Rescue Work, Church and Sunday Schools.

COMPOSED AND EDITED
BY

FLORA B. NELSON, FANNIE BIRDSALL, AND
T. H. NELSON, EVANGELISTS.

PUBLISHED BY
PENTECOST BAND PUBLISHING CO.,
INDIANAPOLIS, IND.

PREFACE.

WE TRUST that "GARDEN OF SPICES" will prove to be all that its name implies, a real center of musical aroma and refreshing odors. It is a providential production, which inspiration called forth amid the busy toils of the harvest field. The book will stand on its own merits; the authors humbly ask but a perusal of its pages, and pray that God may make it a blessing to many. The profits of this book will all be used in non-salaried mission work.

NOTICE:--The Words and Music of nearly every piece in "GARDEN OF SPICES" are copyrighted. Permission to use the same must be obtained in writing from owners of copyright.

Garden of Spices.

1. Christ is Here.

Thos. H. Nelson.   Flora Birdsall Nelson.

1. Hark! the her-ald an-gels sing, Christ is here, Christ is here; Glo-ry to Im-man-uel King, Christ the Lord is here; Tho' to pen-i-tents re-vealed, Mak-ing way to heav-en clear, Yet to sin-ners He's con-cealed, Christ the Lord is here.
2. Waft the ti-dings o'er the sea, Christ is here, Christ is here, Come to set the pris-oners free, Christ the Lord is here; He's the God that reigns on high, Still a Sa-vior ev - er near; Swell the an-them to the sky, Christ the Lord is here.
3. Whis-per in the hour of grief, Christ is here, Christ is here; Here to bring a blest re-lief, Christ the Lord is here. Loud pro-claim the ti-dings grand, Tell each slave of sin and fear, Je-sus breaks each sin-ful band; Christ the Lord is here.
4. Shout a-bove the din of war, Christ is here, Christ is here; Roll the glorious notes a-far, Christ the Lord is here. Hark! ye is-lands of the sea, And ye dis-tant lands give ear, Swell the glo-rious ju - bi - lee, Christ the Lord is here.
5. Tell it on the rag-ing main, Christ is here, Christ is here; Shout o'er moun-tain for-est, plain, Christ the Lord is here; Sing it in the bri-dal hall, Chant it softly o'er the bier, Make the mes-sage plain to all, Christ the Lord is here.

Copyright, 1899, by T. H. Nelson.

3. The Savior With Me.

LIZZIE EDWARDS.   JNO. R. SWENEY.
DUET.

1. I must have the Sav-ior with me, For I dare not walk a-lone,
2. I must have the Sav-ior with me, For my faith, at best, is weak;
3. I must have the Sav-ior with me, In the on - ward march of life,
4. I must have the Sav-ior with me, And His eye the way must guide,

I must feel His pres-ence near me, And His arm a-round me thrown.
He can whisper words of comfort That no oth - er voice can speak.
Thro' the tempest and the sunshine, Thro' the bat-tle and the strife.
Till I reach the vale of Jor-dan, till I cross the roll - ing tide.

CHORUS.

Then my soul............ shall fear no ill,   Let Him
Then my soul shall fear no ill, fear no ill,

lead............ me where He will,   I will
Let Him lead me where He will, where He will,

go............ with-out a mur-mur, And His foot-steps fol-low still.
I will go

Used by per. of John J. Hood, owner of copyright.

6. Thou Art Coming.

T. H. NELSON. FLORA B. NELSON.

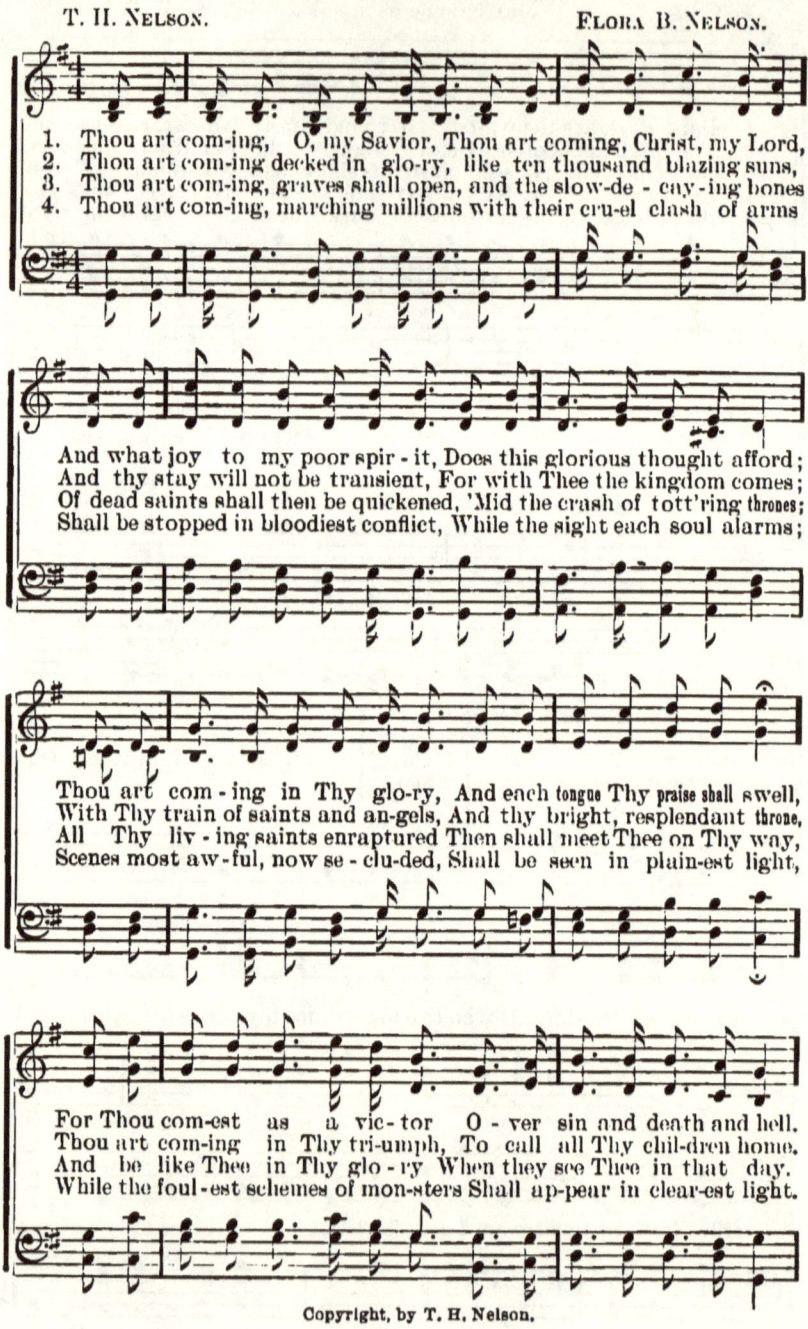

1. Thou art com-ing, O, my Savior, Thou art coming, Christ, my Lord,
2. Thou art com-ing decked in glo-ry, like ten thousand blazing suns,
3. Thou art com-ing, graves shall open, and the slow-de-cay-ing bones
4. Thou art com-ing, marching millions with their cru-el clash of arms

And what joy to my poor spir-it, Does this glorious thought afford;
And thy stay will not be transient, For with Thee the kingdom comes;
Of dead saints shall then be quickened, 'Mid the crash of tott'ring thrones;
Shall be stopped in bloodiest conflict, While the sight each soul alarms;

Thou art com-ing in Thy glo-ry, And each tongue Thy praise shall swell,
With Thy train of saints and an-gels, And thy bright, resplendant throne,
All Thy liv-ing saints enraptured Then shall meet Thee on Thy way,
Scenes most aw-ful, now se-clu-ded, Shall be seen in plain-est light,

For Thou com-est as a vic-tor O-ver sin and death and hell.
Thou art com-ing in Thy tri-umph, To call all Thy chil-dren home.
And be like Thee in Thy glo-ry When they see Thee in that day.
While the foul-est schemes of mon-sters Shall ap-pear in clear-est light.

Copyright, by T. H. Nelson.

Thou Art Coming--Concluded.

CHORUS.

Thou art com-ing, Je-sus, Sa-vior, not a man of sor-rows now,

But a King of kings e-ter-nal and with glo-ry on Thy brow;

How it hastes on wings of an-gels, does this blest mil-len-nial day;

May we all be watch-ing, read-y, Lord, to meet Thee on Thy way.

5. Thou art com-ing! not a sor-row, nor a tear, regret, or pain
Shall be felt by those confiding in the merits of Thy name;
They will share with Thee Thy triumph, while e-ternal ages roll,
O, the joy, the bliss, the glo-ry! how the thought transports the soul.

7. He Leadeth Me.

1. He leadeth me! oh! blessed thought,
Oh! words with heavenly comfort fraught;
Whate'er I do, where'er I be,
Still 'tis God's hand that leadeth me.

REF.—He leadeth me! He leadeth me!
By His own hand He leadeth me;
His faithful follower I would be,
For by His hand He leadeth me.

2. Sometimes 'mid scenes of deepest gloom,
Sometimes where Eden's bowers bloom,
By waters still, o'er troubled sea,
Still 'tis His hand that leadeth me.

3. Lord, I would clasp Thy hand in mine,
Nor ever murmur nor repine—
Content, whatever lot I see—
Since 'tis my God that leadeth me.

4. And when my task on earth is done,
When, by Thy grace the victory's won,
E'en death's cold wave I will not flee,
Since God through Jordan leadeth me.

8. Earth's Vanities.

Vivian A. Dake.   Fannie Birdsall.

1. I have sought pleas-ure the wide world around, Drank its cup deeply, but none have I found; Sweet for a moment, then bitter as gall, Flash like a me-teor, then dark-ness o'er all. Van-i-ty all, yea, much lighter than air, Bri-ers for ros-es, for peace, heav-iest care;
2. Friendships were mine with the fairest of earth, Heart knit to heart of true merit and worth, Gone, and I'm left with the per-ish-ing clod; Cords snap'd a-sun-der—pass un-der the rod. Low 'mid the ash-es of sor-row I lie, cov-ered with sack-cloth and ready to die;
3. Tread-mills of du-ty that nev-er are done; Con-flicts and bat-tles, but vic-to-ries none; Troubles like bil-lows roll over my head, Fear-ing, yet wish-ing to lie with the dead. Wishing 'twere morning as fast speeds the night, Wish-ing 'twere evening when breaks morning light;
4. My heart is wea-ry of din and of strife, Wea-ry of liv-ing this un-mean-ing life, Sat-is-fied never, no peace and no rest, Warring waves ev-er beat fierce on my breast; Discord, con-fu-sion wher-ev-er I go; Life is so emp-ty, a van-i-ty show. Oh, must I ev-er in
5. Hark! 'tis a voice like the waves of the sea, Breaks on my soul with glad ti-dings for me; "Come unto me" all ye weary and worn, Heav-i-ly la-den, your bur-den I've borne; Cast it all down at the foot of the cross, Joy for your sorrow and gain for all loss, Plen-ty for pov-er-ty,

Copyright, 1899, by T. H. Nelson.

Earths' Vanities--Concluded.

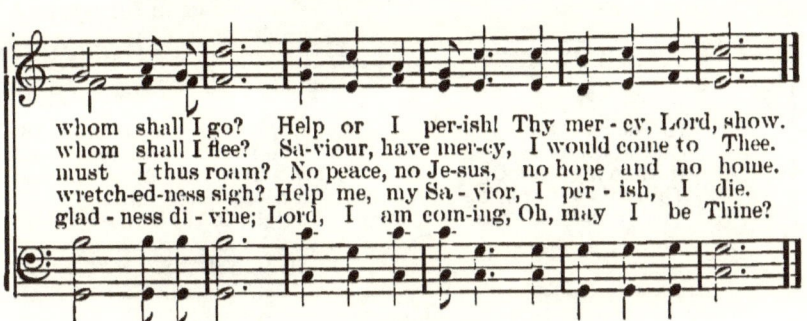

whom shall I go? Help or I perish! Thy mer-cy, Lord, show.
whom shall I flee? Sa-viour, have mer-cy, I would come to Thee.
must I thus roam? No peace, no Je-sus, no hope and no home.
wretch-ed-ness sigh? Help me, my Sa-vior, I per-ish, I die.
glad-ness di-vine; Lord, I am com-ing, Oh, may I be Thine?

6. Now I have found what my soul long has craved;
Glory to Jesus! I'm saved, I am saved,
Saved from my sor-row and striving and sin,
Saved from my foes from without and within;
Heaven has come with its sweetness and rest,
Satisfied ever, continually blest;
Well-springs of joy, floods of glory divine,
Shout the glad news, Lord—eternally thine.

9. Jesus, Savior, Pilot Me.

EDWARD HOPPER. J. E. GOULD.

1. Je-sus, Sav-ior, pi-lot me, O-ver life's tem-pest-uous sea;
D.C.—Chart and com-pass came from thee; Je-sus, Sav-ior, pi-lot me.

2. As a moth-er stills her child, Thou canst hush the o-cean wild;
D.C.—Wondrous Sovereign of the sea, Je-sus, Sav-ior, pi-lot me.

3. When at last I near the shore, And the fear-ful breakers roar,
D.C.—May I hear thee say to me, "Fear not, I will pi-lot thee!"

Un-known waves before me roll, Hid-ing rocks and treacherous shoal;
Boisterous waves o-bey thy will, When thou say'st to them "Be still!"
'Twixt me and the peace-ful rest, Then while lean-ing on thy breast,

Fifty Million Heathen—Concluded.

Chorus.

hea-then per-ish year-ly with-out God.
hea-then who die year-ly with-out God.
hea-then per-ish year-ly with-out God.
hea-then per-ish year-ly with-out God.
blood-washed souls die, shouting the praise of God.

A-rouse! a-rise! O heed the sighs of the hosts now in dark-ness lost, And re-mem-ber the blood of the Son of God was the price their re-demp-tion cost.

11. The Half was Never Told.

1. I know I love Thee better Lord,
   Than any earthly joy;
   For Thou hast given me the peace
   Which nothing can destroy.

   ### Chorus.

   The half has never yet been told,
   Of love so full and free;
   The half has never yet been told,
   The blood it cleanseth me.

2. I know that Thou art nearer still,
   Than any earthly throng;
   And sweeter is the thought of Thee,
   Than any lovely song.

3. Thou hast put gladness in my heart;
   Then well may I be glad,
   Without the secret of Thy love
   I could not but be sad.

4. O, Savior, precious Savior, mine!
   What will Thy presence be?
   If such a walk of joy can crown
   Our walk on earth with Thee.

By and By--Concluded.

Savior shall behold, And we'll strike the harps of gold, by and by.

13. Purity.

Victor Strange.   Flora B. Nelson.

1. I want a prin - ci - ple with - in,
2. The spring of all my ac - tions, Lord,

That loves to do the right, That loves to do the right;
Thy blood must pur - i - fy, Thy blood must pur - i - fy;

That ev - er shuns the thing un-clean, And walks as in Thy sight.
My hopes are hang-ing on Thy word, Speak, Sav-ior, or I die.

3. From every evil tendency
   I pant to be set free,
And joined to all the living, Lord,
   By being joined to Thee.

4. Self-will and vanity I hate,
   And lying lips despise;
And on Thee, O, my God, I wait,
   With tears and groans and sighs.

5. A blessing will not satisfy,
   I will not let Thee go,
Till Thou my heart dost purify,
   And God and heav'n bestow.

6. Thus, in the image of my Lord,
   My soul doth long to be;
Made pure in His all-cleansing blood,
   From every stain set free.

Copyright, by T. H. Nelson.

A White Robe--Concluded.

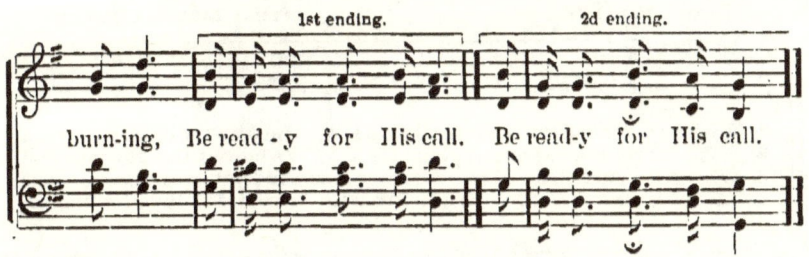

burn-ing, Be read-y for His call. Be read-y for His call.

15. Make Me Like Thee.

T. H. NELSON.   FANNIE BIRDSALL.

1. Make me like Thee Oh Lord, Cleansed in Thy prec-ious blood,
2. Thy gra-cious love im-part, Pour on my thirst-y heart
3. Tho' fond-est friends may die, Tho' cher-ished hopes may fly,

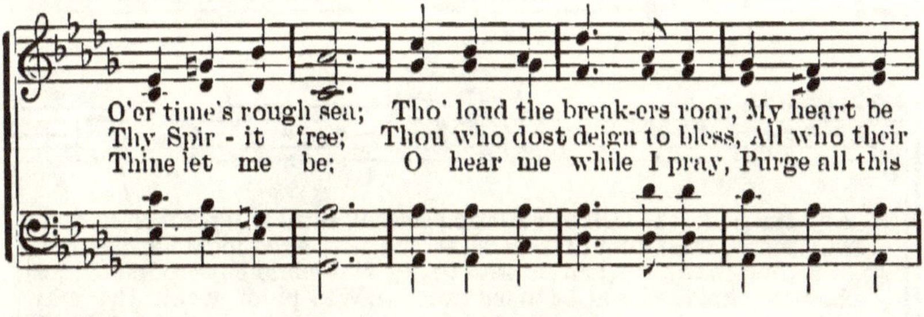

O'er time's rough sea; Tho' loud the break-ers roar, My heart be
Thy Spir-it free; Thou who dost deign to bless, All who their
Thine let me be; O hear me while I pray, Purge all this

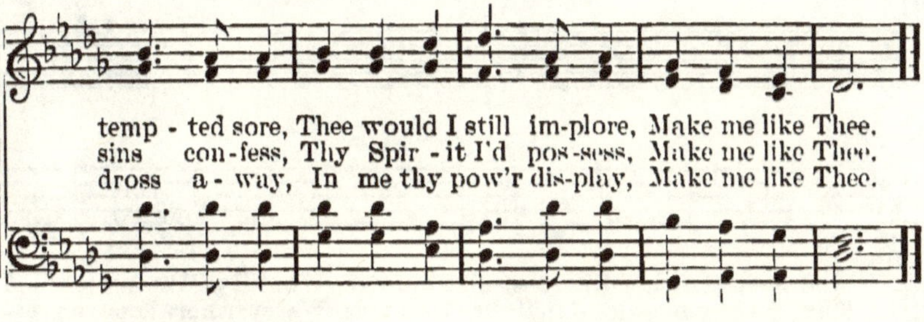

temp-ted sore, Thee would I still im-plore, Make me like Thee.
sins con-fess, Thy Spir-it I'd pos-sess, Make me like Thee.
dross a-way, In me thy pow'r dis-play, Make me like Thee.

4. Tho' persecutions rise,
   Storm clouds o'er-spread my skies,
     Thy power I'd see;
   Rough tho' the path I tread,
   Vexations 'round me spread,
   By thee I'd still be led,
     Make me like thee.

5. When life's last hour is fled,
   When death's dark vale I tread,
     Thee would I see;
   Fall at thy glorious feet,
   Lost in thy love so sweet,
   And feel my soul complete,
     Savior like thee!

Copyright, by T. H. Nelson.

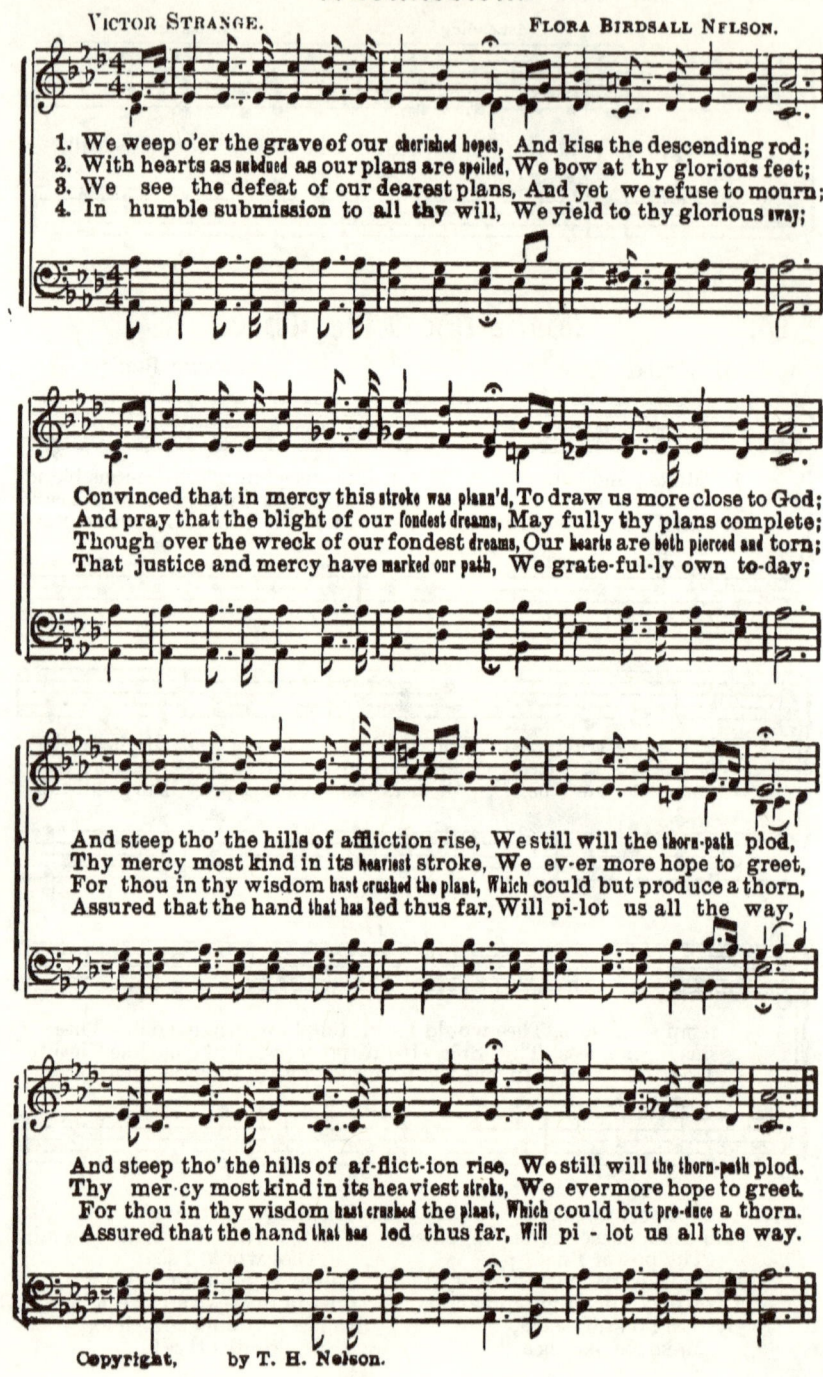

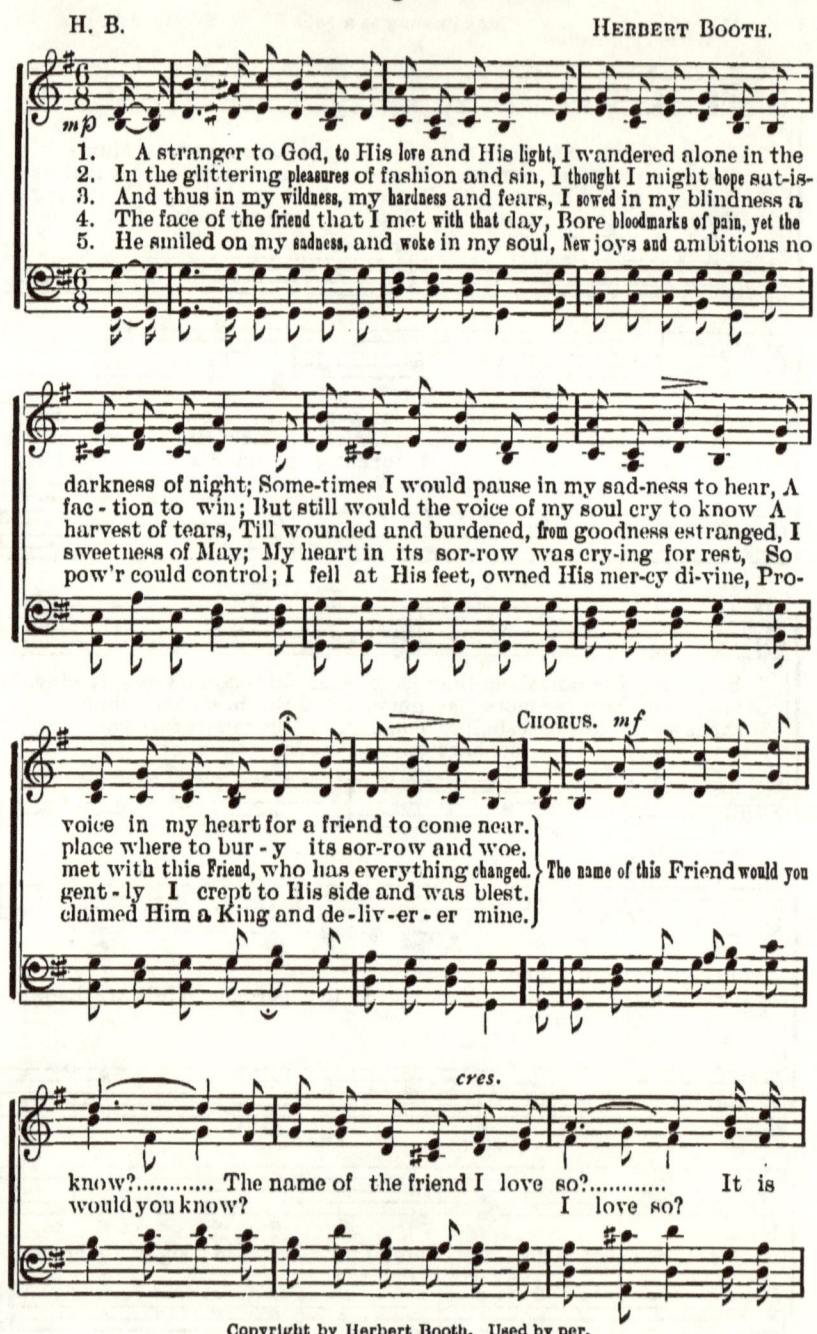

A Stranger to God--Concluded.

Jesus' blest name !and it kindles a flame Of love in my heart here below.

19. Jesus, Lover of My Soul.

CHARLES WESLEY.   Tune—MARTYN, 7, D.

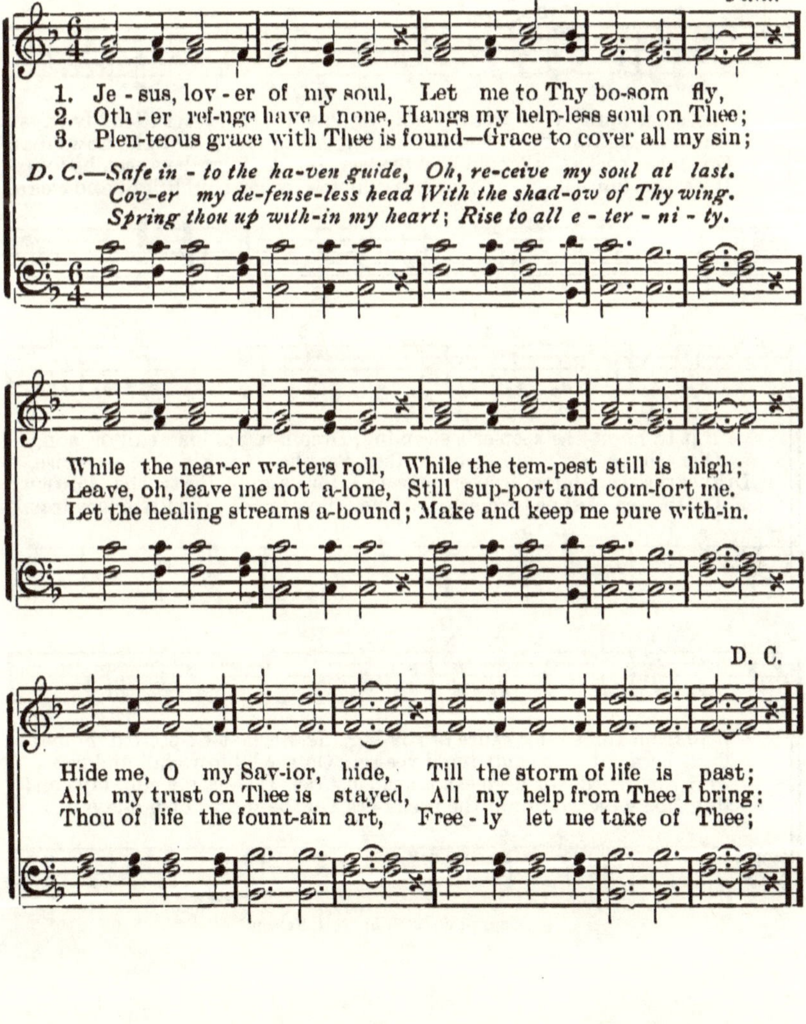

FINE.

1. Je-sus, lov-er of my soul, Let me to Thy bo-som fly,
2. Oth-er ref-uge have I none, Hangs my help-less soul on Thee;
3. Plen-teous grace with Thee is found—Grace to cover all my sin;

D. C.—*Safe in-to the ha-ven guide, Oh, re-ceive my soul at last.*
Cov-er my de-fense-less head With the shad-ow of Thy wing.
Spring thou up with-in my heart; Rise to all e-ter-ni-ty.

While the near-er wa-ters roll, While the tem-pest still is high;
Leave, oh, leave me not a-lone, Still sup-port and com-fort me.
Let the healing streams a-bound; Make and keep me pure with-in.

D. C.

Hide me, O my Sav-ior, hide, Till the storm of life is past;
All my trust on Thee is stayed, All my help from Thee I bring;
Thou of life the fount-ain art, Free-ly let me take of Thee;

20. The Lighthouse.

A light-house keeper, who had watched anxiously for the return of his son from a long voyage, one night let his lights go out. In the morning the first object that met his gaze, was the dead body of his son, which was washed ashore from a wrecked vessel.

T. H. NELSON.   FANNIE BIRDSALL.

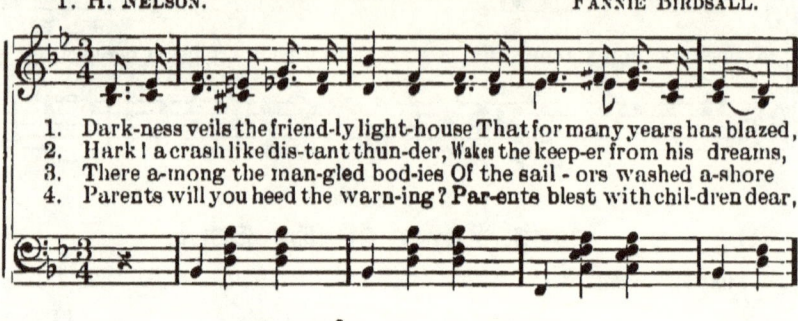

1. Dark-ness veils the friend-ly light-house That for many years has blazed,
2. Hark! a crash like dis-tant thun-der, Wakes the keep-er from his dreams,
3. There a-mong the man-gled bod-ies Of the sail-ors washed a-shore
4. Parents will you heed the warn-ing? **Par-ents** blest with chil-dren dear,

Cheer-ing man-y a wear-y sai-lor Past the rocks, with friend-ly rays;
Quick he lights the friend-ly bea-con; All too late the light now streams;
On the rocks, all cold and life-less Is a form he's seen be-fore;
Does the fam-il-y al-tar bea-con Throw its light out bright and clear?

But to-night the keep-er's sleep-ing, Dream-ing of his sail-or son,
O'er the an-gry, sul-len wa-ters, Sees he to his dire sur-prise,
Draws the trem-bling keep-er near-er. Looks a-gain, the truth is known;
On the sea of time some loved one, If your al-tar fire burns low,

Who from three long years of rov-ing, Is at last ex-pec-ted home.
Tim-bers of a shat-tered ves-sel On the bil-lows fall and rise.
And in words of deep-est an-guish, Cries, O God, my son, my son!
May be wrecked a-mid the break-ers, On the shores of end-less woe.

Copyright, 1899, by T. H. Nelson.

The Lighthouse—Concluded.

Who from three long years of rov-ing, Is at last ex-pec-ted home.
Tim-bers of a shat-tered ves-sel On the bil - lows fall and rise.
And in words of deep-est an-guish, Cries, "O God, my son, my son!"
May be wrecked a-mid the break-ers On the shores of end-less woe.

21. Holy, Holy, Holy.

REGINALD HEBER.   Tune: NICEA. 11, 12, 10.

1. Ho-ly, ho-ly, ho - ly, Lord God Al-might-y! Ear - ly in the
2. Ho-ly, ho-ly, ho - ly! all the saints a-dore thee, Casting down their
3. Ho-ly, ho-ly, ho - ly! tho' the dark-ness hide thee, Tho' the eye of
4. Ho-ly, ho-ly, ho - ly! Lord God Al-might-y! All thy works shall

morn - ing our song shall rise to thee; Ho-ly, ho-ly, ho - ly,
gold-en crowns a-round the glas-sy sea; Cher-u-bim and ser-a-phim
sin - ful man thy glo - ry may not see; On-ly thou art ho - ly!
praise thy name, in earth, and sky, and sea; Ho-ly, ho-ly, ho - ly,

mer - ci - ful and might-y, God in Three Persons, blessed Trinity!
fall-ing down be-fore thee, Which wert, and art, and evermore shalt be.
there is none be-side thee, Per-fect in power, in love, and pur-i-ty.
mer - ci - ful and might-y, God in Three Per-sons, blessed Trin-i-ty!

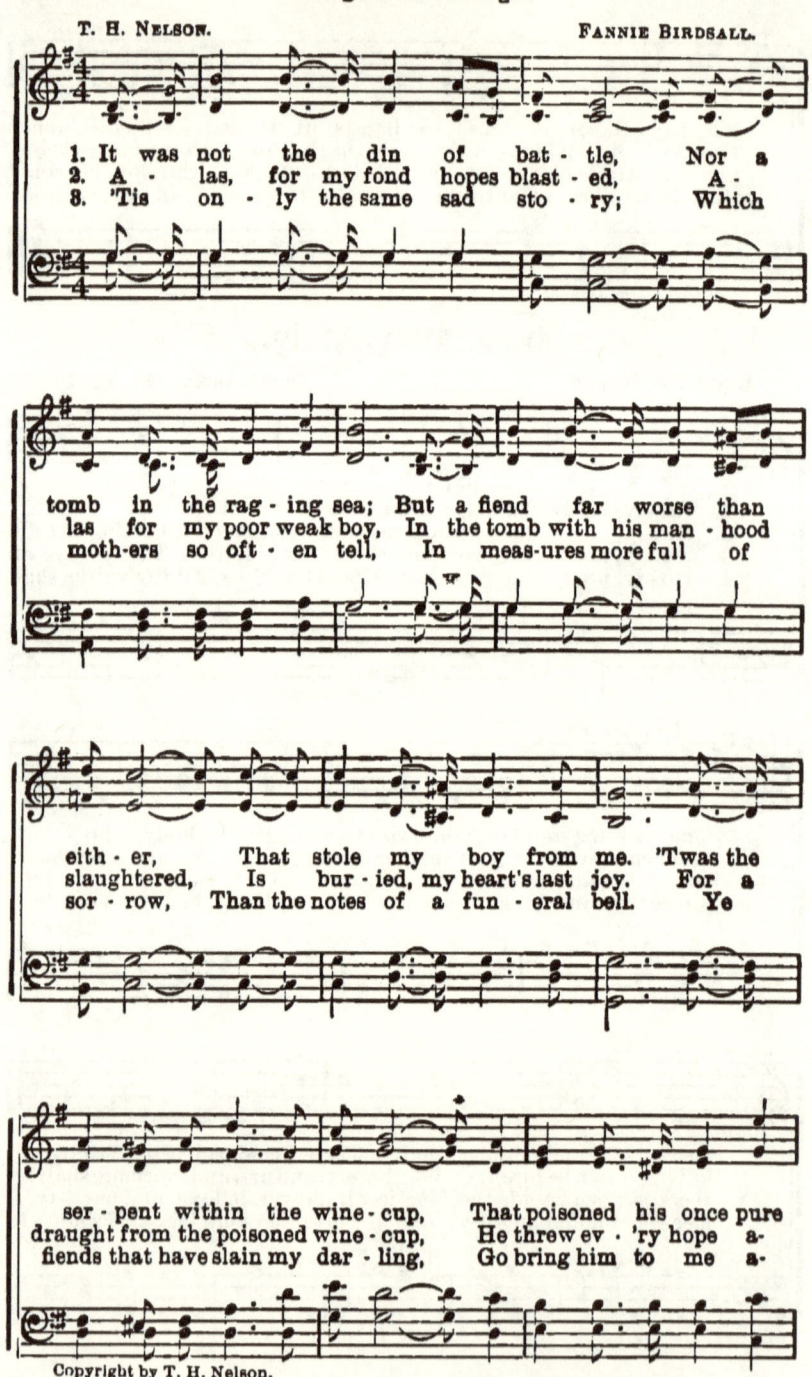

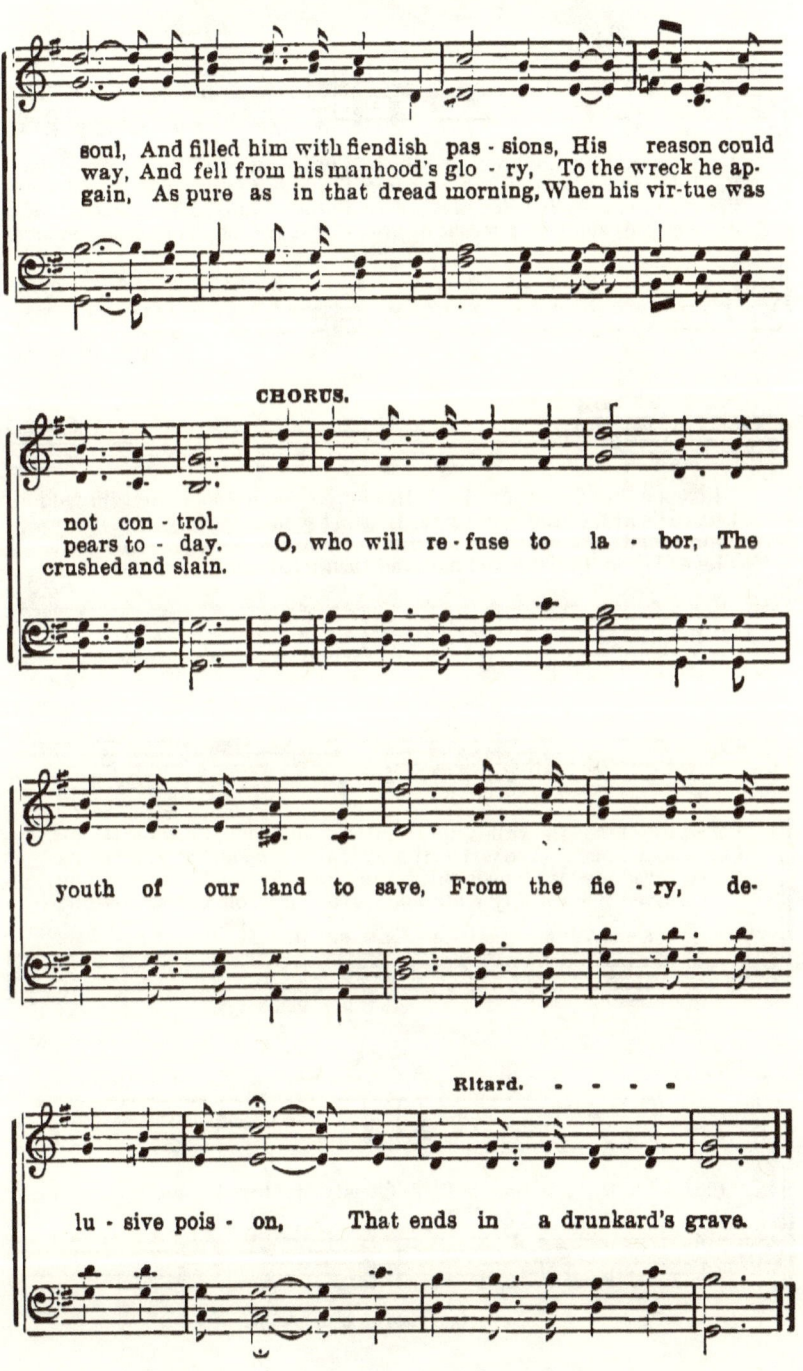

Christ Loved Me--Concluded.

praise Him thro' e - ter - ni - ty, For Christ loved me.

24. The Precious Bible.

FANNIE BIRDSALL.   LOTTIE BIRDSALL.

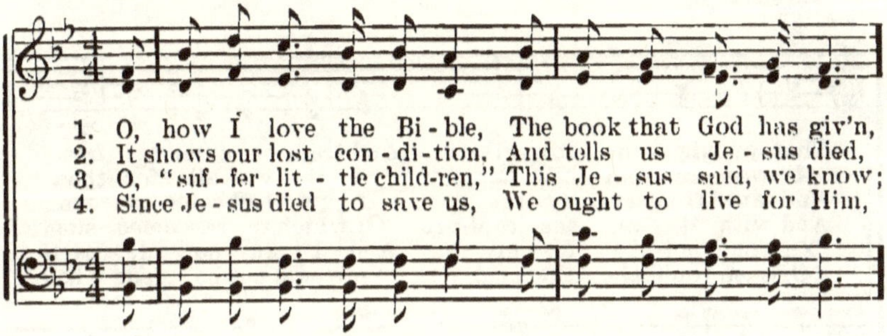

1. O, how I love the Bi - ble, The book that God has giv'n,
2. It shows our lost con - di - tion, And tells us Je - sus died,
3. O, "suf - fer lit - tle chil-dren," This Je - sus said, we know;
4. Since Je - sus died to save us, We ought to live for Him,

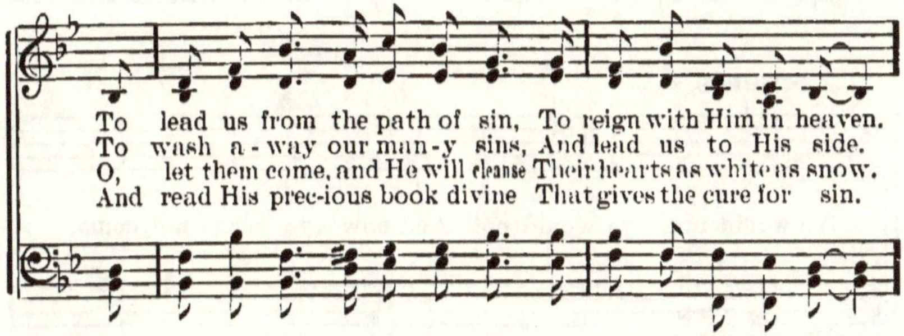

To lead us from the path of sin, To reign with Him in heaven.
To wash a - way our man-y sins, And lead us to His side.
O, let them come, and He will cleanse Their hearts as white as snow.
And read His prec-ious book divine That gives the cure for sin.

CHORUS.

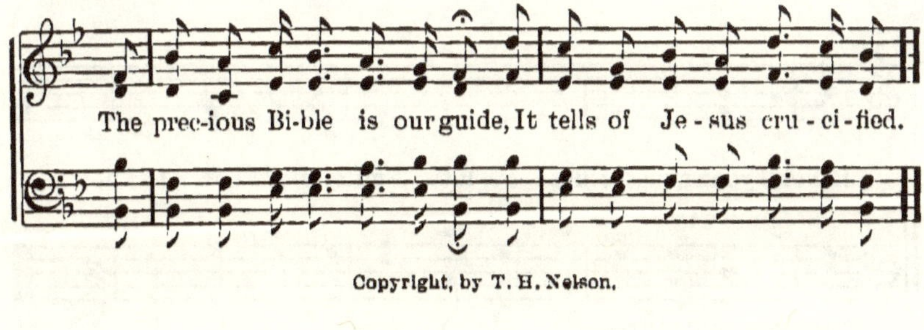

The prec-ious Bi-ble is our guide, It tells of Je - sus cru - ci - fied.

Copyright, by T. H. Nelson.

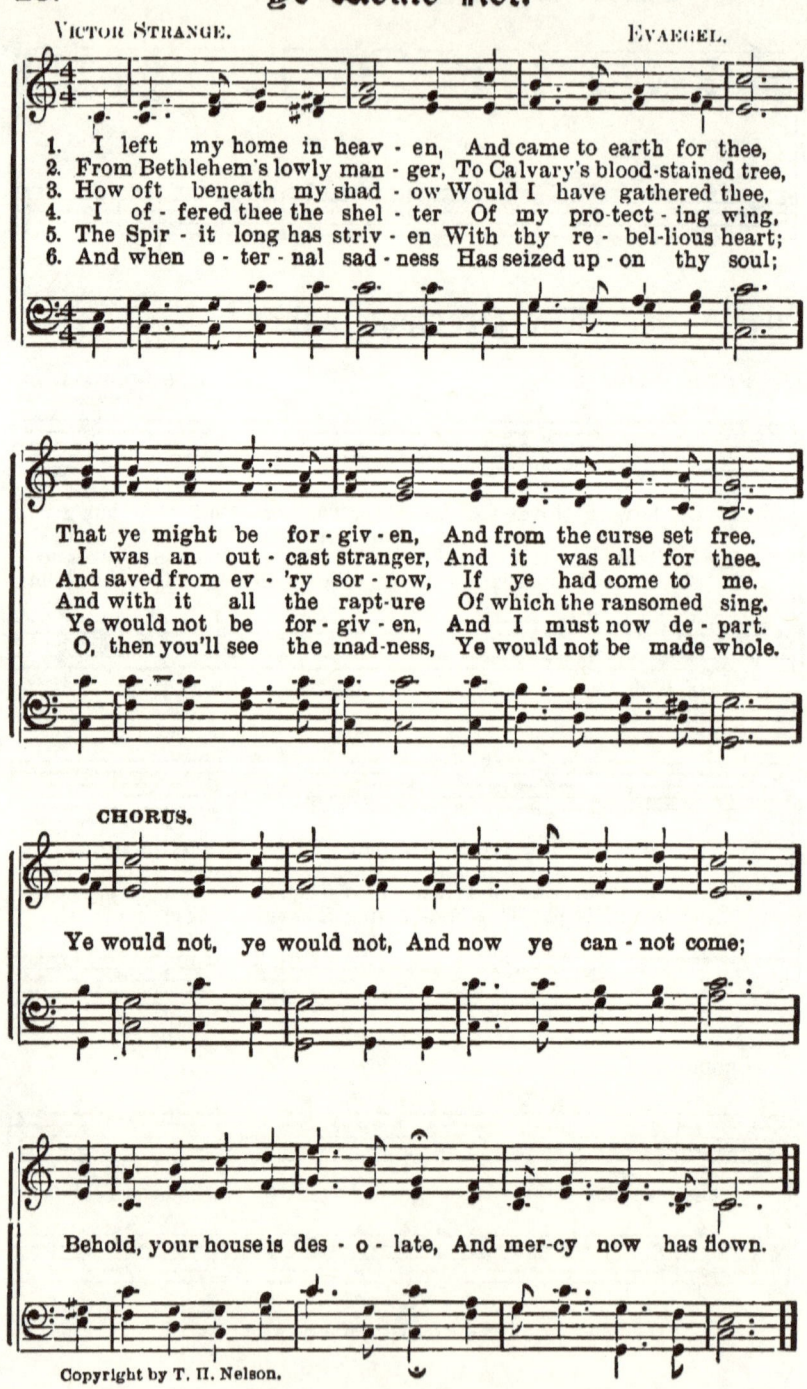

Parting to Meet--Concluded.

more here be-low, Oh, how sad the thought to thee, trav'-ler to e-ter-ni-ty; Part-ing to meet a-gain at the judg-ment.
more here be-low, Oh, how glad the thought to thee, trav'-ler to e-ter-ni-ty; Read-y to meet a-gain at the judg-ment.

28. The Great Physician.

WM. HUNTER.   Arr. by J. H. STOCKTON.

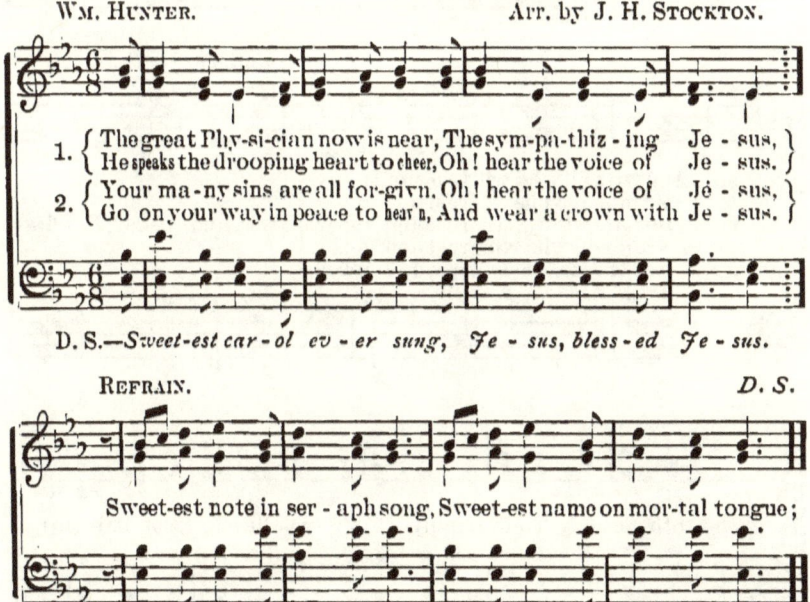

1. { The great Phy-si-cian now is near, The sym-pa-thiz-ing Je-sus,
    He speaks the drooping heart to cheer, Oh! hear the voice of Je-sus. }

2. { Your ma-ny sins are all for-givn, Oh! hear the voice of Je-sus,
    Go on your way in peace to heav'n, And wear a crown with Je-sus. }

D. S.—*Sweet-est car-ol ev-er sung, Je-sus, bless-ed Je-sus.*

REFRAIN.   D. S.

Sweet-est note in ser-aph song, Sweet-est name on mor-tal tongue;

3. All glory to the dying Lamb!
    I now believe in Jesus;
    I love the blessed Savior's name,
    I love the name of Jesus.

4. His name dispels my guilt and fear,
    No other name but Jesus;
    Oh! how my soul delights to hear
    The charming name of Jesus.

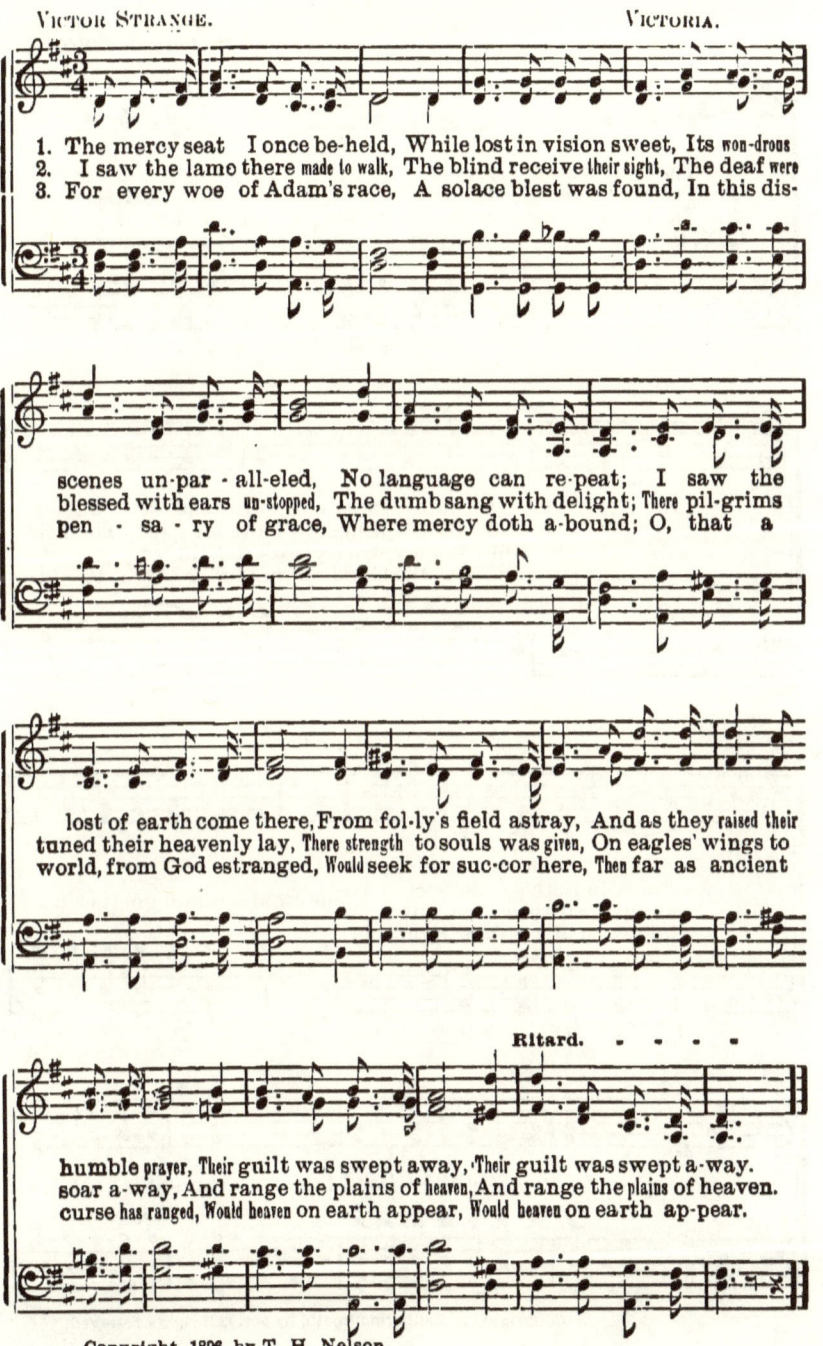

Magdalene--Concluded.

hand-some and pure as the snow;.......... See, where is she now
those who His love now en-joy;.......... O, how He now yearns
change all thy dark-ness to-day;.......... Then come to Him now,

with those wretched com-pan-ions, sink-ing down in dis-hon-or and woe.
from her woes to re-lieve her, and her craving for sin to des-troy.
from thy fol-lies all turning, and walk thee in wis-dom's blest way.

CHORUS.

O, leave these com-pan - ions so reck - less and wretch-ed,

Who cause thee in sin's path to roam; Come back to thy Sa-vior and

loved ones neg-lec-ted, Come to thy fond pa - rents and home.

36. I've Missed It at Last.

VIVIAN A. DAKE. IDA M. DAKE.

1. "I've missed it at last," he re-peat-ed,...... While the shades of de-
2. "The thief on the cross I re-mem-ber,...... Ne'er re-fused till the
3. "I've sold out my soul for a feath-er,...... No hope in the
4. "The spir-it in-sult-ed, re-sist-ed,...... Still plead till the
5. He bur-ied his face in the pil-low,...... With hor-ror his

spair gath-ered fast; "My hopes are for-ev-er de-feat-ed, I have missed,
sum-mer was past, And now in death's chilling December, I have missed,
whirlwind's fierce blast; I'm un-done for-ev-er and ev-er, I have missed
die I had cast, I said 'Go thy way,' I in-sist-ed; He went,
soul all a-ghast, And back from e-ter-ni-ty's bil-low, He shriek'd,

CHORUS.

I have missed it at last!" "I've missed it at last, missed sal-va-tion, From the pure and the ho-ly out-cast; Nev-er more peace to feel—dire dam-na-tion— I've missed, I have missed it at last.

Copyright, by T. H. Nelson.

My New Friend--Concluded.

CHORUS.

Friend is your heart weary and sad?
Do you long for the joys that are dead?
Give Jesus your heart, he'll true comfort impart,
And he'll dry all the tears you would shed.

39 Sweet Hour of Prayer.

1 Sweet hour of pray'r, sweet hour of pray'r,
That calls me from a world of care,
And bids me, at my Father's throne,
Make all my wants and wishes known!
In seasons of distress and grief,
My soul has often found relief,
And oft escaped the tempter's snare,
By thy return, sweet hour of pray'r.

2. Sweet hour of pray'r, sweet hour of pray'r,
To Him, whose truth and faithfulness
Engage the waiting soul to bless:
And since He bids me seek his face,
Believe His word, and trust His grace,
I'll cast on him my every care,
And wait for thee, sweet hour of pray'r.

3. Sweet hour of pray'r, sweet hour of pray'r,
May I thy consolation share,
Till, from Mount Pisgah's lofty height,
I view my home, and take my flight;
This robe of flesh I'll drop and rise
To seize the everlasting prize;
And shout, while passing thro' the air,

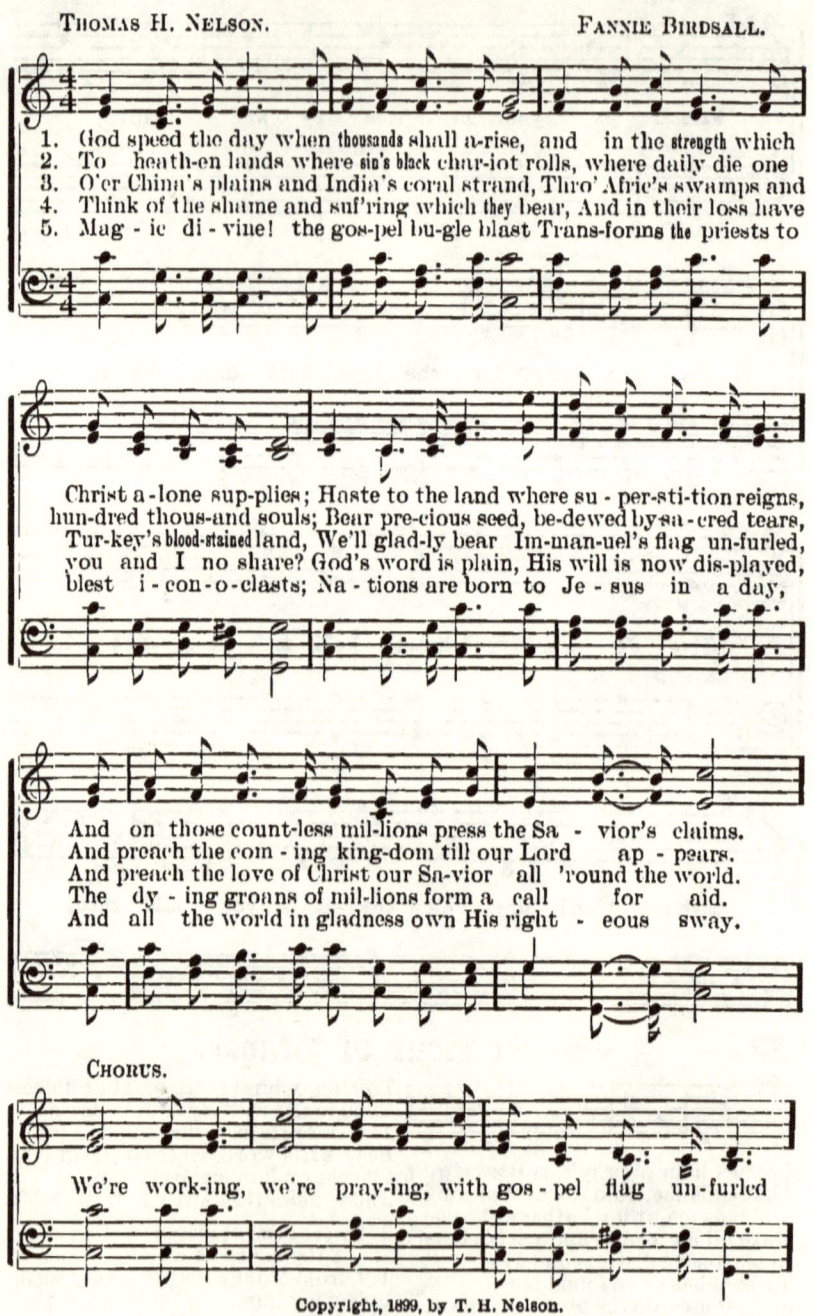

Missionary Battle Song--Concluded.

Till Christ shall reign in tri-umph o'er the whole wide world.

41. True to the End.

VICTOR STRANGE.　　　　　　　　　　VICTORIA.

1. Will you in the fight be true, O, my soul? Will you see the bat-tle thro' O, my soul? When the tide of battle flows, And the hosts of hell oppose, Trusted friends appear as foes, O, my soul.
2. Would you always conquer or be, O, my soul? Gladly take what comes to thee, O, my soul? Curses here lose all their sting, Crosses crowns of glory bring, And thou shalt with rapture sing, O, my soul?
3. Will you when the war is o'er, O, my soul, Sing upon the glo-ry shore, O, my soul? And present the souls you've won, Who like you the race have run, And have reached their final home, O, my soul?
4. In the hour when nature fails, O, my soul, And in death's cold hand she reels, O, my soul; When you're done with toil and prayer, Then you shall the glory share, In the land just o-ver there, O, my soul.
5. Will you tread the plains of light, O, my soul, Never more feel sorrow's blight, O, my soul? In the pal-ace of the King, Where ce-lestial anthems ring, And an-gel-ic choirs sing, O, my soul.

Ritard.

Copyright by T. H. Nelson.

We'll Girdle the Globe.

V. A. Dake.
Ida M. Dake.

O will you to their rescue go, Lost wand'rers down to endless woe?
And grope in sin and nature's night, Forever vainly seeking light.
Till all the earth, from pole to pole, Shall hear Salvation's echoes roll.
Till burning lines of gospel fire, Shall gird the world and mount up higher

Copyright by T. H. Nelson.

We'll Girdle the Globe--Concluded.

CHORUS.

We'll girdle the globe with salvation. With ho - li - ness unto the Lord.

And light shall illumine each nation, The light from the lamp of his word.

45. Luther's Cradle Hymn.

MARTIN LUTHER.   FLORA BIRDSALL NELSON.

1. A - way in a man - ger, no crib for a bed, The lit - tle Lord Je - sus laid down his sweet head; The stars in the heav - en looked forth where He lay, The lit - tle Lord Je - sus, a - sleep on the hay.
2. The cat - tle are low - ing, the poor ba - by wakes, But lit - tle Lord Je - sus, no cry - ing He makes; I love thee, Lord Je - sus, look down from the sky, And stay by my cra - dle to watch lull-a - by.

Copyright, 1899, by T. H. Nelson.

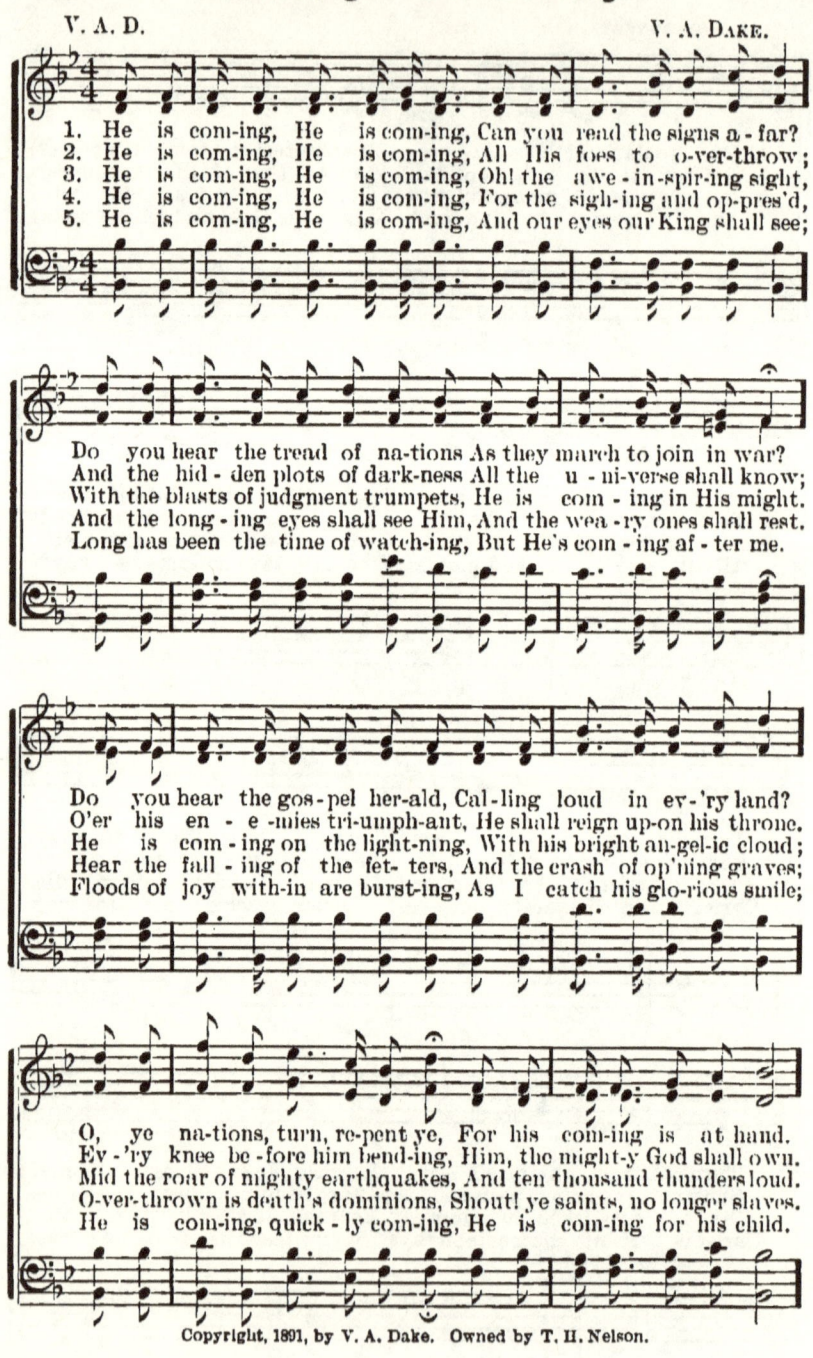

Watch For His Coming--Concluded.

CHORUS.

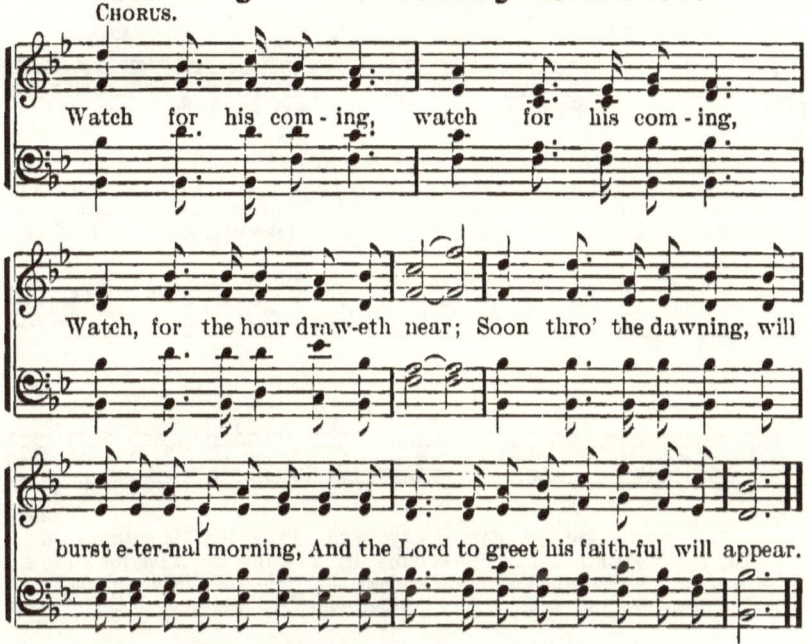

Watch for his com-ing, watch for his com-ing, Watch, for the hour draw-eth near; Soon thro' the dawning, will burst e-ter-nal morning, And the Lord to greet his faith-ful will appear.

49. Must Jesus Bear the Cross Alone?

THOS. SHEPHERD. GEO. N. ALLEN.

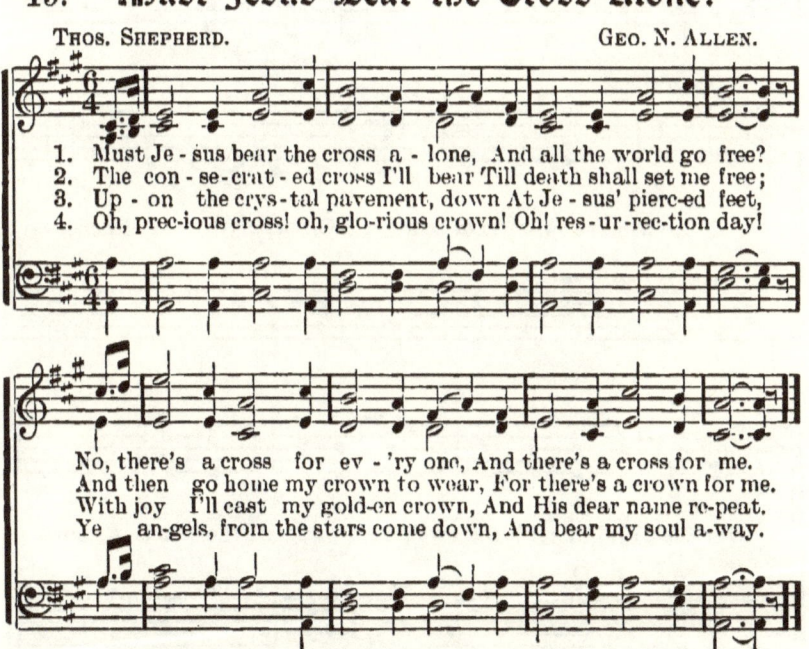

1. Must Je-sus bear the cross a-lone, And all the world go free?
2. The con-se-crat-ed cross I'll bear Till death shall set me free;
3. Up-on the crys-tal pavement, down At Je-sus' pierc-ed feet,
4. Oh, prec-ious cross! oh, glo-rious crown! Oh! res-ur-rec-tion day!

No, there's a cross for ev-'ry one, And there's a cross for me.
And then go home my crown to wear, For there's a crown for me.
With joy I'll cast my gold-en crown, And His dear name re-peat.
Ye an-gels, from the stars come down, And bear my soul a-way.

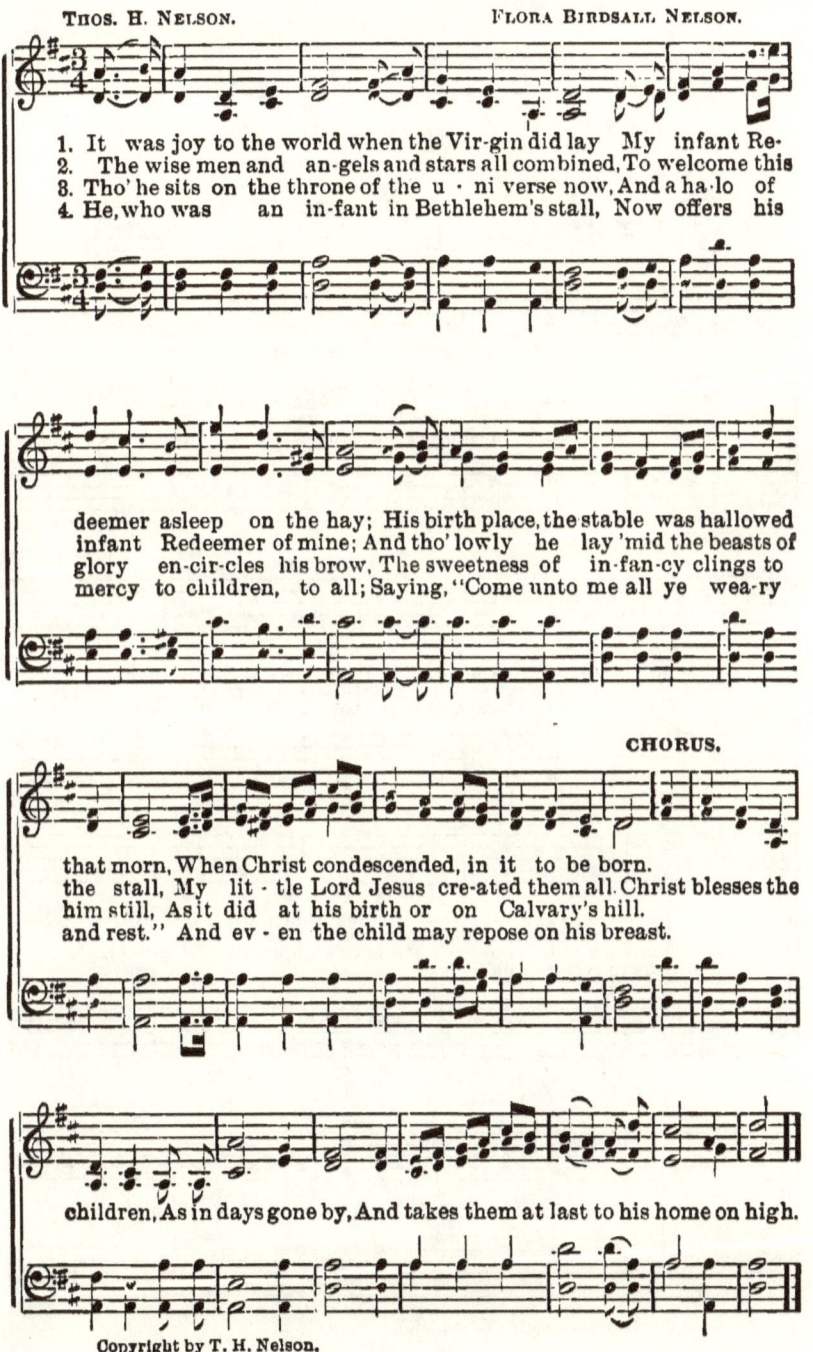

Going Down to the Grave--Concluded.

Come trust in His word, And thou shalt not die.

55 Jesus Calls the Children.

FANNIE BIRDSALL.   FANNIE BIRDSALL.

1. Jesus loves the children. "Let them come." said He; "Do not now forbid them,
2. Jesus calls the children. Calls them to His fold. Lest their feet should wander
3. Jesus saves the children, Saves from ev'ry sin; When they come repenting.
4. Jesus folds the children, In His arms of love; He will safely lead them

CHORUS.

Blessed shall they be."
O'er sin's mountain cold.
Je - sus takes them in.   Hear Him calling, calling, Children come to-day;
To His home a - bove.

Come and with the Sa - vior walk the nar - row way.

The Toils of the Road--Concluded.

With joy I will fol-low to - day;
That my strength shall be as my day;
Will be plain and clear as the day;
Meet my trials with courage, and say,
O, the toils of the road will seem noth - ing When I get to the end of the way, way.

57. My Faith Looks Up to Thee.

RAY PALMER.   LOWELL MASON.

1. My faith looks up to thee, Thou Lamb of Calvary, Savior di-vine,
2. May thy rich grace impart, Strength to my fainting heart, My zeal inspire;

{ Now hear me while I pray;
  Take all my guilt a-way; } Oh, let me, from this day, Be whol-ly thine.
{ As thou hast died for me,
  Oh, may my love to thee } Pure, warm and changeless be, A living fire.

3. While life's dark maze I tread,
And griefs around me spread,
  Be thou my guide;
Bid darkness turn to day,
Wipe sorrow's tears away,
Nor let me ever stray
  From thee aside.

4. When ends life's transient dream,
When death's cold, sullen stream
  Shall o'er me roll;
Blest Savior, then, in love,
Fear and distress remove;
Oh, bear me safe above,
  A ransomed soul.

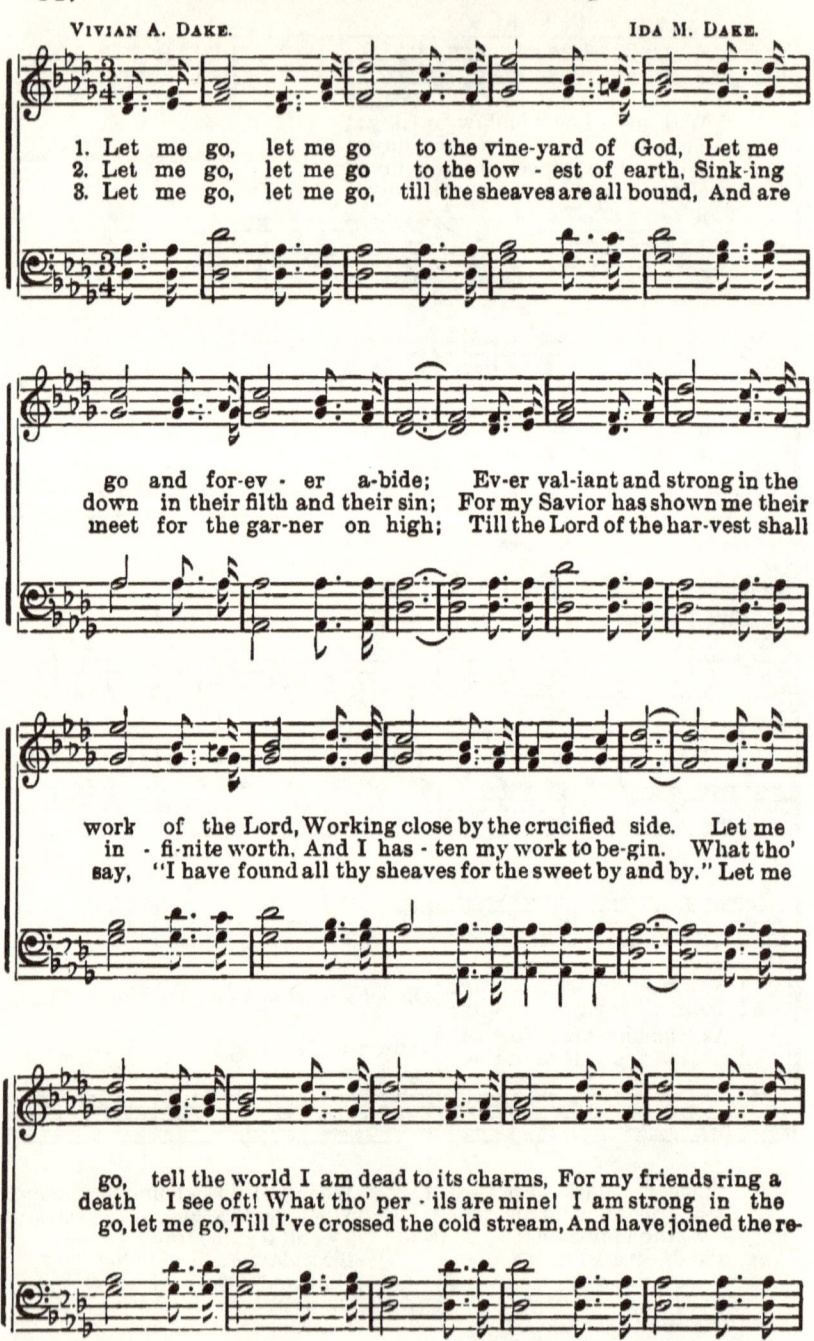

Let Me Go to the Vineyard--Concluded.

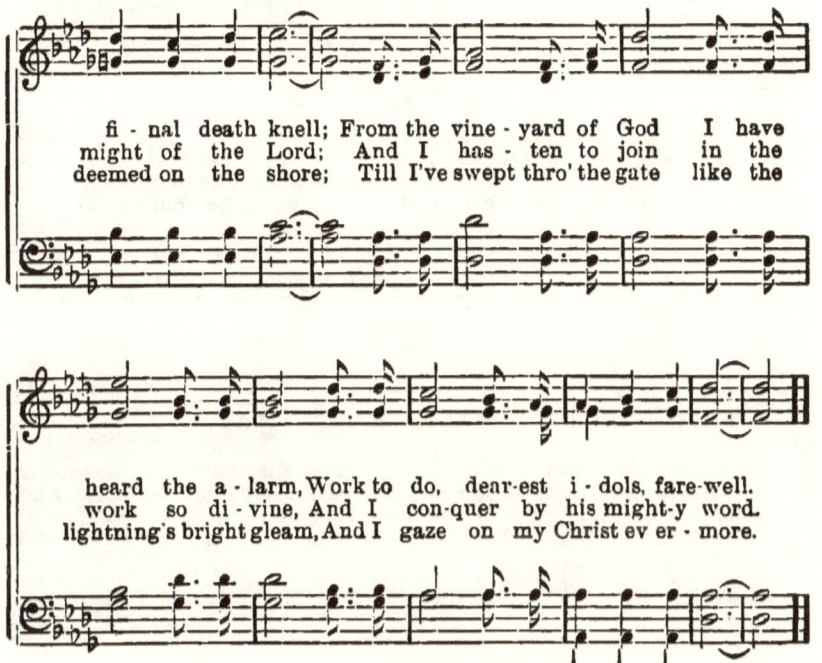

fi - nal death knell; From the vine - yard of God I have
might of the Lord; And I has - ten to join in the
deemed on the shore; Till I've swept thro' the gate like the

heard the a - larm, Work to do, dear-est i - dols, fare-well.
work so di - vine, And I con-quer by his might-y word.
lightning's bright gleam, And I gaze on my Christ ev er - more.

59   Meet Me There.

1. On the happy golden shore,
   Where the faithful part no more,
   When the storms of life are o'er,
     Meet me there;
   Where the night dissolves away
   Into pure and perfect day,
   I am going home to stay;
     Meet me there.

   CHORUS.

   Meet me there, meet me there,
   Where the tree of life is blooming,
     Meet me there;
   When the storms of life are o'er,
   On the happy golden shore,

Where the faithful part no more;
  Meet me there.

2. Here our fondest hopes are vain,
   Dearest links are rent in twain;
   But in heav'n no throb of pain,
     Meet me there;
   By the river sparkling bright,
   In the city of delight,
   Where our faith is lost in sight,
     Meet me there.

3. Where the harps of angels ring,
   And the blest forever sing,
   In the palace of the King,
     Meet me there;
   Where in sweet communion blend
   Heart with heart and friend with friend,
   In a world that ne'er shall end,
     Meet me there.

By per. Wm. J. Kirkpatrick. From "Finest of the Wheat."

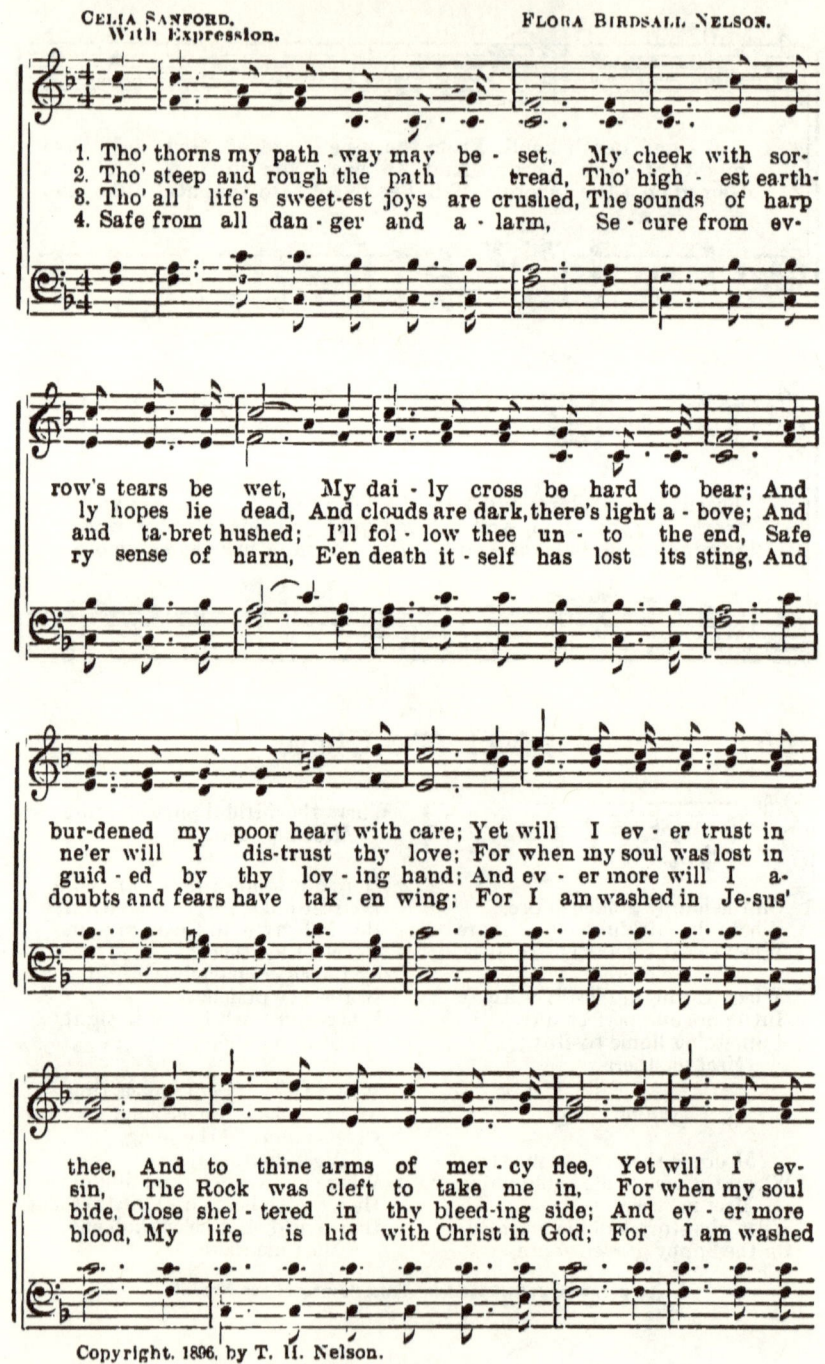

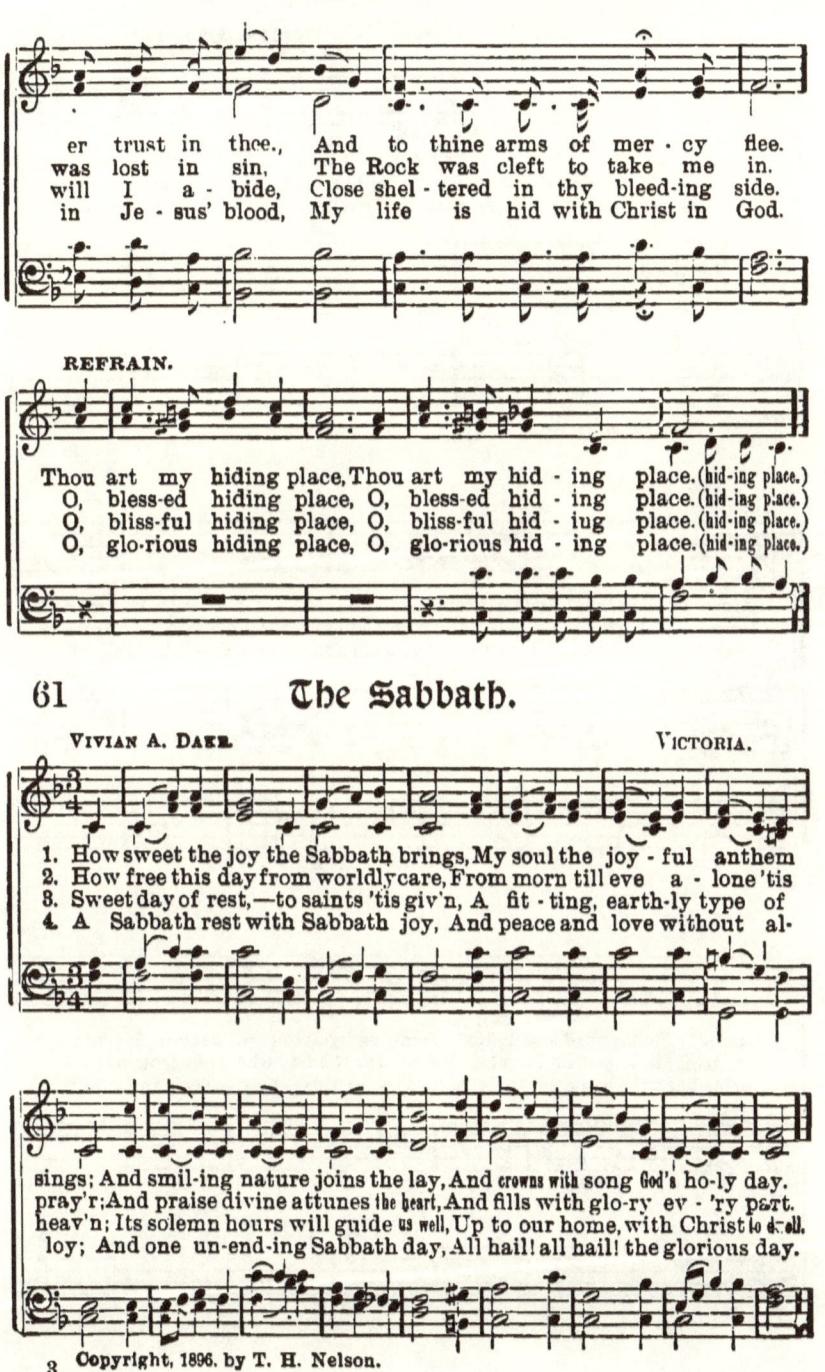

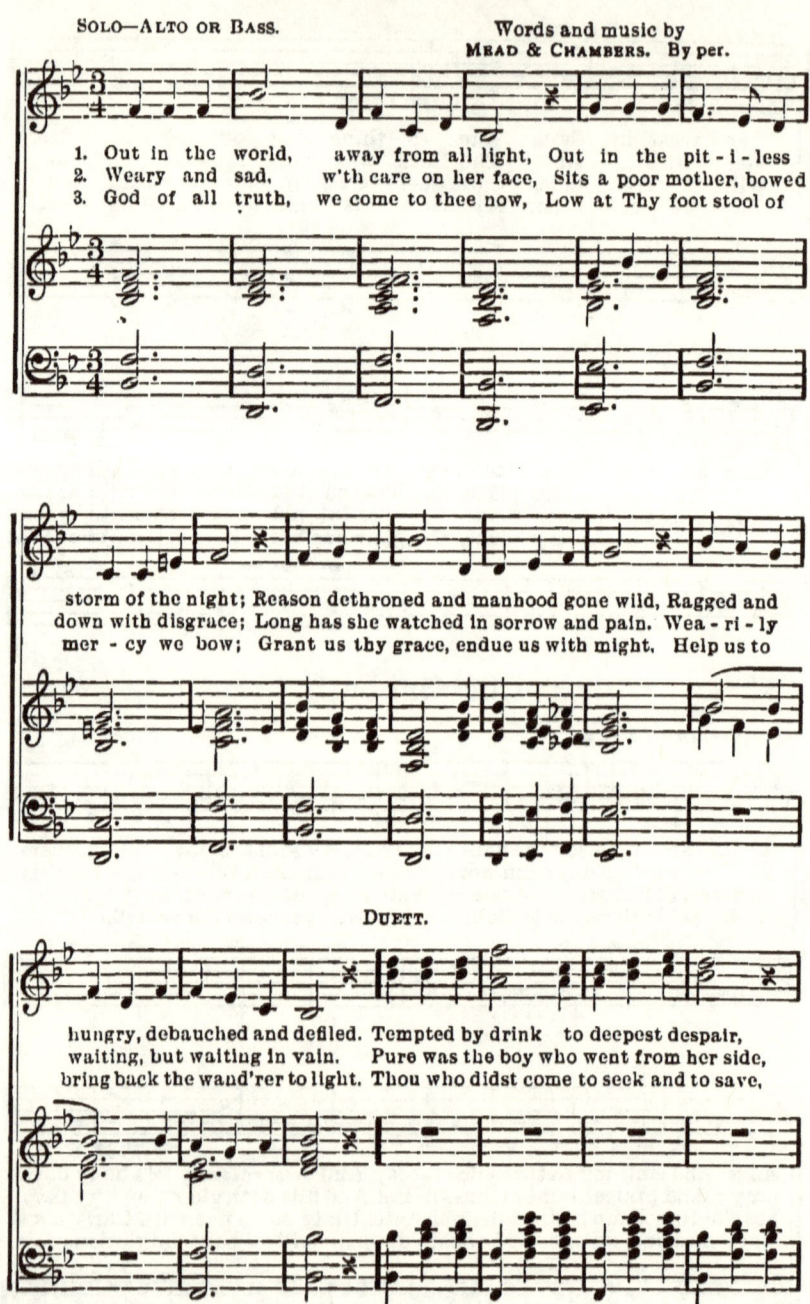

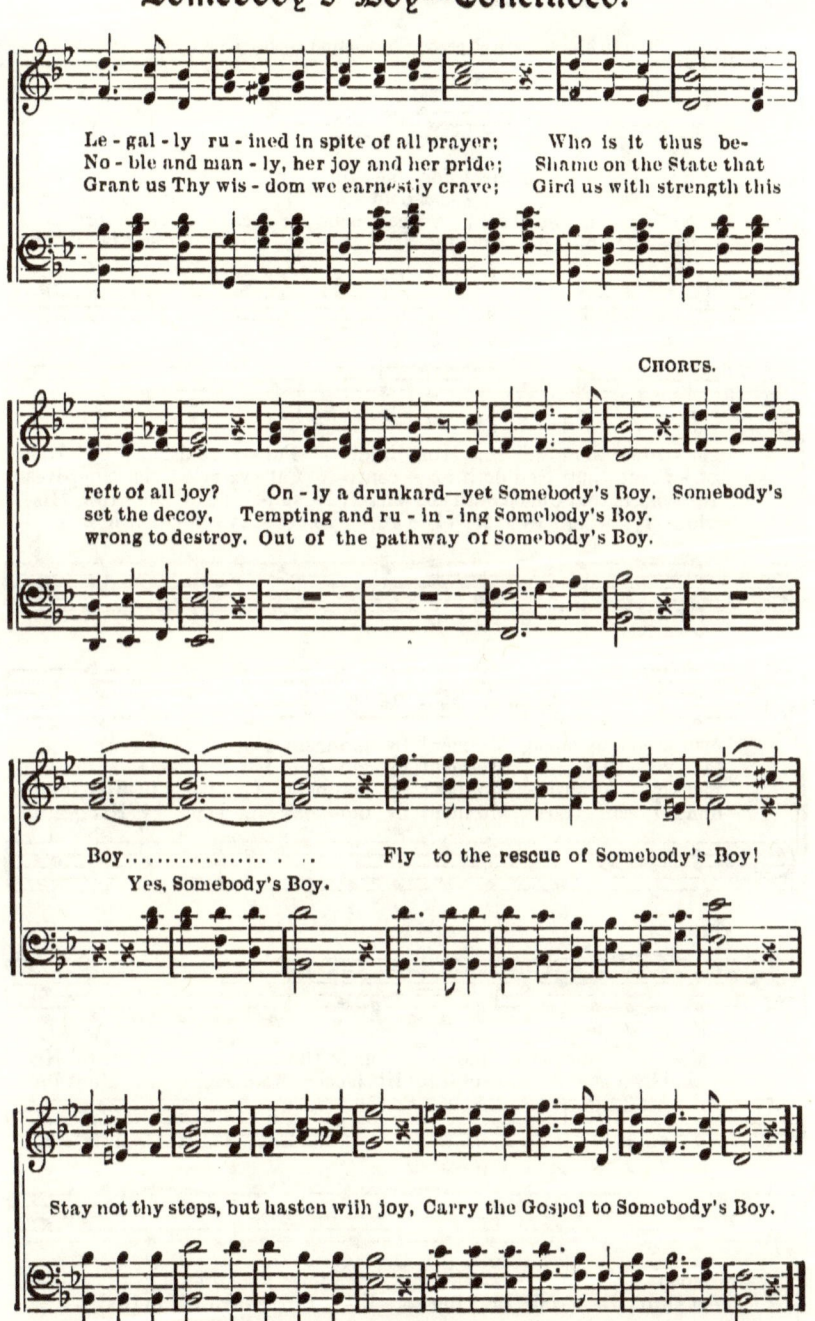

Somebody's Boy—Concluded.

Le - gal - ly ru - ined in spite of all prayer; Who is it thus be-
No - ble and man - ly, her joy and her pride; Shame on the State that
Grant us Thy wis - dom we earnestly crave; Gird us with strength this

CHORUS.

reft of all joy? On - ly a drunkard—yet Somebody's Boy. Somebody's
set the decoy, Tempting and ru - in - ing Somebody's Boy.
wrong to destroy. Out of the pathway of Somebody's Boy.

Boy................... Fly to the rescue of Somebody's Boy!
Yes, Somebody's Boy.

Stay not thy steps, but hasten with joy, Carry the Gospel to Somebody's Boy.

Moment By Moment--Concluded.

64. My Heavenly Home.

WM. HUNTER, D. D. — Arranged.

1. { My heav'nly home is bright and fair; No pain, nor death can en-ter there:
    Its glitt'ring tow'rs the sun outshine; That heav'nly mansion shall be mine. }

Cho. { I'm go-ing home, I'm go-ing home, I'm go-ing home to die no more!
    To die no more, to die no more, I'm go-ing home to die no more! }

2 My Father's house is built on high,
Far, far above the starry sky:
When from this earthly prison free,
That heav'nly mansion mine shall be.

3 Let others seek a home below, [flow,
Which flames devour, or waves o'er-
Be mine a happier lot to own
A heav'nly mansion near the throne.

My Refuge--Concluded.

CHORUS.

I will hide me, I will hide me, Safely from the stormy blast, He will guide me, He will guide me, And receive my soul at last.

I will hide me, I will hide me, I will hide me, stormy blast, He will guide me, He will guide me, at last.

Ritard.

---

68. Work for the Night.

1. Work, for the night is coming,
   Work through the morning hours;
   Work while the dew is sparkling,
   Work 'mid springing flowers;
   Work when the day grows brighter,
   Work in the glowing sun;
   Work, for the night is coming,
   When man's work is done.

2. Work, for the night is coming,
   Work thro' the sunny noon;
   Fill brightest hours with labor;
   Rest comes sure and soon.
   Give every flying minute
   Something to keep in store;
   Work for the night is coming
   When man works no more.

3. Work, for the night is coming,
   Under the sunset skies;
   While their bright tints are glowing,
   Work, for daylight flies.
   Work, till the last beam fadeth,
   Fadeth to shine no more;
   Work, while the night is dark'ning
   When man's work is o'er.

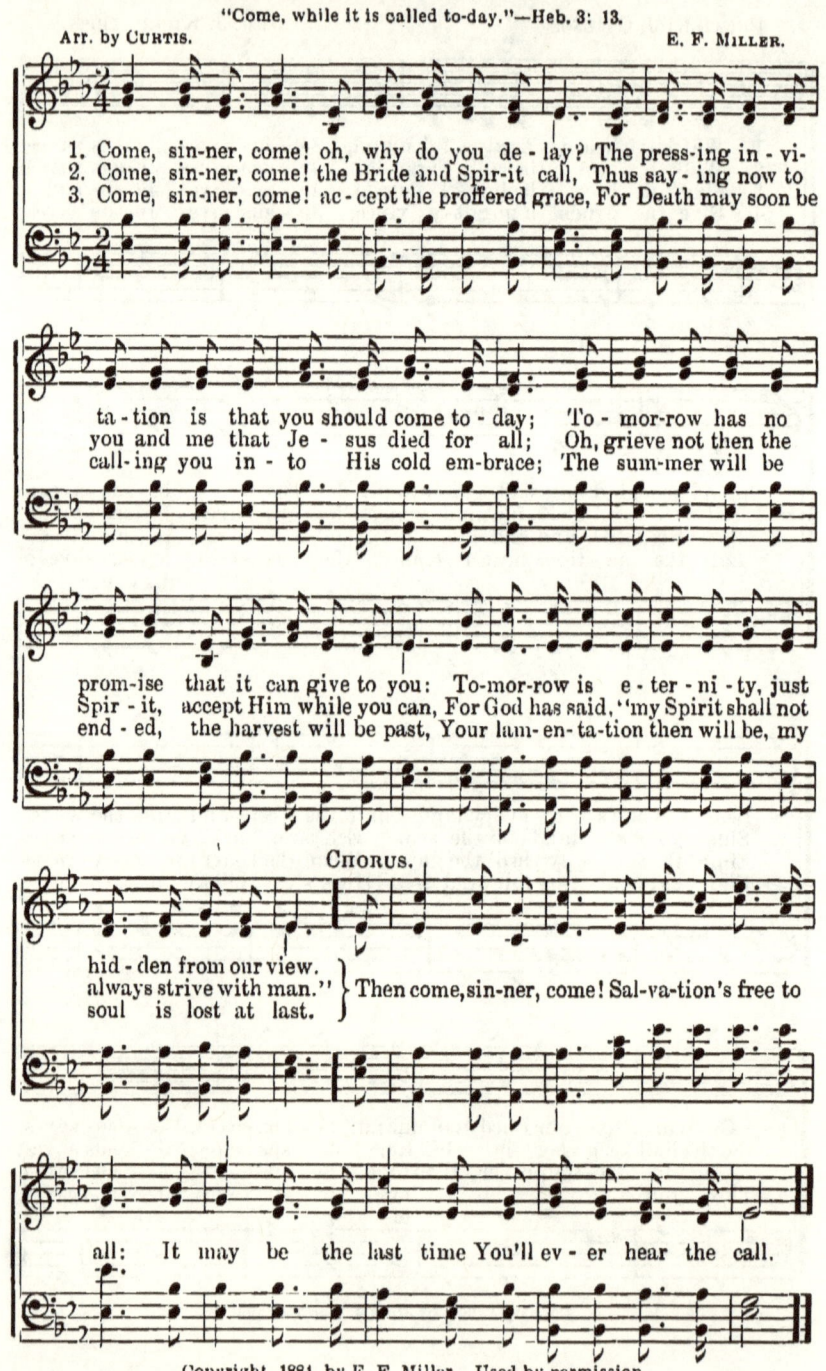

Unanswered Yet—Concluded.

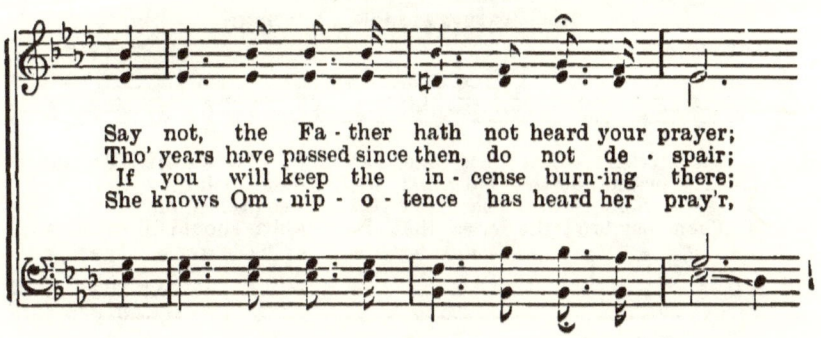

Say not, the Father hath not heard your prayer;
Tho' years have passed since then, do not despair;
If you will keep the incense burning there;
She knows Omnipotence has heard her pray'r,

You shall have your answer, Sometime—somewhere.
God will answer surely, Sometime—somewhere.
You shall see his power, Sometime—somewhere.
Cries, it shall be answered, Sometime—somewhere.

77. The Child of a King.

1. My Father is rich in houses and lands,
He holdeth the wealth of the world in
His hands! [gold,
Of rubies and diamonds, of silver and
His coffers are full,—He has riches untold.

Cho.—I'm the child of a King,
The child of a King;
With Jesus, my Savior,
I'm the child of a King.

2. My Father's own Son, the Savior of men,
Once wandered o'er the earth as the poorest of men;
But now He is reigning forever on high,
And will give me a home in heaven by and by.

3. I once was an outcast stranger on earth,
A sinner by choice, an alien by birth!
But I've been adopted, my name's written down,
An heir to a mansion, a robe and a crown.

4. A tent or cottage, why should I care?
They're building a palace for me over there! [may sing
Though exiled from home, yet still I
"All glory to God, I'm the child of a King.

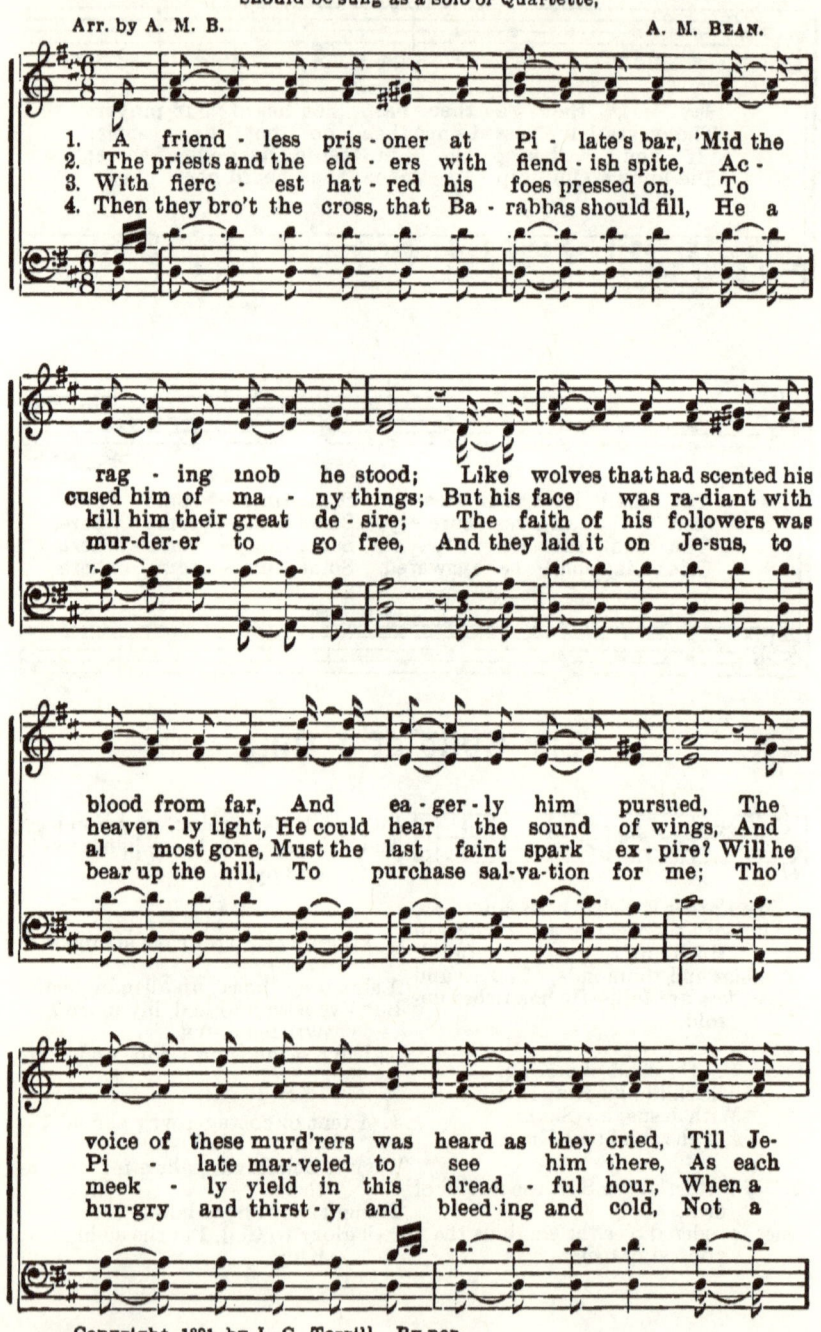

He Answered Never a Word--Concluded.

ru - sa-lem's cit - y was stirred; "Away with him, let him be
wick - ed charge he heard, His mute lips moved as in
mur-der-er is preferred; He who raised the dead, has he
sigh passed his lips that was heard; He trembled a mo-ment, then

cru - ci - fied,
si - lent pray'r,
lost his pow'r?   But he an-swered nev-er a word.
sank to the ground,

5 The rabble with spite and revenge urged them on,
   Till he came to Calvary's height,
  Where they nailed his hands and feet to the cross,
   (O, sinner, look on him to-night!)
  Then raising the cross, oh! what suffering and pain,
   Till the earth and the heavens were stirred,
  But the suffering Jesus with meekness endured,
   And he answered never a word.

79. Companionship with Jesus.

1. Oh, blessed fellowship divine!
    Oh, joy supremely sweet!
   Companionship with Jesus here
    Makes life with bliss replete;
   In union with the purest One
   I find my heaven on earth begun.

REFRAIN.
Oh, wondrous bliss! oh, joy sublime!
 I've Jesus with me all the time!
Oh, wondrous bliss! oh, joy sublime!
 I've Jesus with me all the time!

2. I'm walking close to Jesus' side,
    So close that I can hear
The softest whispers of His love,
 In fellowship so dear,
And feel His great almighty hand
Protects me in this hostile land.

3. I'm leaning on His loving breast,
    Along life's weary way;
   My path, illumined by His smiles,
    Grows brighter day by day;
   No foes, no woes my heart can fear,
   With my almighty Friend so near.

4. I know His sheltering wings of love
    Are always o'er me spread,
   And tho' the storms may fiercely rage;
    All calm and free from dread,
   My peaceful spirit ever sings,
   "I'll trust the covert of Thy wings."

Copyright, by W. J. Kirkpatrick. By per.

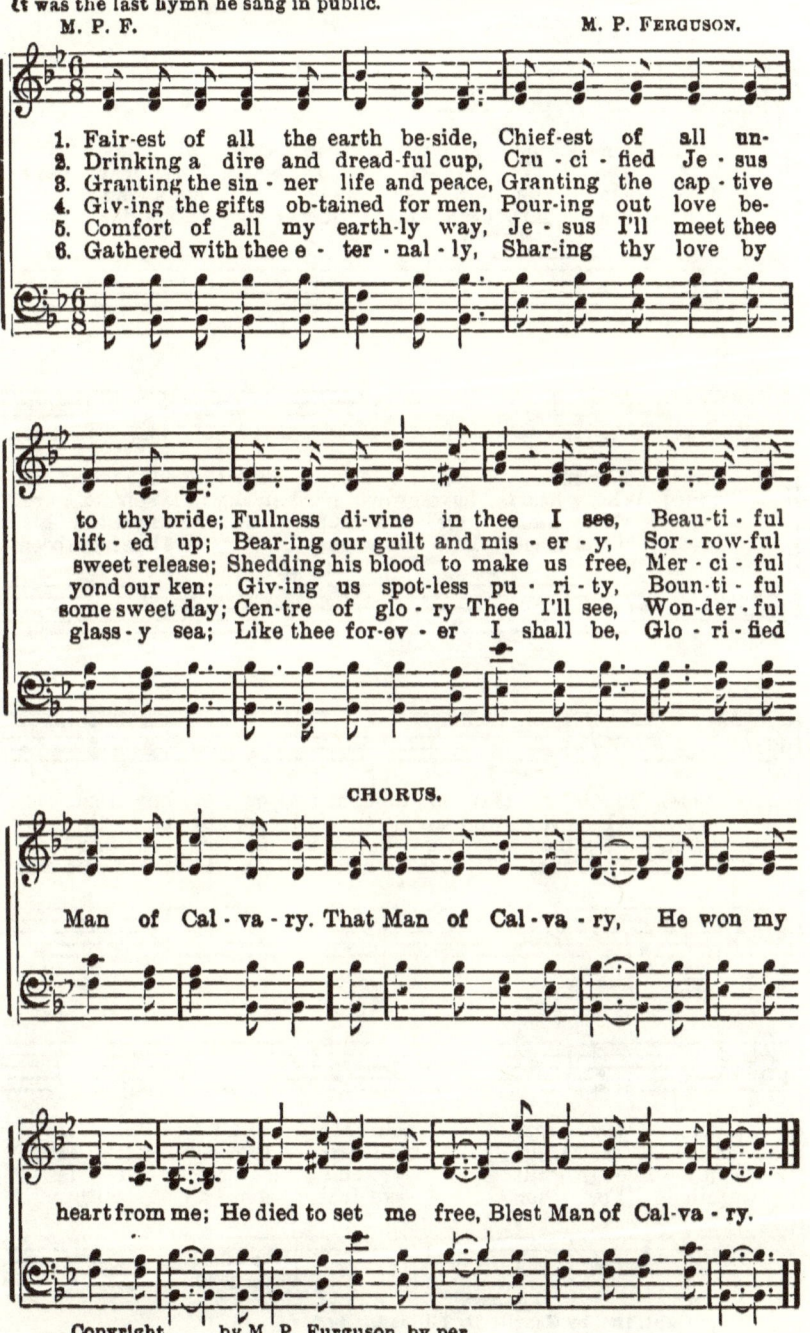

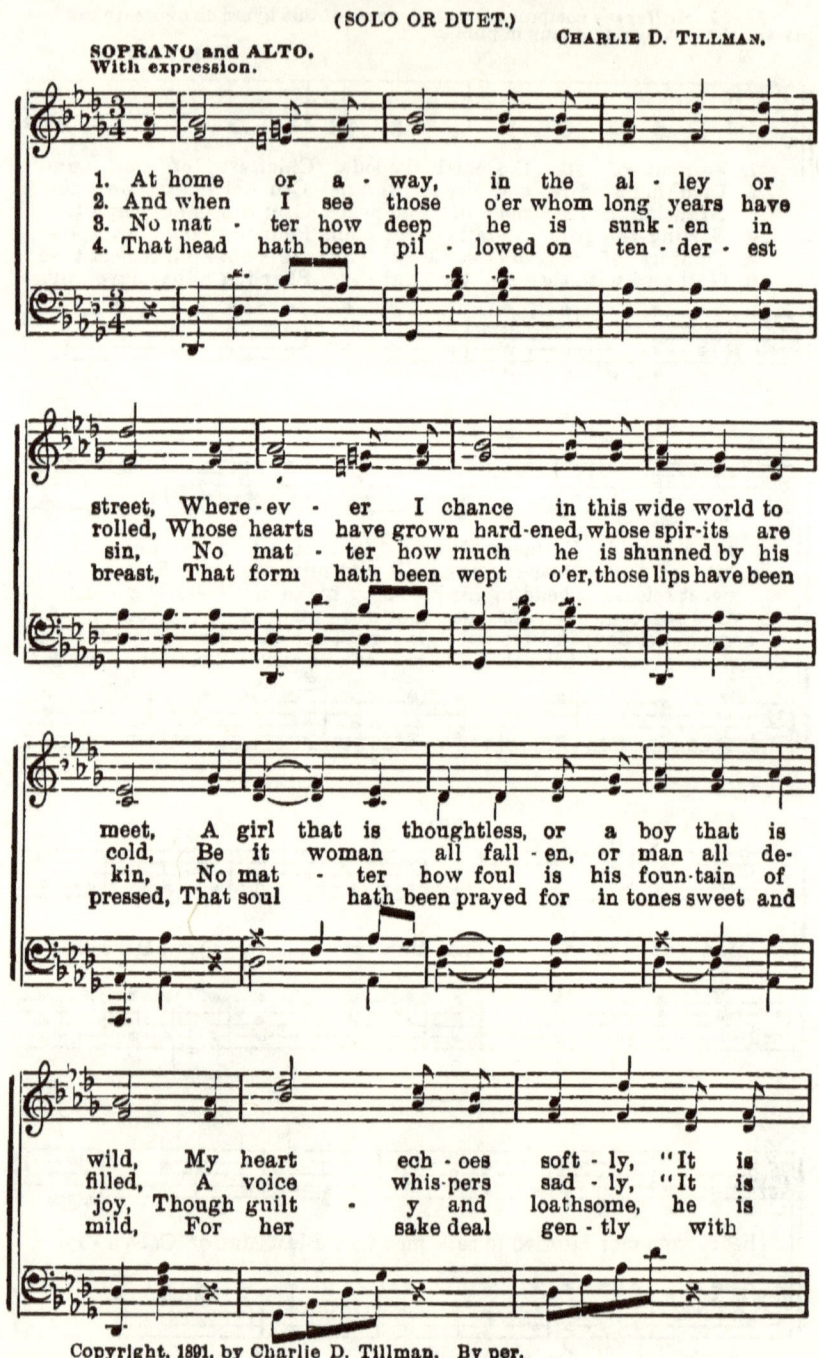

Some Mother's Child—Concluded.

(music)

some moth-er's child," My heart ech-oes soft-ly, "It is
some moth-er's child," A voice whispers sad-ly, "It is
some moth-er's boy," Tho' guilt-y and loathsome, he is
some moth-er's child," For her sake deal gen-tly with

REFRAIN.

some moth-er's child." Some mother's child, some mother's child,
some moth-er's child." Some mother's child, some mother's child,
some moth-er's boy. Some mother's boy, some mother's boy,
some moth-er's child. Some mother's child, some mother's child,

My heart ech-oes soft-ly, "It is some mother's child."
A voice whis-pers sad-ly, "It is some mother's child."
Tho' guilt-y and loathesome, He is some mother's boy.
For her sake deal gen-tly with some mother's child.

83   Alas, and did my Savior Bleed?

1 Alas! and did my Savior bleed?
   And did my Sovereign die?
Would He devote that sacred head
   For such a worm as I?

       CHORUS.

Help me, dear Savior, Thee to own,
   And ever faithful be;
And when thou sittest on thy throne,
   O Lord, remember me.

2 Was it for crimes that I have done
   He groaned upon the tree?
Amazing pity, grace unknown!
   And love beyond degree!

3 Well might the sun in darkness hide,
   And shut his glories in,
When Christ, the mighty Maker, died,
   For man the creature's sin.

4. But drops of grief can ne'er repay
   The debt of love I owe;
Here, Lord, I give myself away,—
   'Tis all that I can do.

Master Wants Workers.

F. J. Stevens.   Fannie Birdsall.

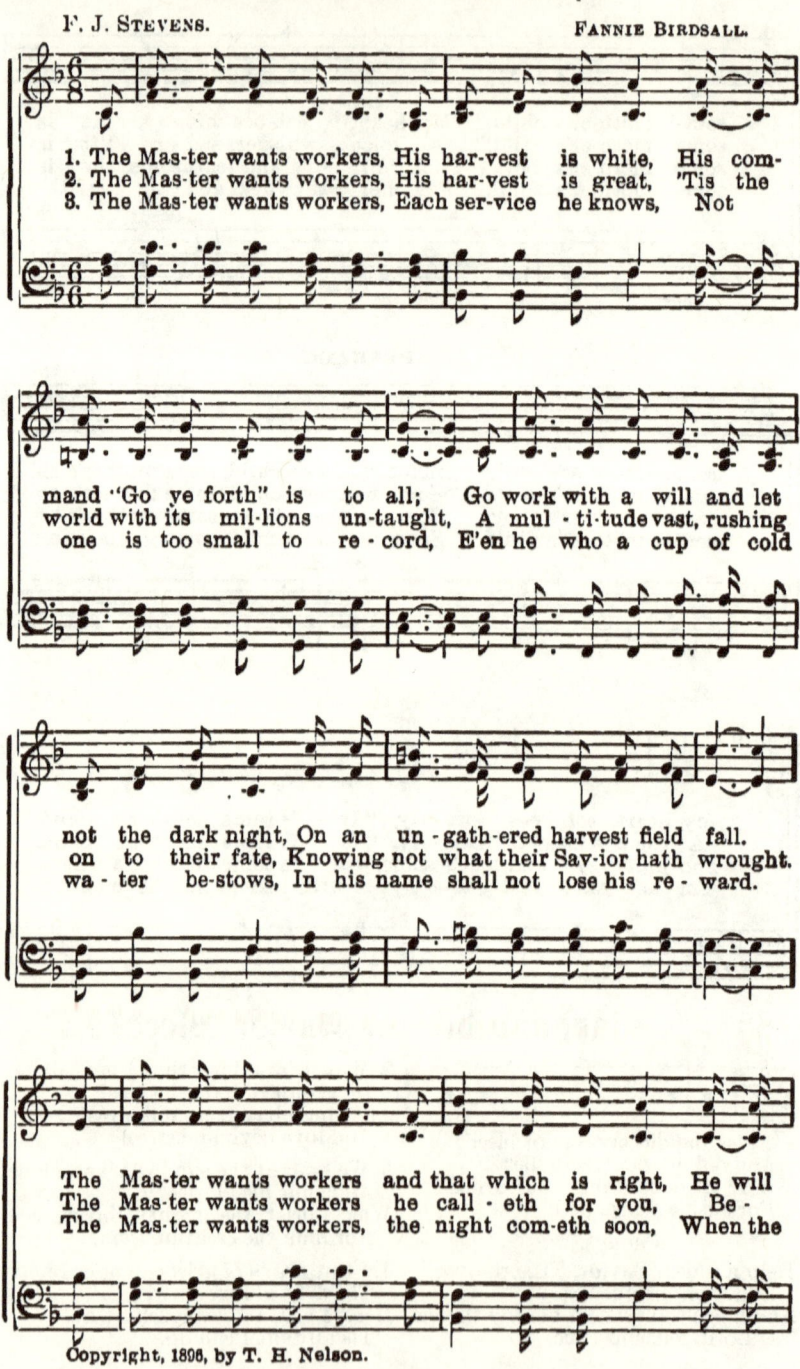

1. The Mas-ter wants workers, His har-vest is white, His com-mand "Go ye forth" is to all; Go work with a will and let not the dark night, On an un-gath-ered harvest field fall.
2. The Mas-ter wants workers, His har-vest is great, 'Tis the world with its mil-lions un-taught, A mul-ti-tude vast, rushing on to their fate, Knowing not what their Sav-ior hath wrought.
3. The Mas-ter wants workers, Each ser-vice he knows, Not one is too small to re-cord, E'en he who a cup of cold wa-ter be-stows, In his name shall not lose his re-ward.

The Mas-ter wants workers and that which is right, He will
The Mas-ter wants workers he call-eth for you, Be-
The Mas-ter wants workers, the night com-eth soon, When the

Copyright, 1896, by T. H. Nelson.

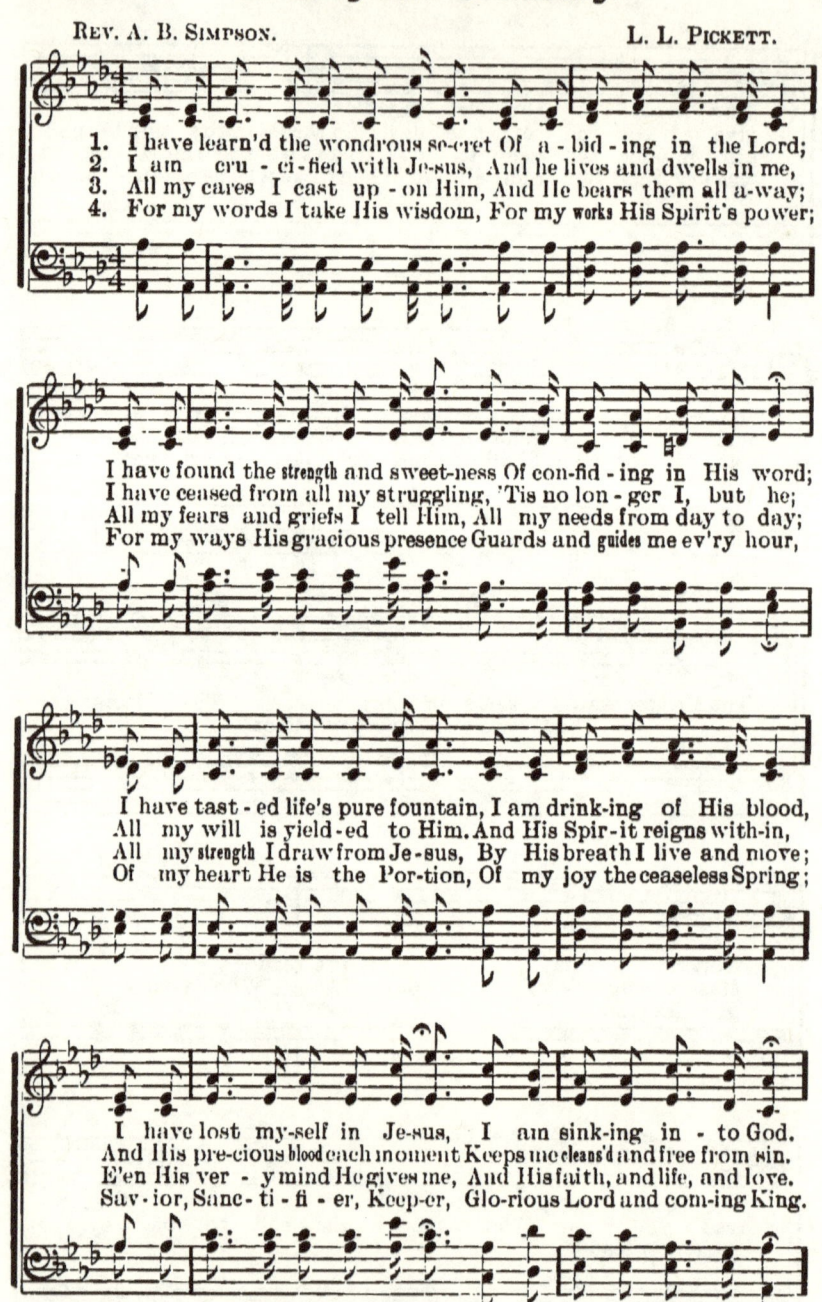

Abiding and Confiding--Concluded.

I'm a-bid - - - - ing in the Lord, And con-
I'm a-bid-ing in the Lord, I'm a-bid-ing in the Lord, And con-

fid - - - ing in His word, And I'm hid - - -
fid-ing in His word, And con-fid-ing in His word, And I'm hiding, safely

- ing, safe-ly hid - - ing, In the bos-om of His love.
hid-ing, I am hid-ing, safely hid-ing.

86. Invitation.

1. Thine iniquity swells like the tide,
   And the day of His vengeance is come;
   Canst thy spirit His coming abide?
   Canst thou bear the impenitent's doom?

   CHORUS:
   Precious soul, linger not!
   Linger not on the storm-covered plain;
   Precious soul, linger not,
   Or thy life will be lost with the slain.

2. Oh, escape to the mountain of God!
   Linger not on the storm-covered plain,
   For the cloud of His wrath spreads abroad,
   And 'tis death to thy soul to remain.

3. There are loved ones who stay with the lost!
   There are treasures to think of and leave;
   But thy soul is of infinite cost:
   Break away from thine idols and live.

4. How the sun rises bright on the soul,
   When our city of refuge we gain!
   How the storm clouds away from us roll,
   And we fear not the fire and the rain.

5. Being justified now by His blood,
   Saved from wrath we shall be, by and by,
   Cleansed from sin in this life giving flood,
   We are ready to live and to die.

Needed--Laborers--Concluded.

Send forth the reap-ers to-day, For this, O Lord, do we pray; do we pray;

Tell the glad news of redemption to all, Shall we not hasten away?

88. Depth of Mercy.

CHAS. WESLEY.   J. STEVENSON.

1. { Depth of mer-cy, can there be Mer-cy still re-serv'd for me?
    Can my God His wrath for-bear, Me, the chief of sin-ners, spare? }

{ God is love, I know, I feel;
   Je-sus weeps and loves me still; } Je-sus weeps, He weeps and loves me still.

2. I have long withstood His grace;
Long provoked Him to His face;
Would not hearken to His calls;
Grieved Him by a thousand falls.

3. Now incline me to relent;
Let me now my sin lament;
Now my foul revolt deplore,
Weep, believe and sin no more.

4. There for me the Saviour stands;
Shows his wounds and spreads his **hands**;
God is love, I know, I feel;
Jesus weeps and loves me still.

90. Power of Other Days.

VICTOR STRANGE.   EVANGEL.

1. Where is the pow'r of oth-er days, Our fath-ers used to feel;
2. Thine own in-dwell-ing pres-ence, Lord, Which thus our fa-thers blest;
3. The gar-land of thy grace im-part, Bid us no lon-ger roam;

The flam-ing fire whose sa-cred blaze Did their de-vo-tions seal?
A - lone can fill the might-y void With-in their chil-dren's breast;
But stamp thine im - age on our hearts And seal us thus thine own;

Where is the con - fi-dence in God That did their souls in-spire,
Then spread thy wings. O, heav'n-ly Dove, A - gain to earth come down,
In this thine own ap-point-ed hour Thy full-ness we would prove,

And made them sing of cleans-ing blood, While flood and flame rose higher?
And with the di - a - dem of love, Our soul-less du-ties crown.
Dis - play a - new thy glo-rious power, And fill our hearts with love.

Copyright, 1899, by T. H. Nelson.

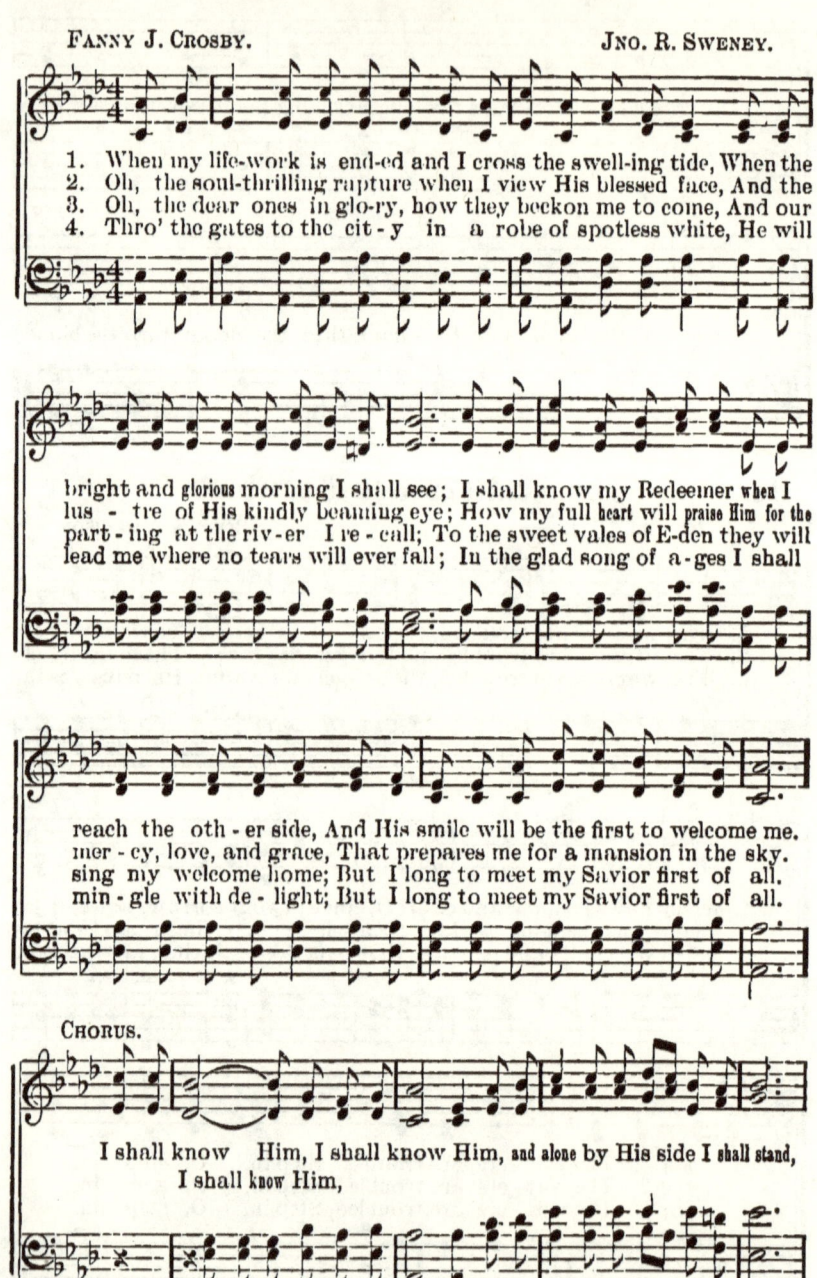

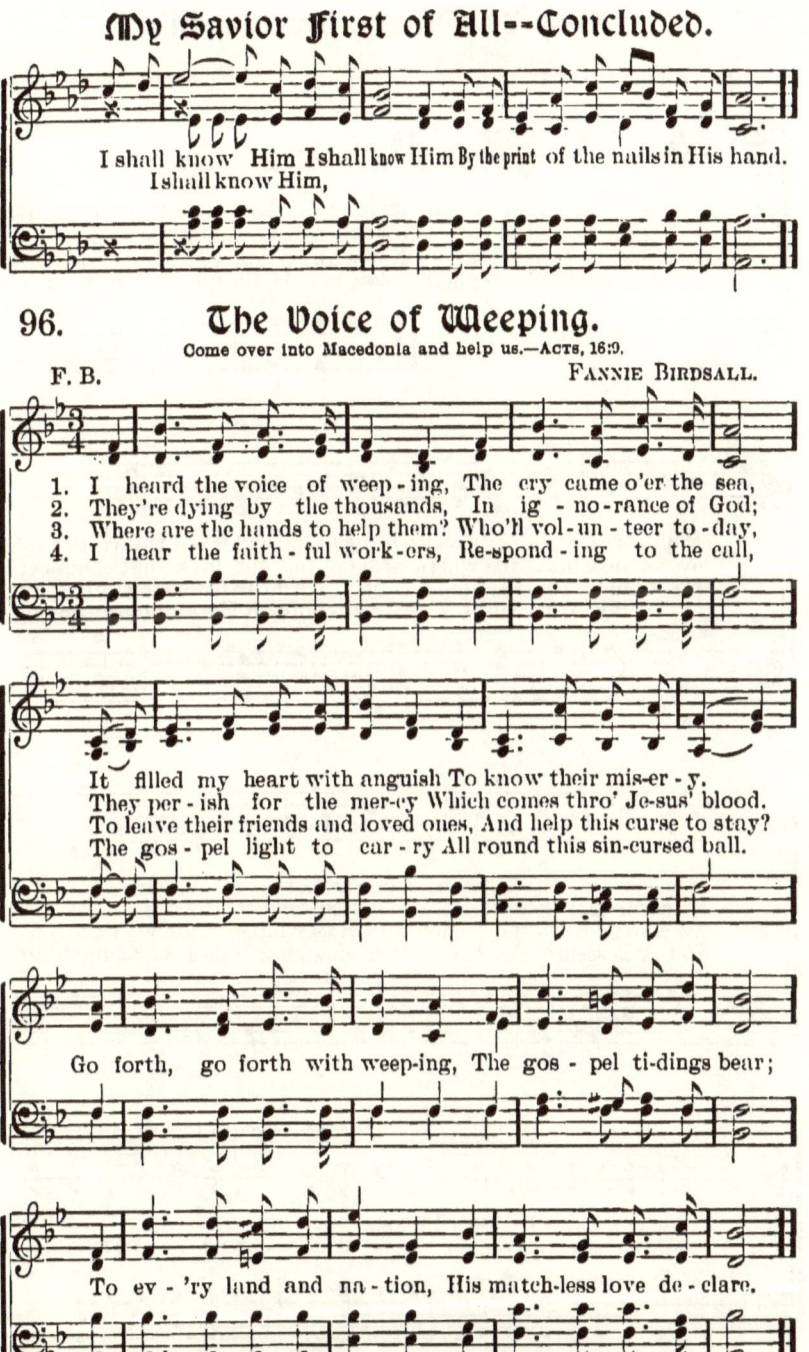

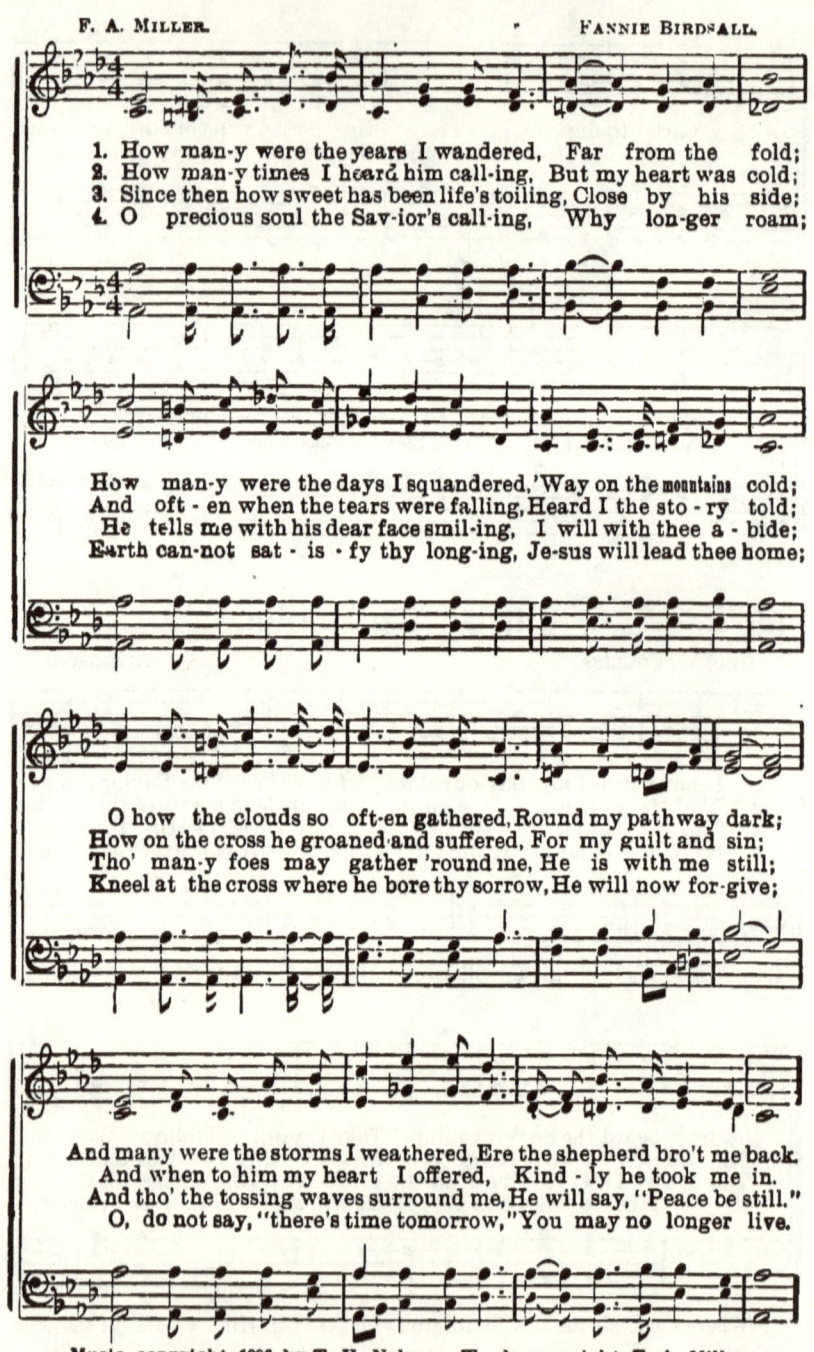

The Wanderer's Return--Concluded.

Wan-der-er, if you but knew what glory, Fills this heart of mine;
How gladly would you hear my story, Then bow at mercy's shrine.

100 Behold! A Stranger.

JOSEPH GRIGG. H. K. OLIVER.

1. Behold! a Stranger's at the door; He gently knocks, has knocked before;
2. But will He prove a friend indeed? He will, the very Friend you need;
3. Oh; lovely at-ti-tude!—He stands With melting heart and laden hands;
4. Admit Him ere His an-ger burn; His feet depart-ed, ne'er return;

Has waited long, is wait-ing still; You treat no other friend so ill.
The Man of Naz-a-reth—'tis He, With garments dyed at Calvary.
Oh, matchless kindness! and He shows This matchless kindness to His foes.
Admit Him, or the hour's at hand When at His door denied you'll stand.

101. The Coming of The Lord.

A. M. B.   A. M. BEAN. By per.

1. There's an awful time of trouble Such as men have never known, When God shall call the nations, To gather at his throne, And when that time shall come the saints shall lift their heads and cry;
2. Jesus said "you'd know 'twas summer, When you'd see the fig tree bloom, So likewise you'd know the end was near, When he should come again, When at midnight's lonely hour, We should hear that awful cry,
3. How oft we ask each other, I wonder when he'll come; I get so tired of waiting, It surely wont be long, For the angel said he'd come again, The day he went on high;
4. The last they ever saw him, 'Twas up at Bethany; His disciples gathered 'round him, To hear what he might say; He raised his hands to bless them, As a chariot swept by,
5. We soon shall hear the trumpet, That shall peal so loud and long; It will wake the buried nations, In the sea and under ground; When at midnight, startled millions, Will to their windows fly;

The Coming of The Lord--Concluded.

For him we've long been waiting, But his coming draweth nigh.
Go out, ye saints to meet him, For his coming draweth nigh.
And Je-sus said, "keep watching, For my coming draweth nigh.
And took him up to hea-ven, But he's coming by and by.
To see the world on fire, And the Sav-ior drawing nigh.

CHORUS.

For the coming of the Lord, For the coming of the Lord, For the coming of the Lord draweth nigh, When this world shall be on fire, and the dead shall rise a-gain, For the coming of the Lord draweth nigh.

CHORUS. **He Lives For Me--Concluded.**

He lives and I shall nev-er die, He lives to give a home on high;
Let saints their loudest anthems raise In songs of ev-er-last-ing praise.

103. Love Found Me.

H. L. GILMOUR. Arr. by H. L. G.

1. { When out in sin, and darkness lost, Love found me; My fainting soul was
     I heard the Savior's words so blest, Love found me; Come weary, heav-y

tempest toss'd, Love found me; } Oh, 'twas love, love,
la-den rest, Love found me. } Oh, 'twas love, 'twas wondrous love,

CHORUS.

Love that moved the mighty God, Love, love, 'twas love found me.

2. The Spirit rous'd me from my sleep,
   Conviction seiz'd me strong and deep,
   Although I long withstood His grace,
   He wooed me to His kind embrace,

3. I'll praise Him while He gives me breath,
   Love, etc.
   For saving from an endless death,

Christ is my advocate above,
I'm yoked to Him in perfect love,

4. And when I reach the gold paved street,
   Love, etc.
   I'll sit adoring at His feet,
   And sing hosannas round the throne,
   Where I shall know as I am known.

Copyright, 1890, by H. L. Gilmour, by per.

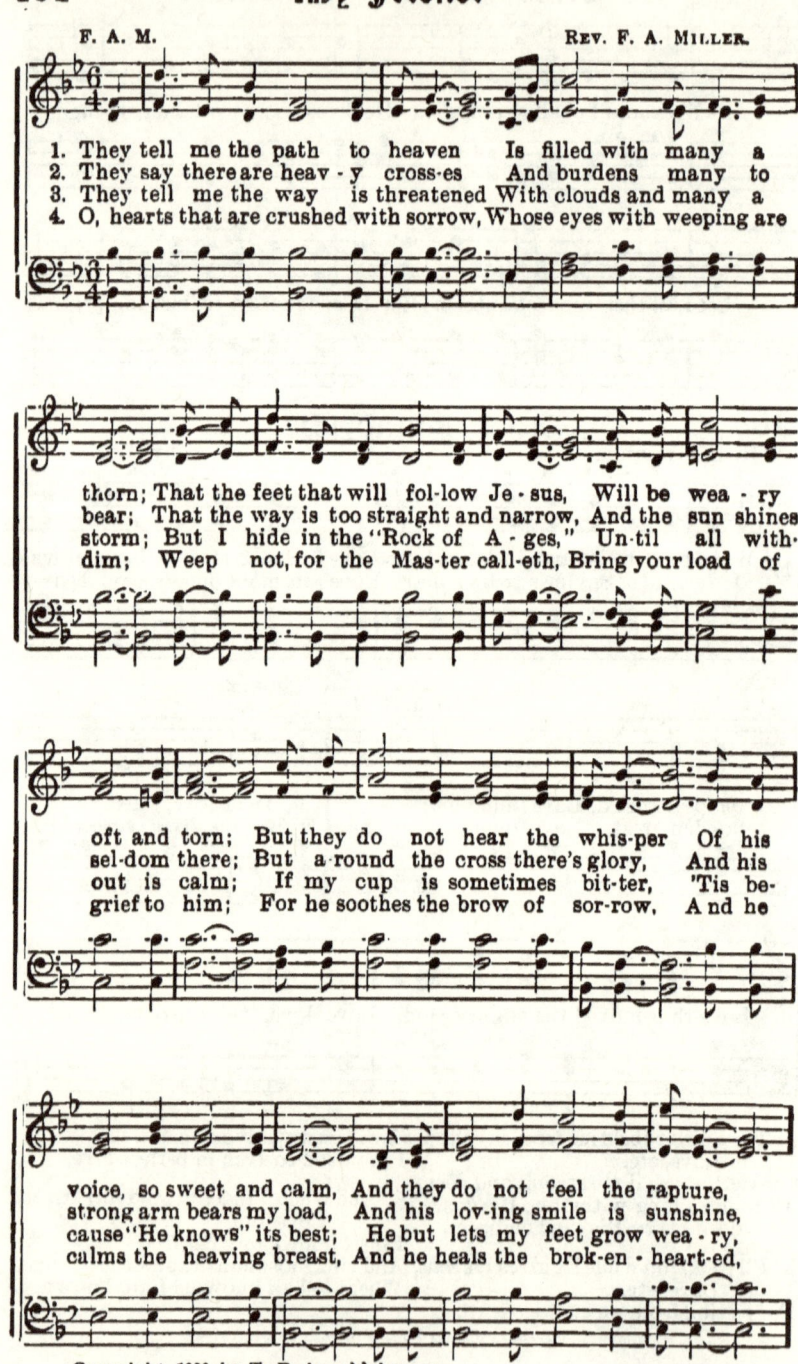

My Friend--Concluded.

105. **What a Friend.**

1. What a Friend we have in Jesus,
   All our sins and griefs to bear!
What a privilege to carry
   Everything to God in prayer!
Oh, what peace we often forfeit,
   Oh, what needless pain we bear,
All because we do not carry
   Everything to God in prayer!

2. Have we trials and temptations?
   Is there trouble anywhere?
We should never be discouraged
   Take it to the Lord in prayer.
Can we find a friend so faithful
   Who will all our sorrows share?
Jesus knows our every weakness,
   Take it to the Lord in prayer.

3. Are we weak and heavy laden,
   Cumbered with a load of care?—
Precious Savior, still our refuge,—
   Take it to the Lord in prayer.
Do thy friends despise, forsake thee?
   Take it to the Lord in prayer;
In His arms He'll take and shield thee;
   Thou wilt find a solace there.

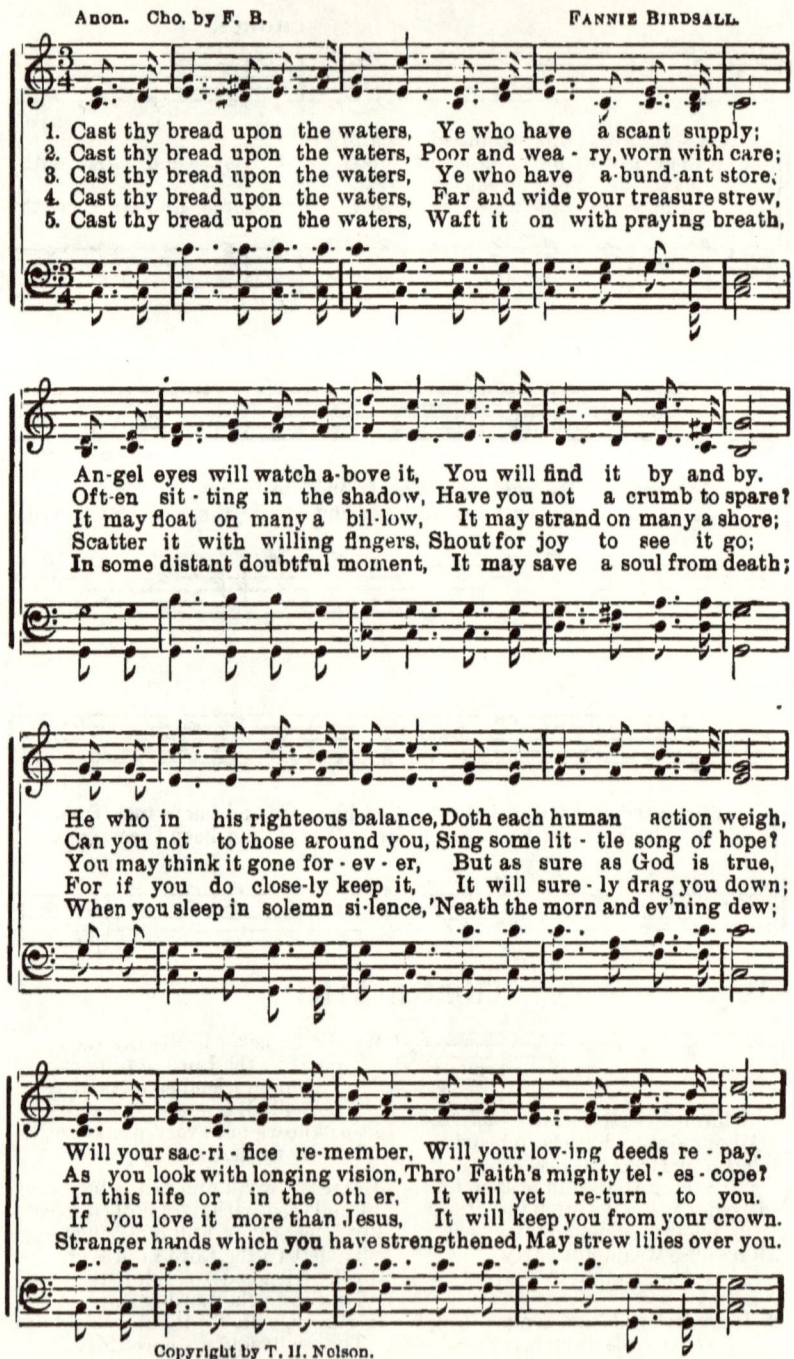

Cast Thy Bread--Concluded.

CHORUS.

Cast thy bread up-on the waters, Send it with a glad a-men;
In this life or in the other, It shall come to you a-gain.

107 Come ye That Love the Lord.

ISAAC WATTS.   Arranged.

1. Come ye that love the Lord, And let your joys be known;
2. Let those re-fuse to sing Who nev-er knew our God;
3. Then let our songs abound, And ev'-ry tear be dry;

CHO.—I'm glad sal-va-tion's free, I'm glad sal-va-tion's free;

Join in a song with sweet accord, While ye surround the throne.
But children of the heav'nly King May speak their joys abroad.
We're marching thro' Immanuel's ground To fair-er worlds on high.

Sal-va-tion's free for you and me, I'm glad sal-va-tion's free.

My Sacrifice--Concluded.

Then mag-ni-fy the Sa - vior, For His gra-cious fa - vor;
His matchless name, love the same
Tell to all the earth abroad, That Je - sus saves.
Jesus comes to save.

114. Joy to the World.

ISAAC WATTS. Tune, ANTIOCH. C. M.

1. Joy to the world! The Lord has come; Let earth re-ceive her King;
{ Let ev' ry heart }
{ pre - pare Him room, } And heaven and na - ture sing, And
And heaven and nature
heaven and nature sing, And heaven, And heaven and na - ture sing.
sing, And heaven and nature sing.

2. Joy to the world! the Savior reigns;
Let men their songs employ,
While fields and floods, rocks, hills and plains,
Repeat the sounding joy.

3. He rules the world with truth and grace,
And makes the nations prove
The glories of His righteousness,
And wonders of His love.

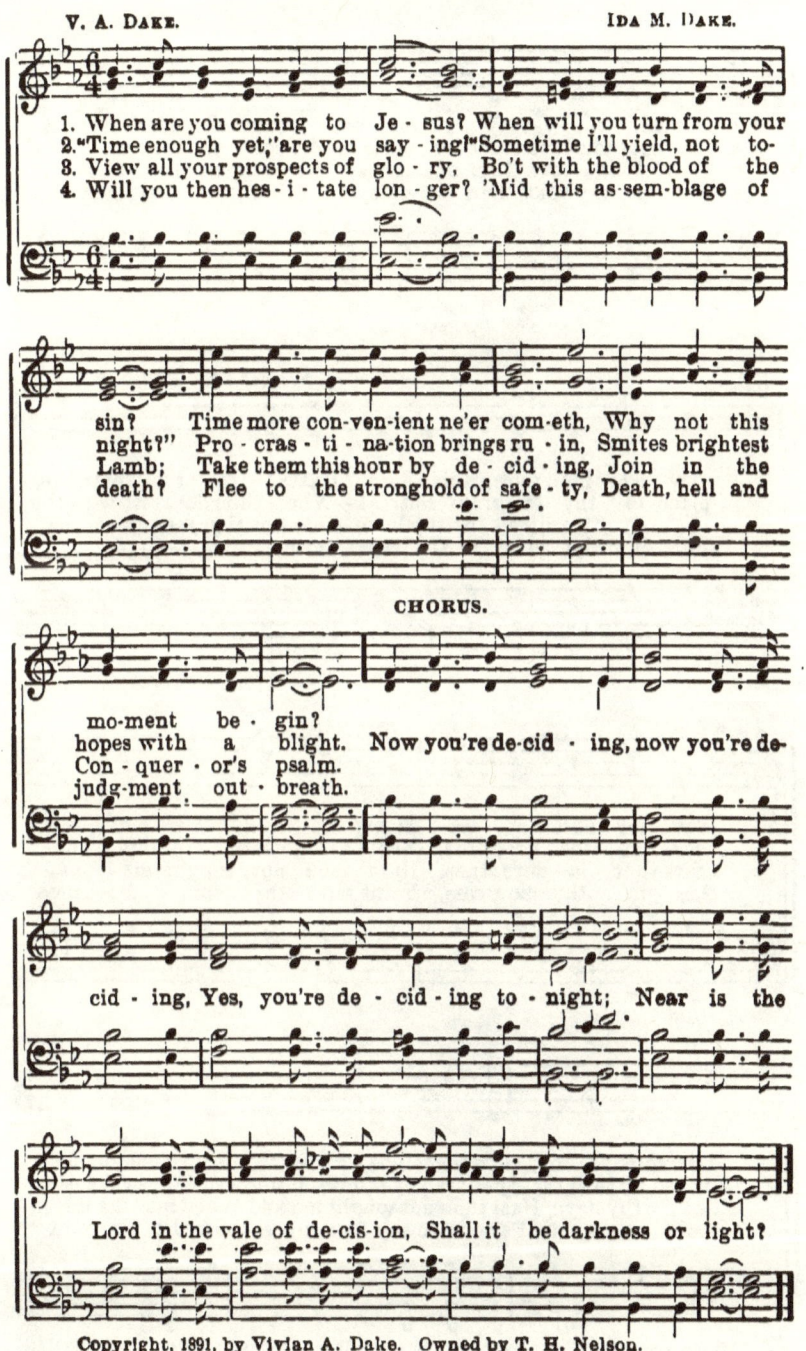

Only for Souls--Concluded.

sin's dark blight, Souls all ex-posed to e-ter-nal night, O, haste to the res-cue for time swift-ly rolls, On-ly for souls, on-ly for souls.

---

120   **Satisfied.**

1 All my life long I had panted
  For a draught from some cool spring
That I hoped would quench the burn-
    ing
Of the thirst I felt within.

CHORUS.

Hallelujah! I have found it—
  What my soul so long has craved!
Jesus satisfies my longings;
  Through his blood I now am saved.

2 Feeding on the husks around me,
  Till my strength was almost gone;
Longed my soul for something better
  Only still to hunger on.

3 Poor I was and sought for riches,
  Something that would satisfy;
But the dust I gathered round me
  Only mocked my soul's sad cry.

4 Well of water ever springing—
  Bread of life so rich and free—
Untold wealth that never faileth—
  My Redeemer is to me.

                          Clara Tear.

123. At Evening Time it Shall be Light.

Thomas H. Nelson.   Flora B. Nelson.

Copyright, 1899, by T. H. Nelson.

At Evening Time--Concluded.

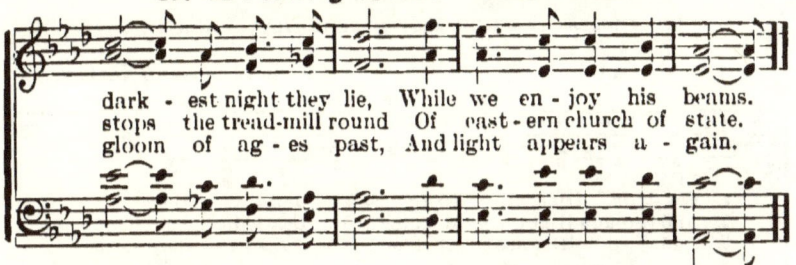

dark - est night they lie, While we en - joy his beams.
stops the tread-mill round Of east - ern church of state.
gloom of ag - es past, And light appears a - gain.

4. The swarthy sons of India
  Shall soon His praises sing,
  And bring the Ganges worshipers
  To Christ, the Lord and King.
  Australia's devil worshippers
  At peace with God shall be,
  For light must break on every land
  And island of the sea.

5 Ye favored nations of the west,
  On whom this light now shines,
  Come, help us to reflect the flame
  To darkened eastern climes;
  Send on the finest of your flocks,
  The child that sweetest sings,
  And ye, who have no child, send gold
  For missionary wings.

124 Christ For The World.

EMLICE GIARDINI.

1. "Christ for the world," we sing; The world to Christ we bring
2. "Christ for the world," we sing; The world to Christ we bring
4. "Christ for the world," we sing; The world to Christ we bring

With love and zeal; The poor, and them that mourn, The faint and
With fervent prayer; The wayward and the lost, By rest - less
With joy - ful song; The newborn souls, whose days, Reclaimed from

o - ver-borne, Sin-sick and sor-row-worn, Whom Christ doth heal.
pas - sion toss'd, Redeemed at countless cost, From dark de - spair.
er - ror's ways, Inspired with hope and praise, To Christ be - long.

Chorus of Praise--Concluded.

CHORUS.

Let the mor-ning stars sing, Let the loud an-thems ring,
Let all that hath breath catch the word, - - - -
Let the worlds join the song, Let cre - a - tion's vast throng,
Swell the an - thems of praise to the Lord.

Copyrighted by Thomas H. Nelson, 1896.

126 **Redeemed.**

I know that the light of His presence
With me doth continually dwell.

1 Redeemed, how I love to proclaim it,
Redeemed by the blood of the Lamb;
Redeemed thro' His infinite mercy,
His child and forever I am.

REF.—Redeemed, redeemed,
Redeemed by the blood of the Lamb,
Redeemed, redeemed,
His child and forever I am.

2 Redeemed, and so happy in Jesus,
No language my rapture can tell,

3 I think of my blessed Redeemer,
I think of Him all the day long,
I sing, for I cannot be silent,
His love is the theme of my song.

3 I know there's a crown that is wait-ing
In yonder bright mansion for me,
And soon, with the spirits made perfect,
At home with the Lord I shall be.

By per. Wm. J. Kirkpatrick. From "Finest of the Wheat."

129. Coming Back Again.

ARRANGED FOR THIS WORK.

1. How sweet are the tidings that greet the pilgrim's ear, As he wan-ders an ex-ile from home; Soon, soon shall the King in His glo-ry ap-pear, and soon will the king-dom come.
2. The mos-sy old graves where the pil-grims slept, Will be o-pened as wide as be-fore; And the mill-ions that sleep in the might-y deep, Shall live on this earth once more.
3. Then we'll meet all the loved ones in that E-den home, Sweet songs of re-demp-tion we'll sing; From the north, from the south, all the ransomed shall come To worship their heavenly King.
4. Our bless-ed Re-deem-er is com-ing a-gain, And we'll meet Him ere long in the air. O, be faith-ful, be hope-ful, be joy-ful till then, And a crown of bright glo-ry we'll wear.

CHORUS.

He is coming, coming, com-ing soon, I know, Coming back to this earth a-gain, And the

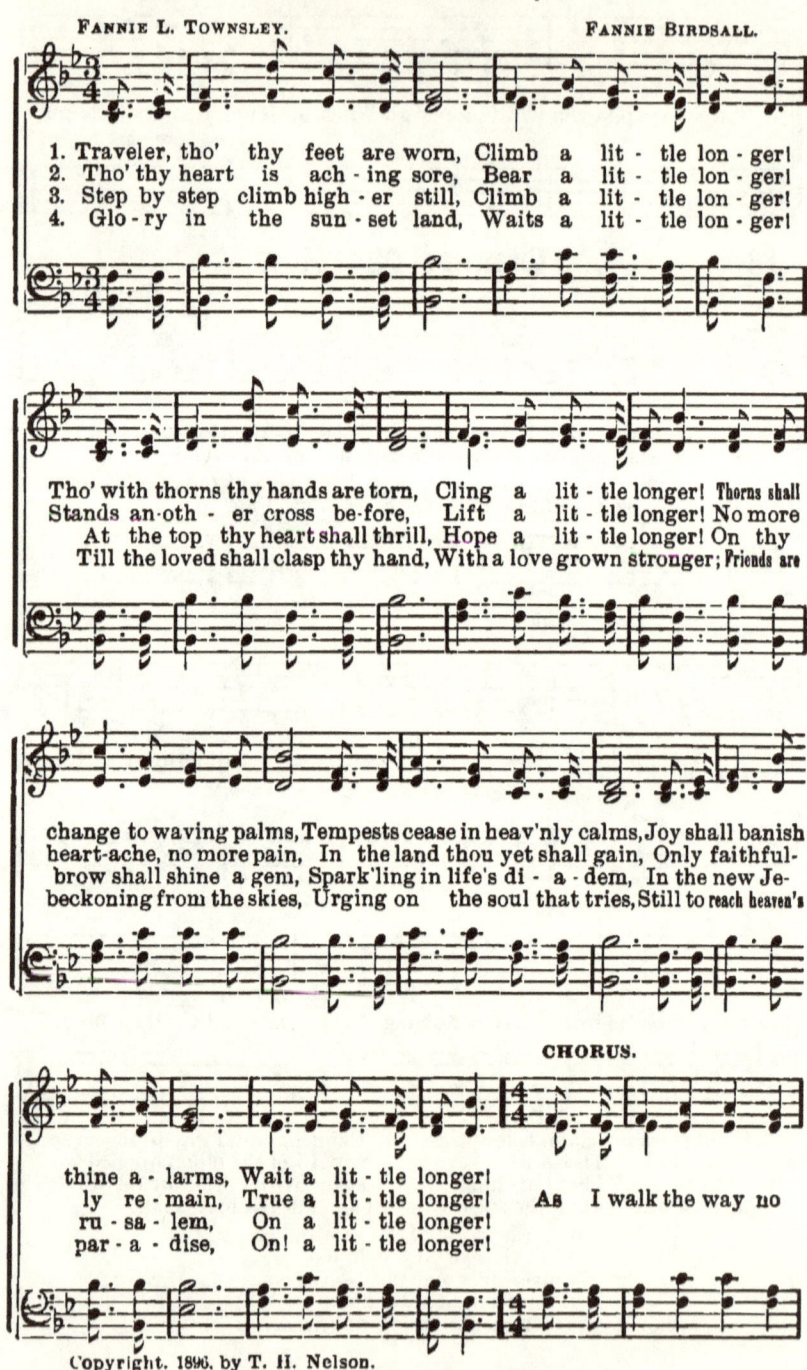

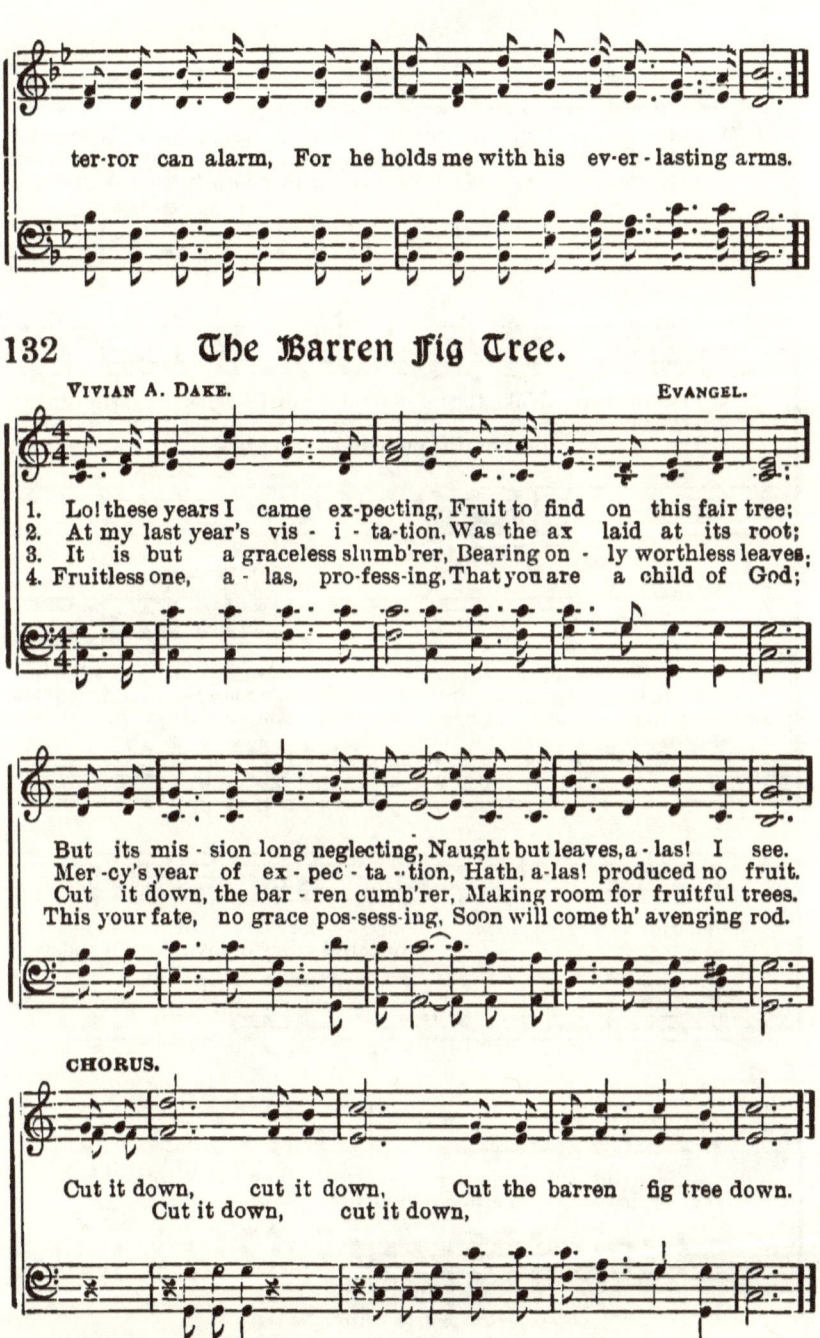

My Beloved--Concluded.

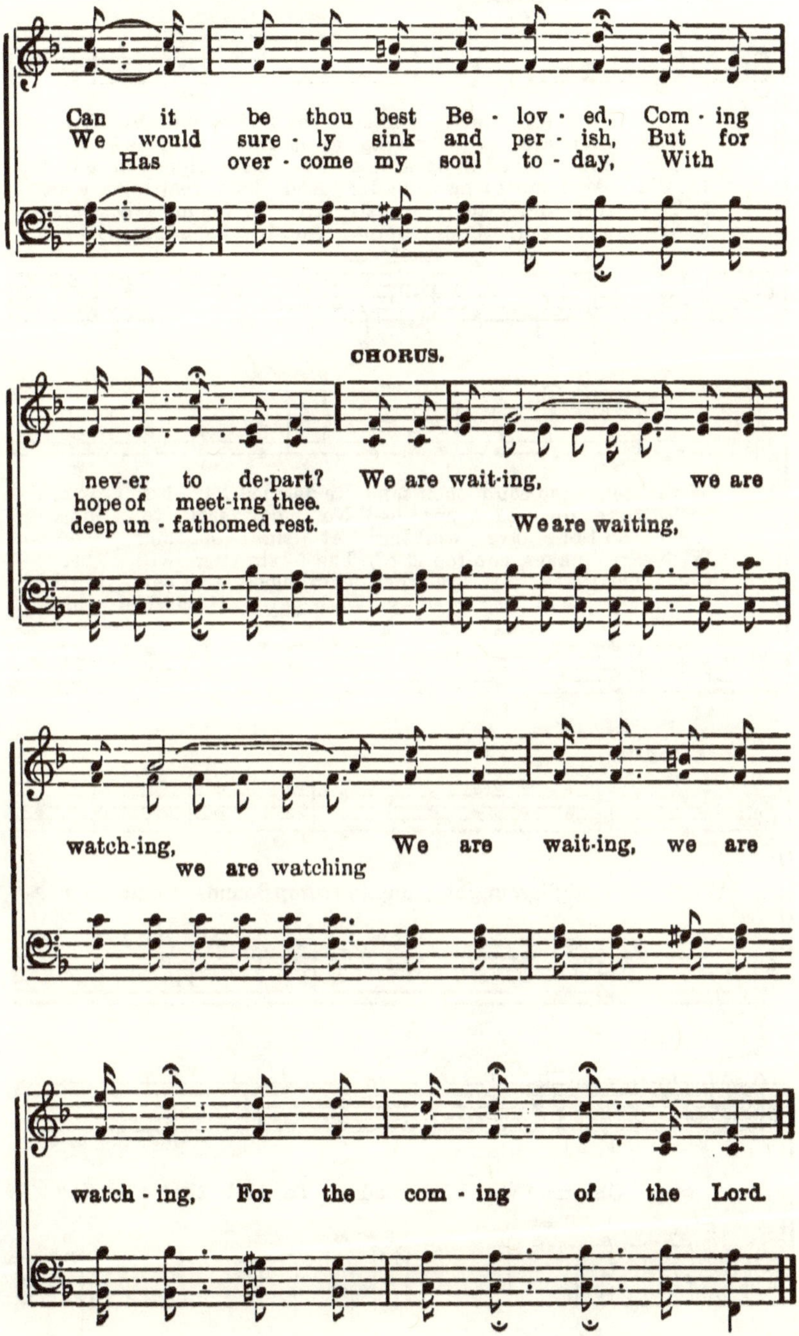

Can it be thou best Beloved, Coming
We would surely sink and perish, But for
Has overcome my soul today, With

CHORUS.

nev-er to depart? We are waiting, we are
hope of meeting thee.
deep unfathomed rest. We are waiting,

watching, We are waiting, we are
we are watching

watching, For the coming of the Lord.

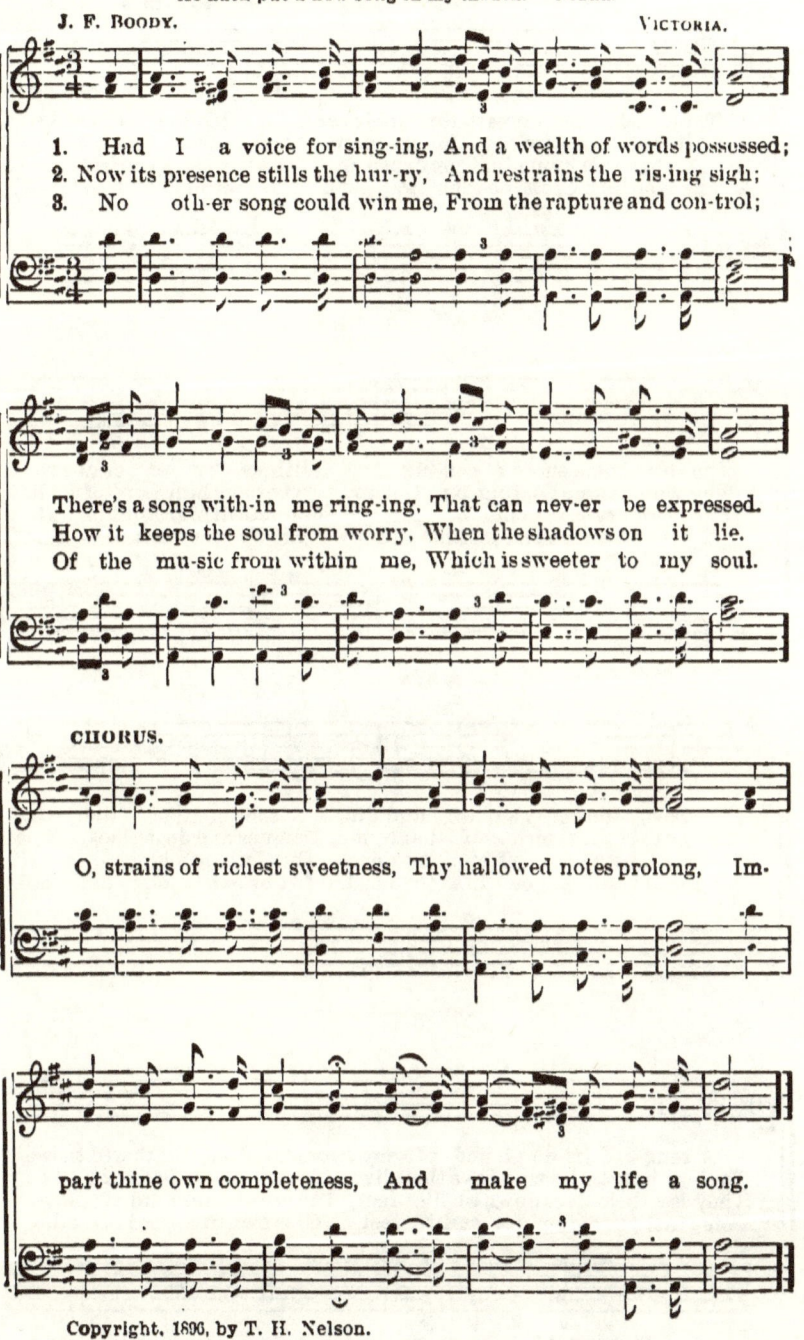

Crown Him.

138

L. M. LATIMER.   FANNIE BIRDSALL.

1. They hushed their breath that noble band, To catch the last fare-well,
2. "All hail the pow'r of Je-sus' name," And clear as bu-gle call,
3. A bat-tle hymn that song sped on, The world for Christ the call,
4. The Southern Cross be-gins to bend The morning dawns at last;

The dear home shore re-ced-ing fast With ev-'ry o-cean swell.
The words came floating on the air, "O crown him Lord of all."
For ev-'ry is-land of the sea Shall crown him Lord of all.
I-dol and shrine and mosque and tow'r At Je-sus' feet are cast.

A-bove the cit-y's noise and din, A song rose on the air,
They caught the spir-it of that hymn, Dan-ger and death looked small
On Af-ric's far off sun-ny slopes, By Chi-na's king-ly wall,
Tri-umph-ant Zi-on lift thy head, Let ev-'ry bur-den fall,

A song of tri-umph and of joy, From loved ones gathered there.
To those brave ones who gave their lives, To crown him Lord of all.
They lay their lives down at his feet, To crown him Lord of all.
Come cast your tro-phies at his feet, And crown him Lord of all.

Copyright by T. H. Nelson.

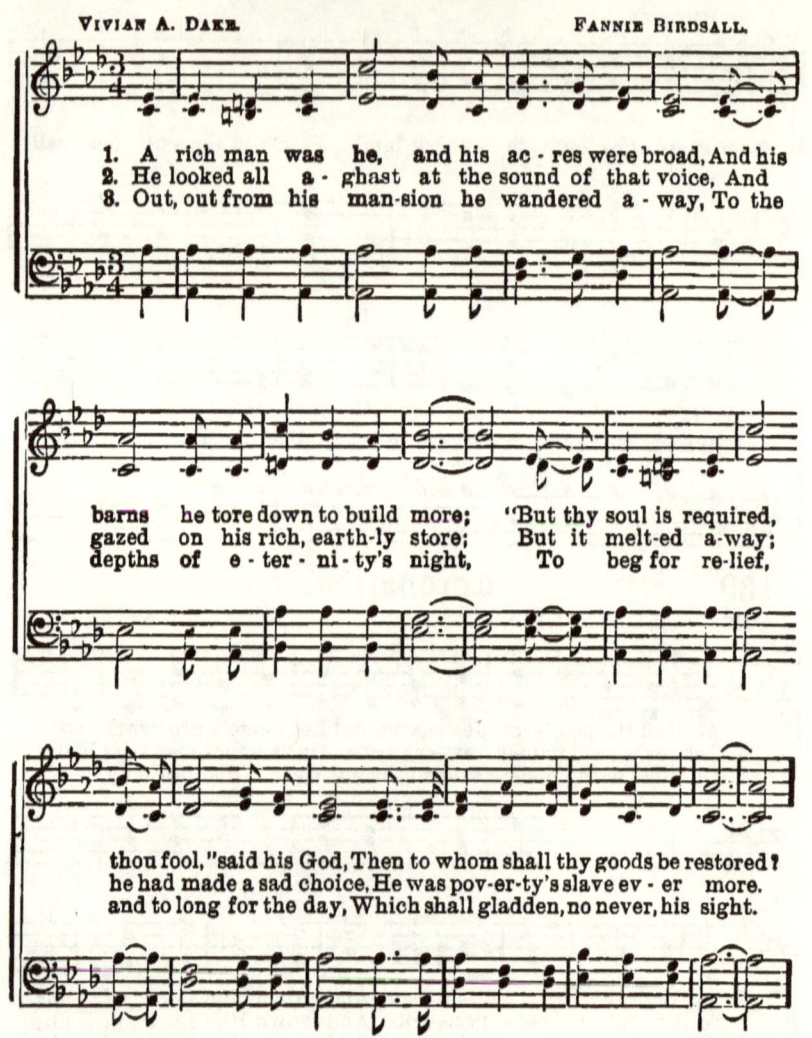

Eternity's Beggar--Concluded.

warning, he turned it a-way; O, sin-ner! then list to the voice of thy God, And turn to the Lord while you may.

Ritard.

141 The Fullness.

T. H. NELSON. FLORA BIRDSALL NELSON.

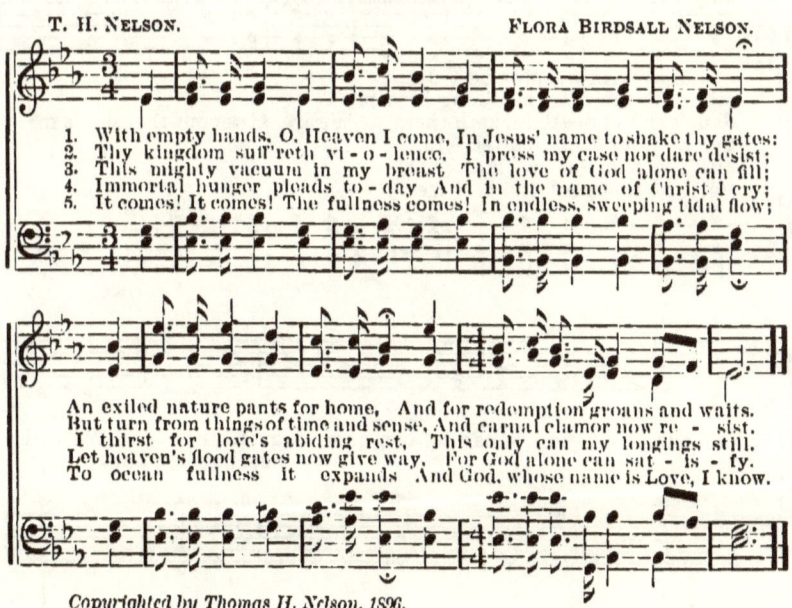

1. With empty hands, O, Heaven I come, In Jesus' name to shake thy gates:
2. Thy kingdom suff'reth vi-o-lence, I press my case nor dare desist;
3. This mighty vacuum in my breast The love of God alone can fill;
4. Immortal hunger pleads to-day And in the name of Christ I cry;
5. It comes! It comes! The fullness comes! In endless, sweeping tidal flow;

An exiled nature pants for home, And for redemption groans and waits.
But turn from things of time and sense, And carnal clamor now re-sist.
I thirst for love's abiding rest, This only can my longings still.
Let heaven's flood gates now give way, For God alone can sat-is-fy.
To ocean fullness it expands And God, whose name is Love, I know.

Copyrighted by Thomas H. Nelson, 1896.

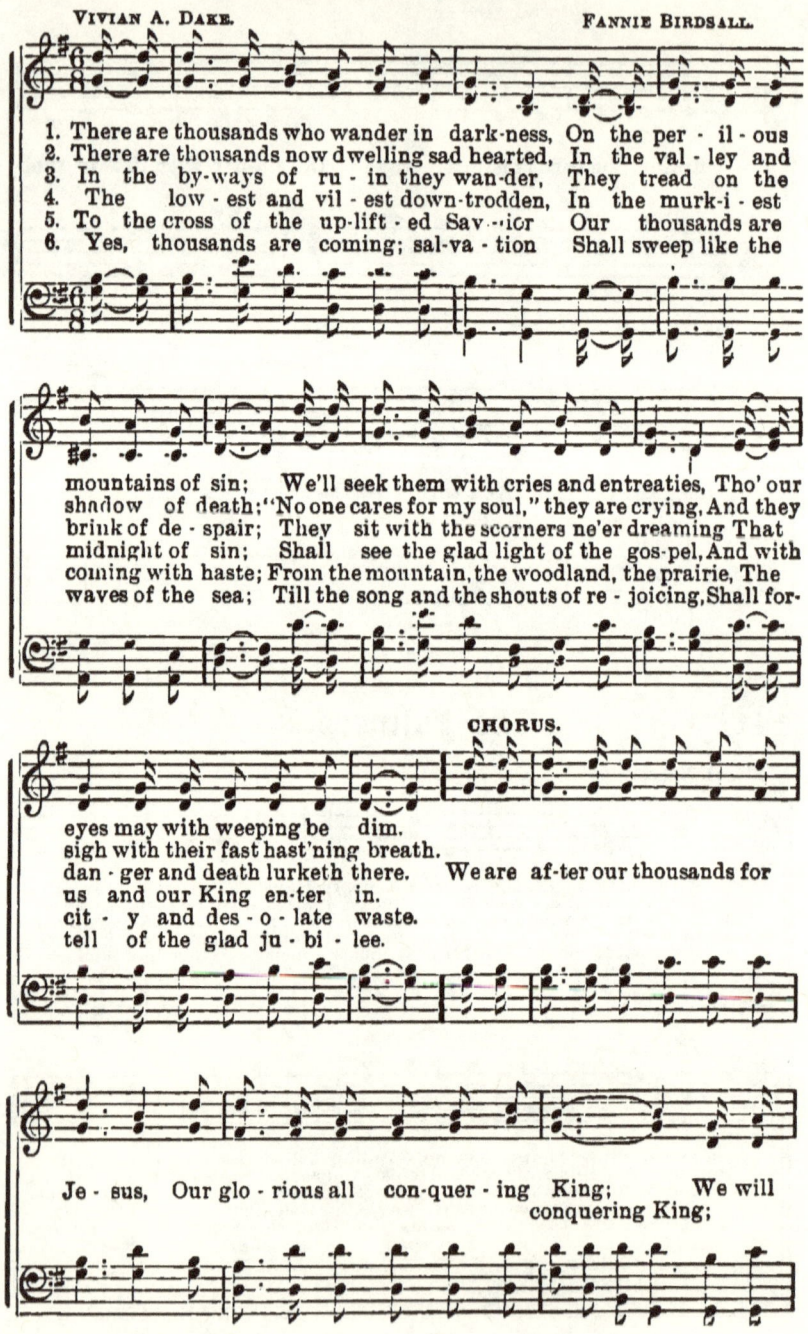

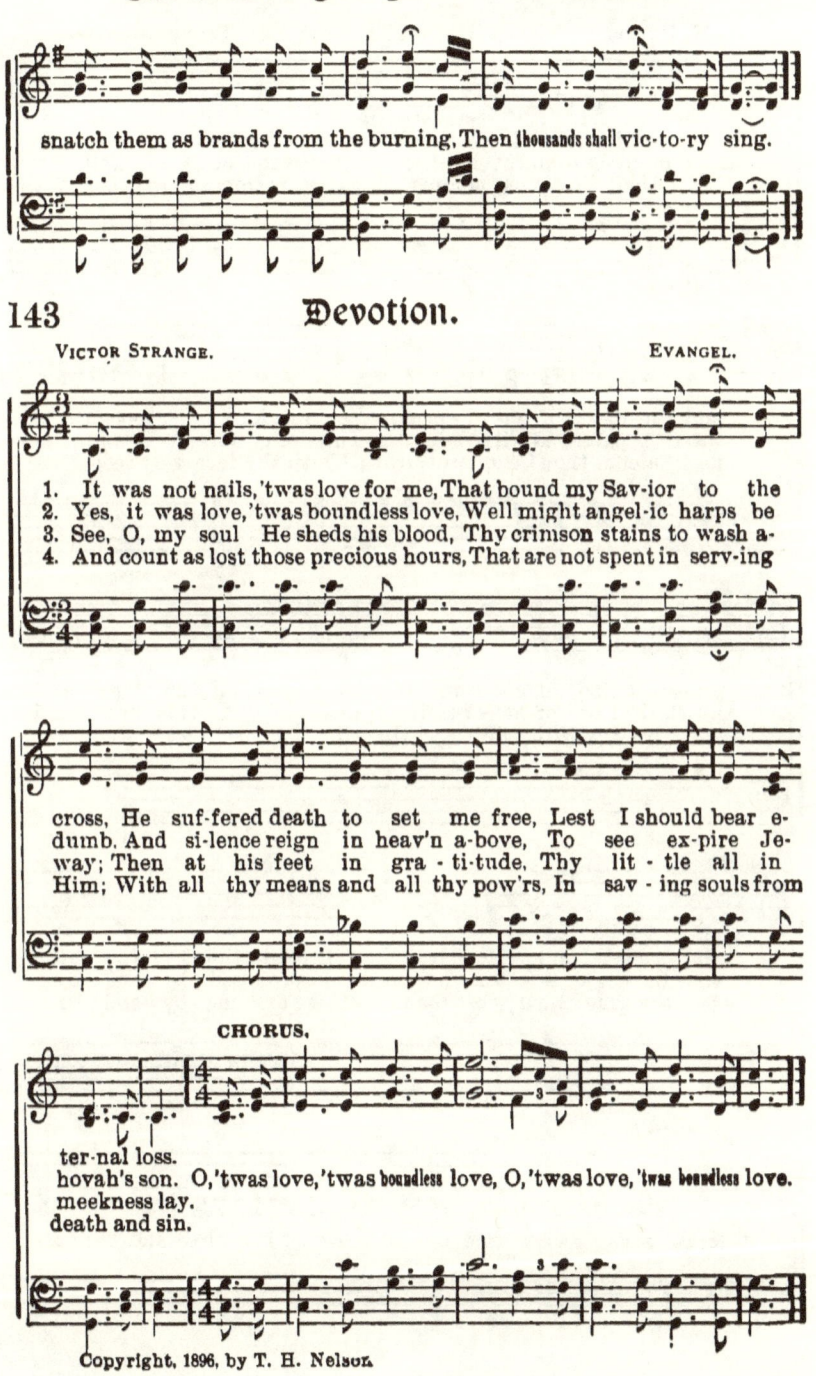

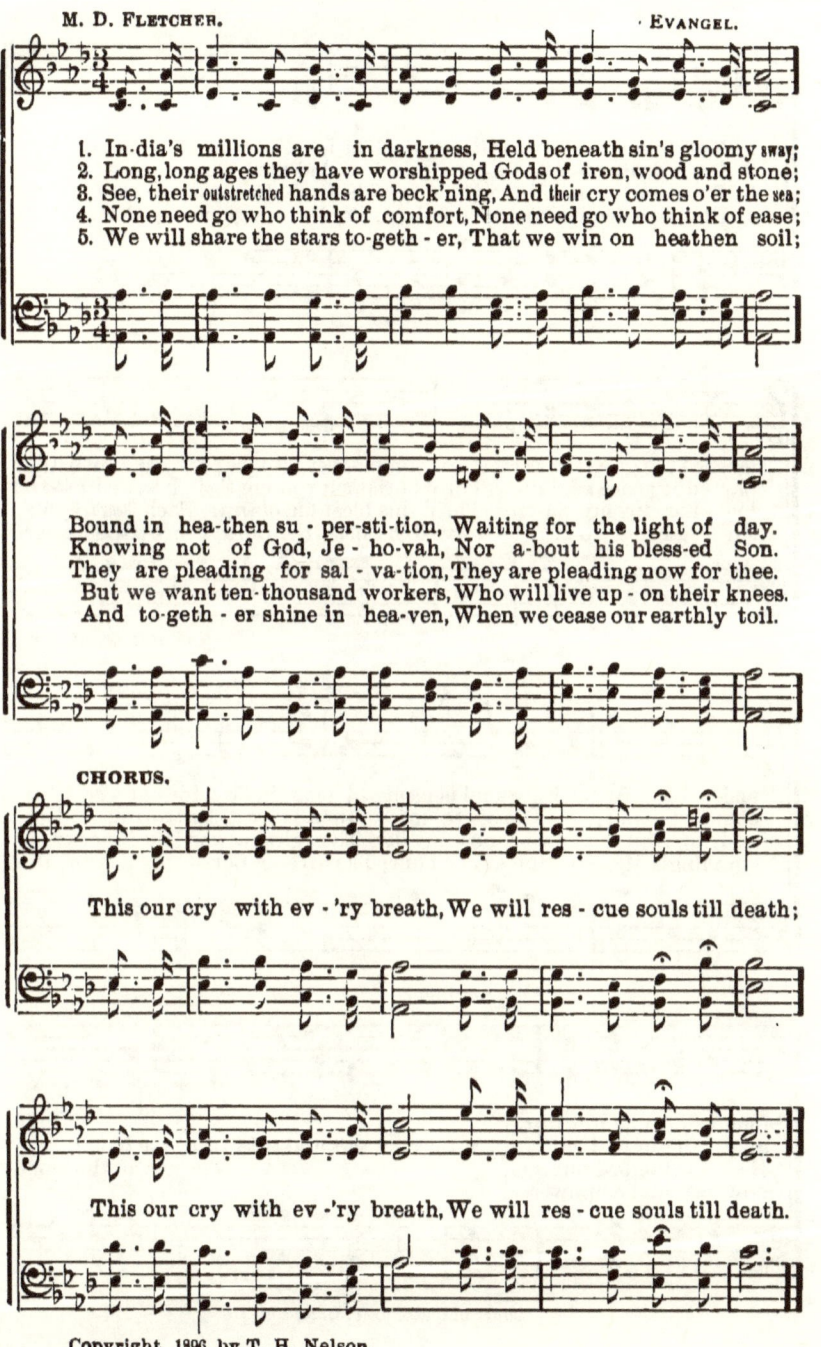

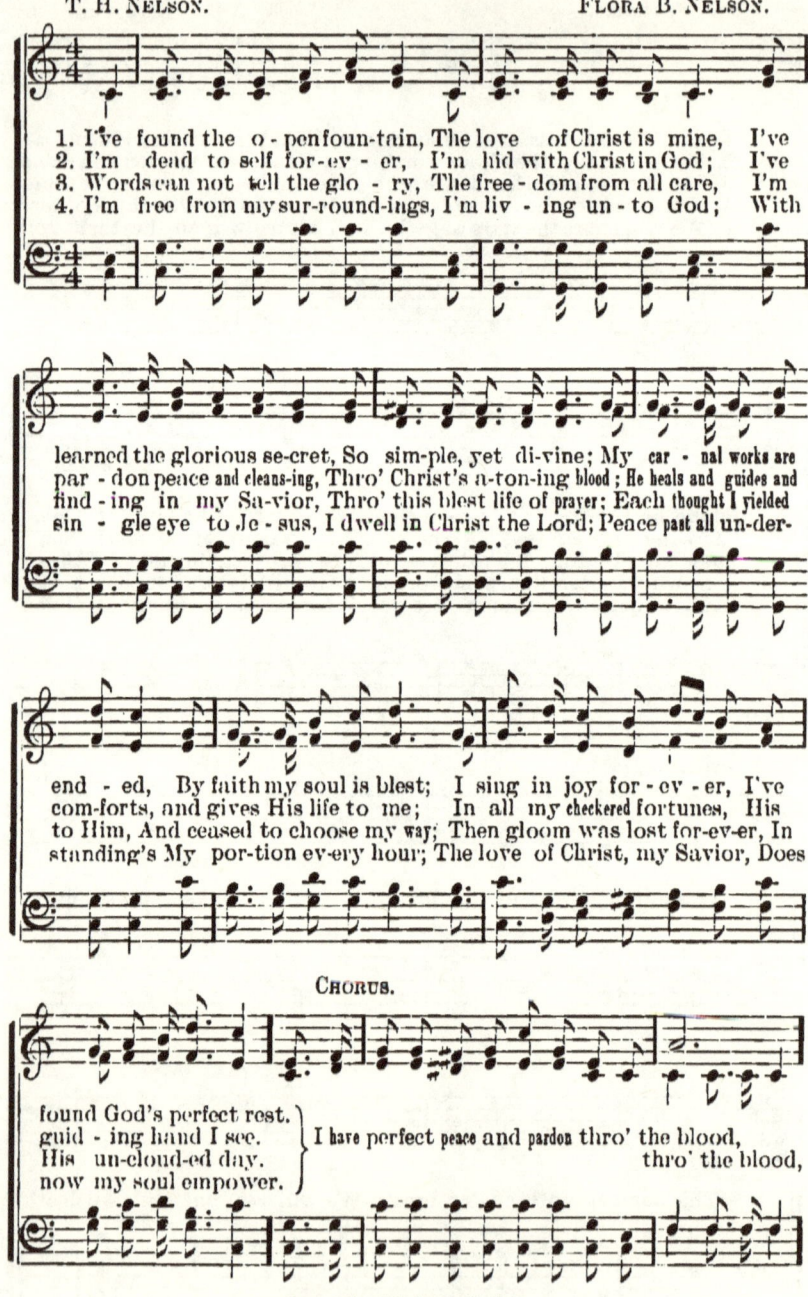

The Open Fountain--Concluded.

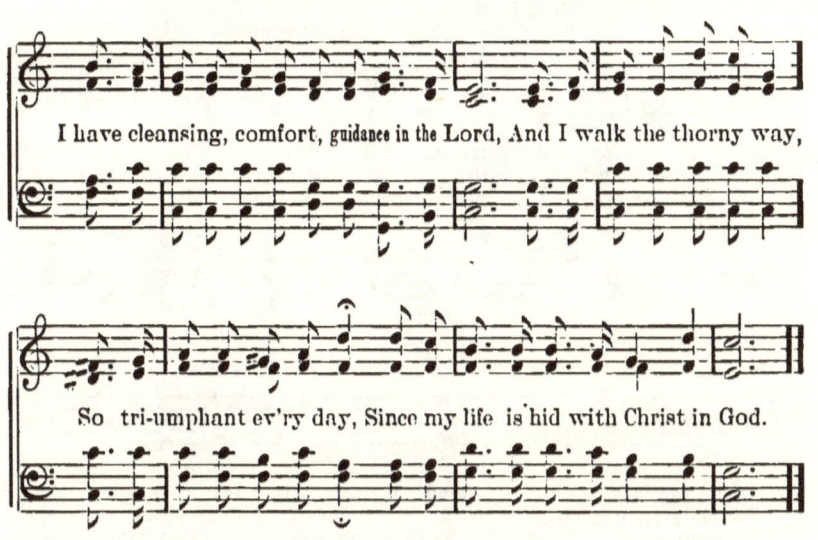

149. My Soul, Be On Thy Guard.

GEORGE HEATH.   DR. LOWELL MASON.

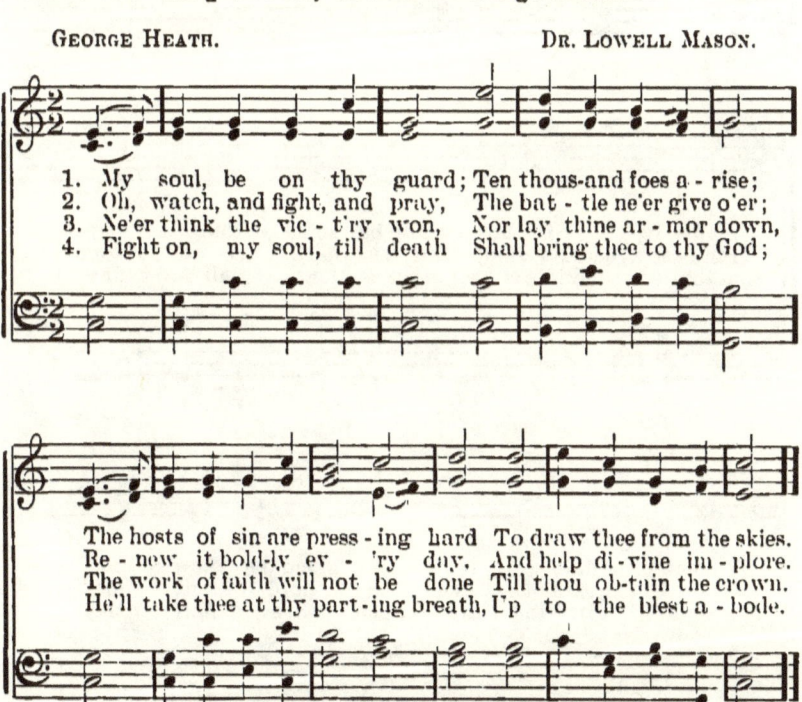

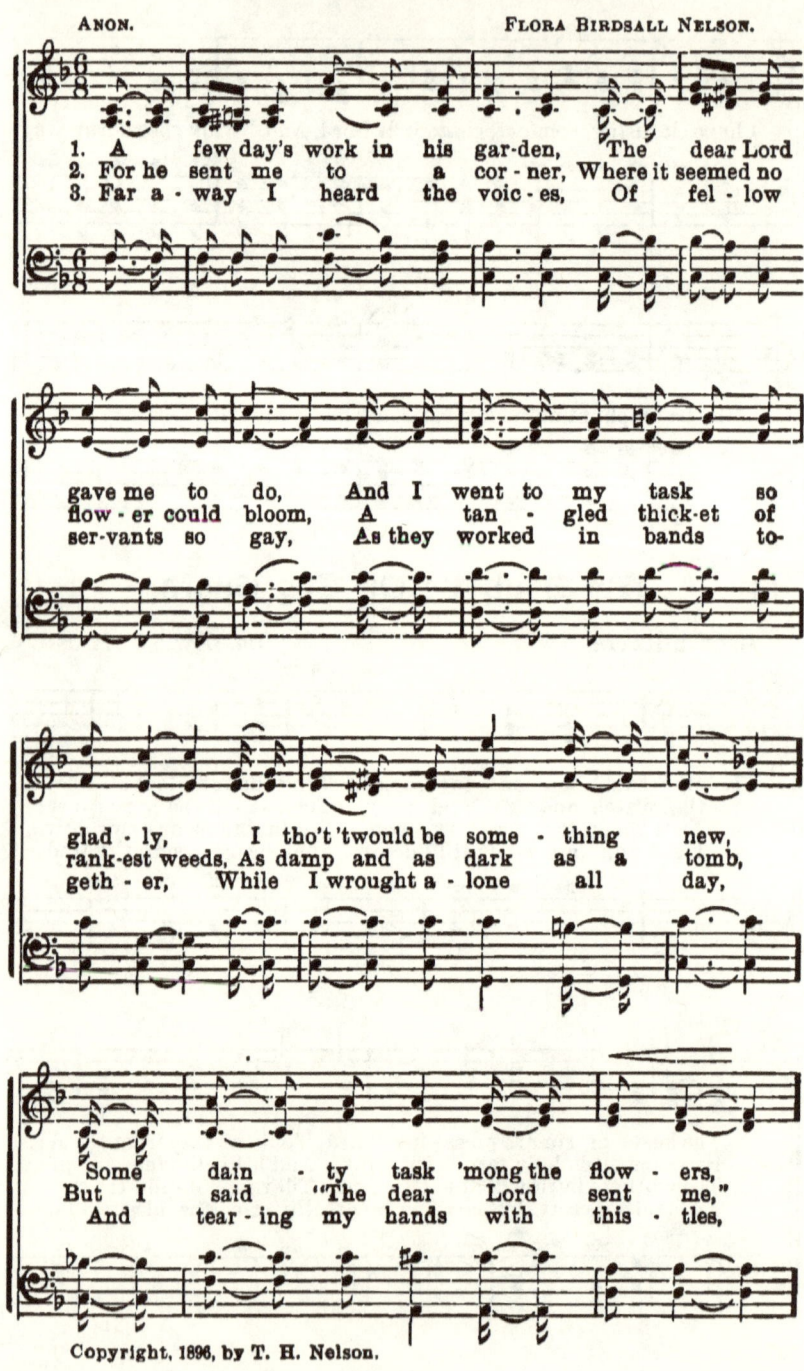

The Lord's Garden--Concluded.

That would show my skill and taste, But a-las! I sat
So in tears the task be-gun, In clean-ing
With heart so heav-y and sad, And nev-er a

Ritard.

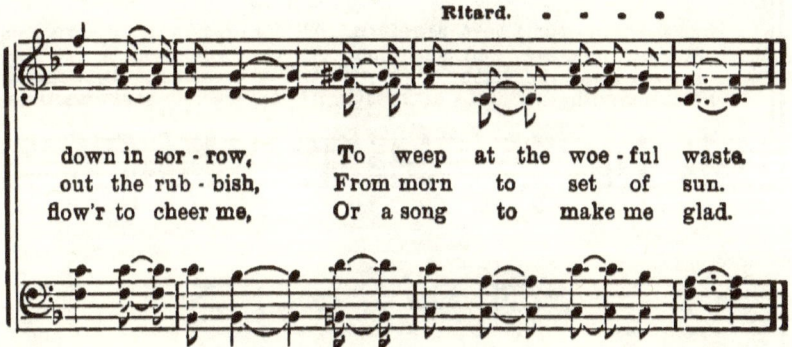

down in sor-row, To weep at the woe-ful waste.
out the rub-bish, From morn to set of sun.
flow'r to cheer me, Or a song to make me glad.

4 But slowly the task grew lighter,
  As I cleared the rubbish away,
And the soft brown earth lay open,
  To the light and warmth of day;
The Master came down at the nightfall,
  And gave me a smile so sweet,
I knew he was pleased with the service,
  Though so rough and incomplete.

5 For he said, "Dear heart, be patient,
  I bring you some seeds to sow,
In the soft brown soil, for watching
  To see that they thrive and grow."
So my heart grew light and gladsome,
  For the corner, dark and wild,
Where I'd wrought in tears and sadness,
  In growing loveliness smiled.

6 I watched and tended my corner,
  I gave it most faithful care,
In pruning and training the tender plants,
  Till they bloomed with fragrance rare.
The Master came to his garden,
  Again at set of sun,
And I ran with joy to meet him,
  For he said, "Dear child, well done,

7 For this dark, benighted corner,
  Was a grievous sight to see;
What you have wrought in toil and pain,
  Was a blessed work for me."
Forgotten was all the sorrow,
  Forgotten the lonely hours;
As I stood beside the Master,
  Who smiled upon the flowers.

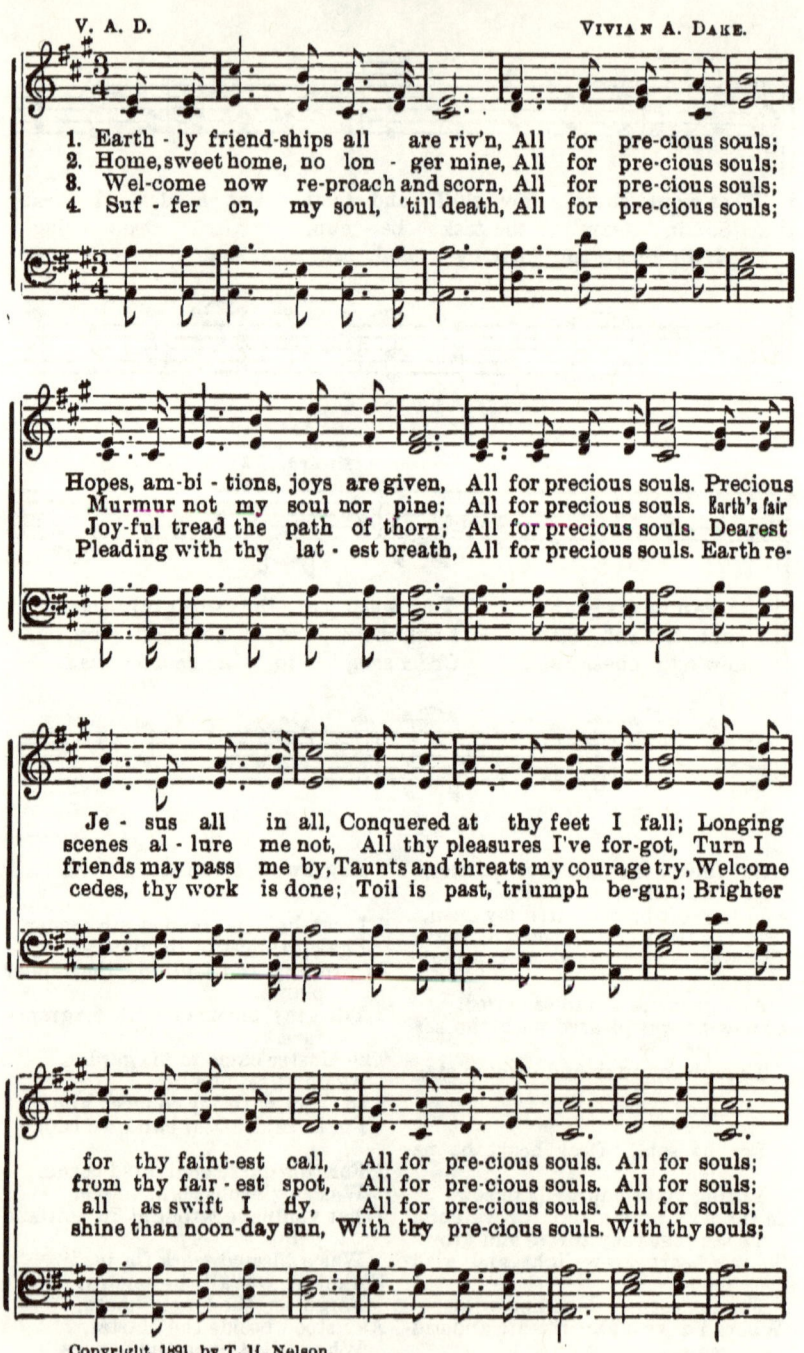

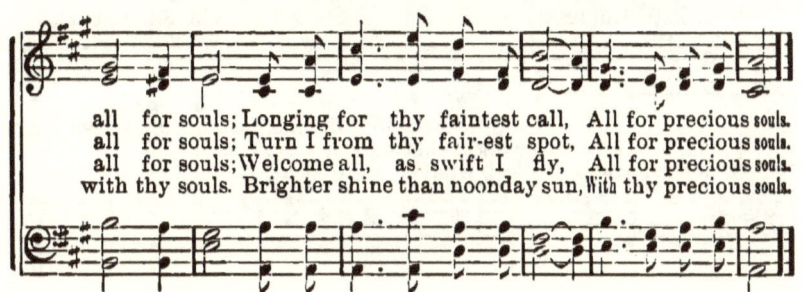

All for Precious Souls—Concluded.

all for souls; Longing for thy faintest call, All for precious souls.
all for souls; Turn I from thy fair-est spot, All for precious souls.
all for souls; Welcome all, as swift I fly, All for precious souls.
with thy souls. Brighter shine than noonday sun, With thy precious souls.

152 **All My Springs.**

T. H. NELSON.   VICTORIA.

1. All my springs are found in Thee, Low - ly
2. All my springs are found in Thee, Peace and
3. All my springs are found in Thee, Break earth's
4. All my springs are found in Thee, When the
5. All my springs are found in Thee, Though the

Lamb of God, Thou didst die to
joy and love; Thou dost ev - er
tend - 'rest tie; Joy - ful still my
world - lings frown, Far be - yond the
wild waves roar; Thou canst still the

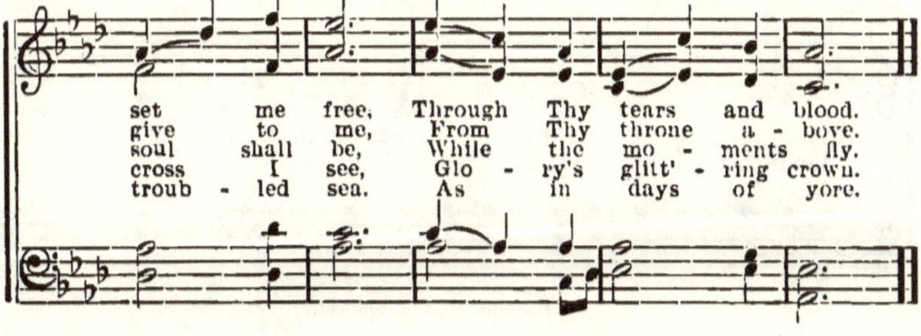

set me free, Through Thy tears and blood.
give to me, From Thy throne a - bove.
soul shall be, While the mo - ments fly.
cross I see, Glo - ry's glitt' - ring crown.
troub - led sea. As in days of yore.

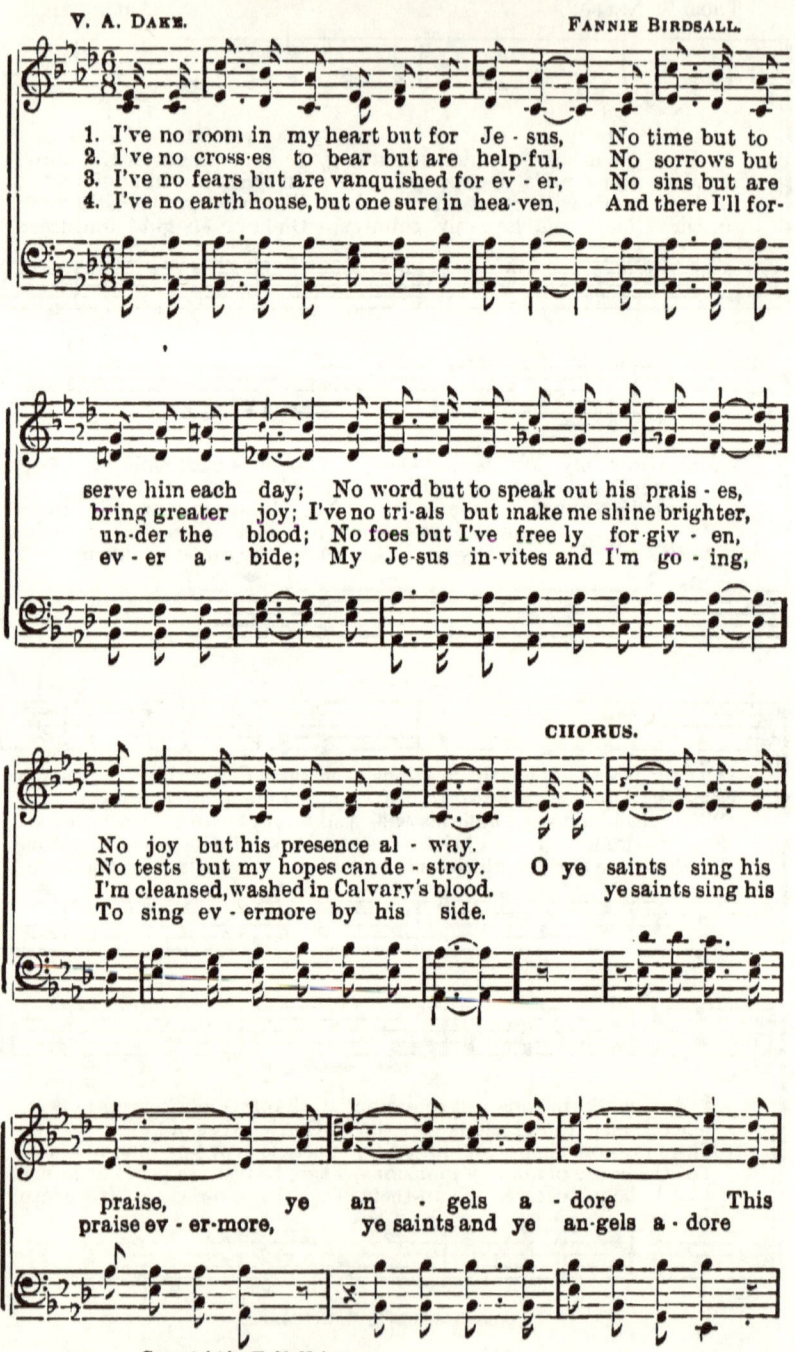

Room in My Heart--Concluded.

glo-ry-crowned King, who shall reign, who shall reign ever more.
this glory crowned King,

156   Almost But Lost.

A. F. GROW.   EVANGEL.

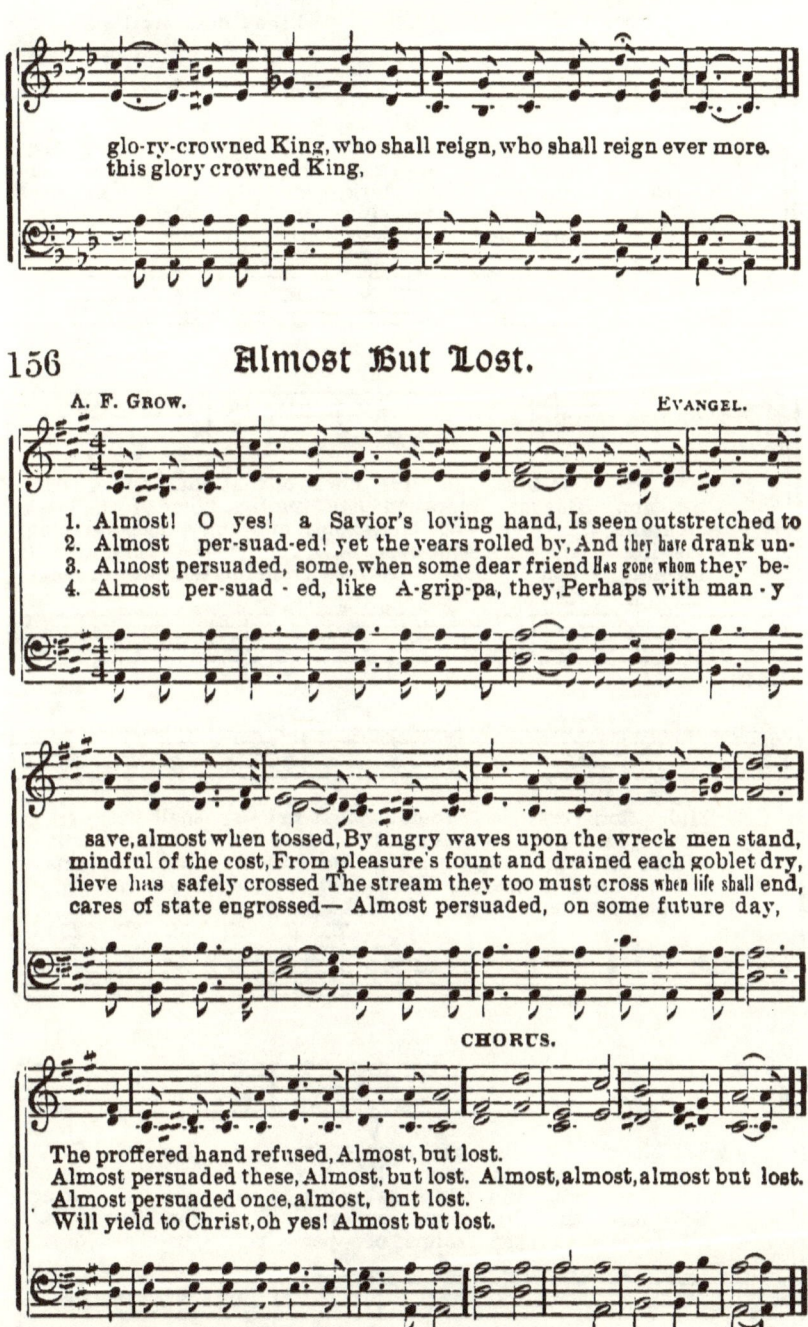

1. Almost! O yes! a Savior's loving hand, Is seen outstretched to
2. Almost per-suad-ed! yet the years rolled by, And they have drank un-
3. Almost persuaded, some, when some dear friend Has gone whom they be-
4. Almost per-suad-ed, like A-grip-pa, they, Perhaps with man-y

save, almost when tossed, By angry waves upon the wreck men stand,
mindful of the cost, From pleasure's fount and drained each goblet dry,
lieve has safely crossed The stream they too must cross when life shall end,
cares of state engrossed— Almost persuaded, on some future day,

CHORUS.

The proffered hand refused, Almost, but lost.
Almost persuaded these, Almost, but lost. Almost, almost, almost but lost.
Almost persuaded once, almost, but lost.
Will yield to Christ, oh yes! Almost but lost.

Copyright, 1896, by T. H. Nelson.

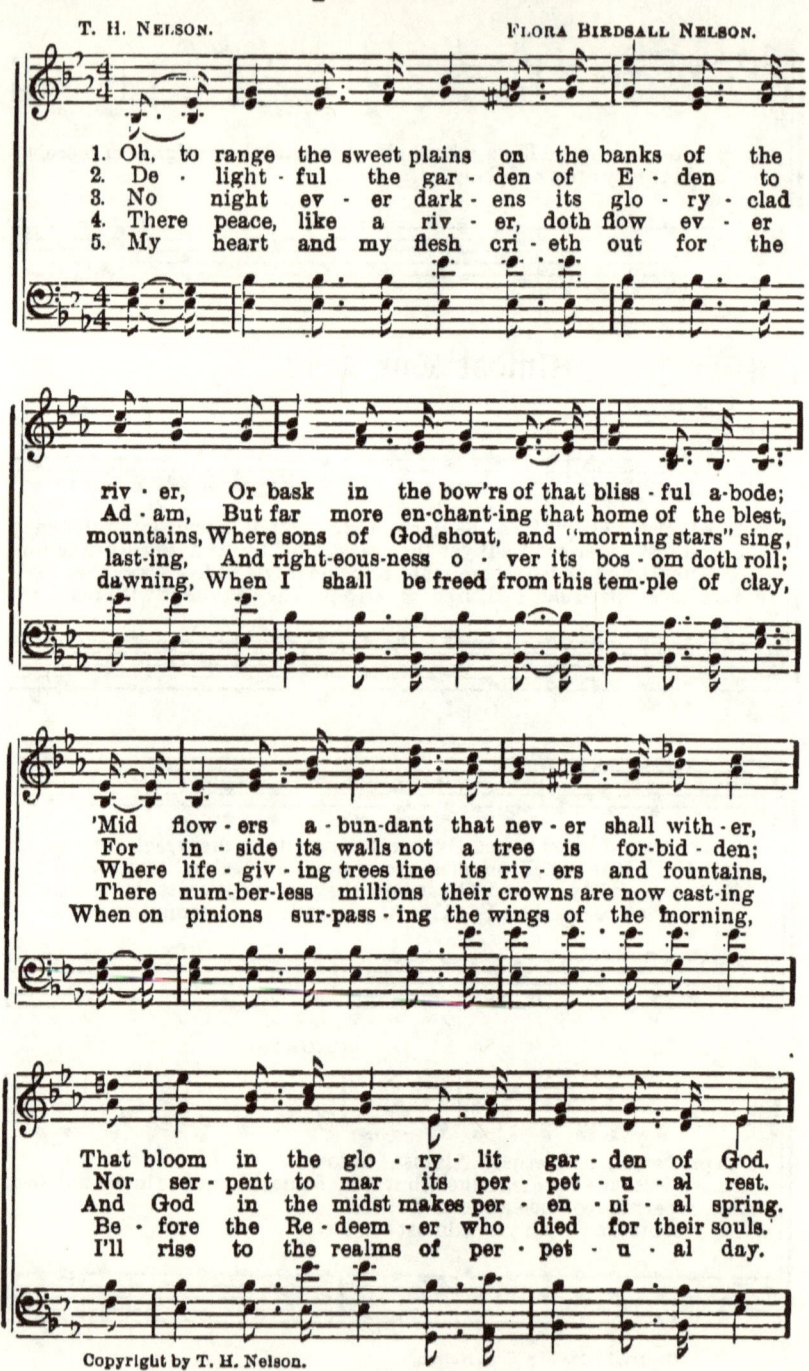

The Paradise of God--Concluded.

CHORUS.

Fight on then, my soul, in the war nev-er wea-ry,
For soon all thy con-flicts on earth shall be o'er; And
thou shalt be crown'd with a gar-land of vict-'ry,
And shine as the sun on that glo-ry-lit shore.

158 It Reaches Me.

1 Oh, this uttermost salvation!
  'Tis a fountain full and free,
Pure, exhaustless, ever flowing,
  Wondrous grace! it reaches me!

Cho.—It reaches me! it reaches me!
  Wondrous grace! it reaches me!

Pure, exhaustless, ever flowing,
  Wondrous grace! it reaches me!

2 How amazing God's compassion?
  That so vile a worm should prove
This stupendous bliss of heaven,
  This unmeasured wealth of love!

3 Jesus, Savior, I adore thee!
  Now thy love I will proclaim;
I will tell the blessed story,
  I will magnify thy name!

Mary D. James.

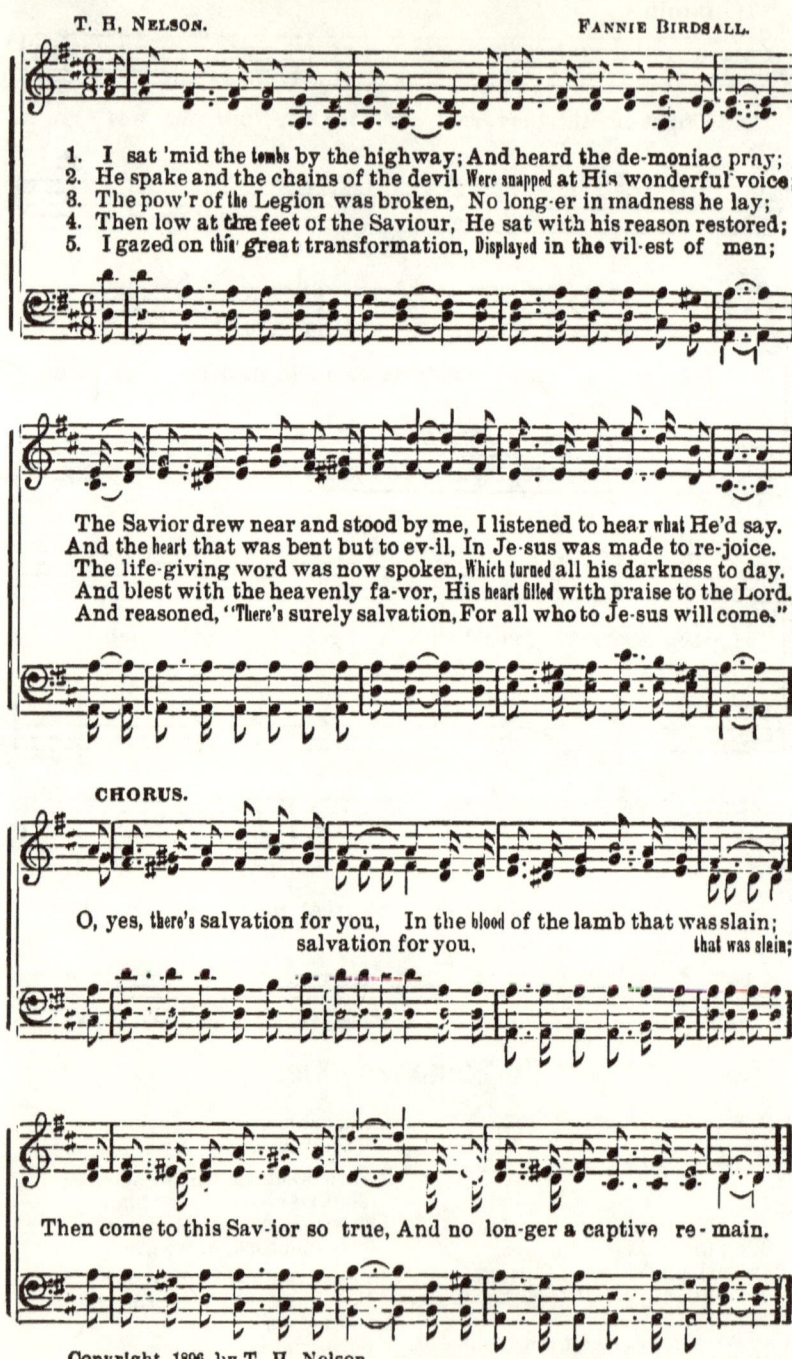

Church Militant Hymn--Concluded.

soundeth? 'tis cre - a - tion, groaning for its lat - ter day!
up, thou drow-sy sol-dier, worlds are charging to the shock.
ev -'ry nerve and sin-ew tell on a - ges— tell for God!

CHORUS.

Up ye sol - diers, worlds are charg-ing,
drow-sy sol-diers, yes, worlds are charging,

heav'n be - hold-ing, thou hast but an hour to fight.
yes, heav'n be-hold-ing,

162 The Cleansing Wave.

From the "Guide to Holiness."

MRS. PHŒBE PALMER.

1 Oh, now I see the crimson wave,
   The fountain deep and wide;
Jesus, my Lord, mighty to save,
   Points to his wounded side.

CHO.—The cleansing stream, I see, I see!
   I plunge and oh, it cleanseth me!
Oh, praise the Lord, it cleanseth me!
   It cleanseth me, yes, cleanseth me.

2 I see the new creation rise,
   I hear the speaking blood;
It speaks! polluted nature dies!
   Sinks 'neath the cleansing flood.

3 I rise to walk in heaven's own light,
   Above the world and sin,
With heart made pure, and garments white,
   And Christ enthroned within.

4 Amazing grace! 'tis heav'n below
   To feel the blood applied;
And Jesus, only Jesus know,
   My Jesus crucified.

163. Wilt Thou be Made Whole?

W. J. K.
Wm. J. Kirkpatrick.

1. Hear the footsteps of Jesus, He is now passing by, Bearing balm for the wounded, Healing all who apply; As He spake to the suff'rer Who lay at the pool, He is saying this moment, "Wilt thou be made whole?"
2. 'Tis the voice of that Savior, Whose merciful call Freely offers salvation To one and to all; He is now beck'ning to Him Each sin-tainted soul, And lovingly asking, "Wilt thou be made whole?"
3. Are you halting and struggling, O'er-powered by your sin, While the waters are troubled Can you not enter in? Lo, the Savior stands waiting To strengthen your soul, He is earnestly pleading, "Wilt thou be made whole?"
4. Blessed Savior, assist us To rest on Thy word; Let the soul-healing power On us now be outpoured: Wash away ev'ry sin-spot, Take per-fect control, Say to each trusting spirit, "Thy faith makes thee whole."

REFRAIN.

Wilt thou be made whole? Wilt thou be made whole? O come, weary suff'rer, O come, sin-sick soul; See, the life-stream is flowing, See the

Copyrighted by Wm. J. Kirkpatrick. By per.

What a Sinner I Have Been--Concluded.

CHORUS.

He has saved from ev-'ry sin, He has slain the foes within,

And has giv'n me peace and gladness in my soul; Oh, I'll

trust him for my bread, And his heal-ing oil to shed

On my bod-y while 'tis day, and keep me whole.

166   **The Joyful Sound.**

1 Salvation! O the joyful sound!
  What pleasure to our ears!
  A sovereign balm for every wound,
  A cordial for our fears.

2 Salvation! let the echo fly
  The spacious earth around,
  While all the armies of the sky
  Conspire to raise the sound.

3 Salvation! O Thou bleeding lamb!
  To Thee the praise belongs;
  Salvation shall inspire our hearts,
  And dwell upon our tongues.

167. The Judgment.

"For we must all appear before the judgment seat of Christ."—2nd Cor., v. 10.

VICTOR STRANGE.   FANNIE BIRDSALL.

1. When the stars from heav'n are fall-ing, And the moon appears as blood, And the sun in darkness hides his face a-way;
2. When the roar of Judgment thunder, Shall a-wake the sleep-ing dead, And the great white throne of jus-tice shall ap-pear;
3. When be-fore the face of Je-sus, Earth and hea-ven flee a-way, And the dead both small and great be-fore him stand;
4. When the books shall all be opened, And the Judge shall see the same, Find-ing writ-ten there men's works of sin and strife;

When the judgment scene ap-pall-ing, With its aw-ful glo-ry flood, Shall ap-pear, and with it bring the judgment day.
When the rocks are cleft a-sun-der By Je-ho-vah's might-y tread, And the hearts of men are fail-ing them for fear.
When the hand of ter-ror seiz-es men In that approaching day, When the an-gel stands on both the sea and land.
And they call for rocks and mountains As Je-ho-vah speaks their names, And for-ev-er blots them from the book of life.

Ritard.

Copyright by T. H. Nelson.

CHORUS.

When that aw-ful hour of reck'ning is at hand,
And time does to E-ter-ni-ty ex-pand,
When the day of wrath is come, And the Judge sits on his throne, O, who shall be a-ble then to stand?

168 The Solid Rock.

1 My hope is built on nothing less,
  Than Jesus' blood and righteousness;
  I dare not trust the sweetest frame,
  But wholly lean on Jesus' name.

Cho.—On Christ the solid rock I stand;
  All other ground is sinking sand,
  All other ground is sinking sand.

2 When darkness veils His lovely face,
  I rest on His unchanging grace;
  In every high and stormy gale,
  My anchor holds within the veil.

3 When He shall come with trumpet sound,
  O may I then in Him be found;
  Dressed in His righteousness alone,
  Faultless to stand before the throne.

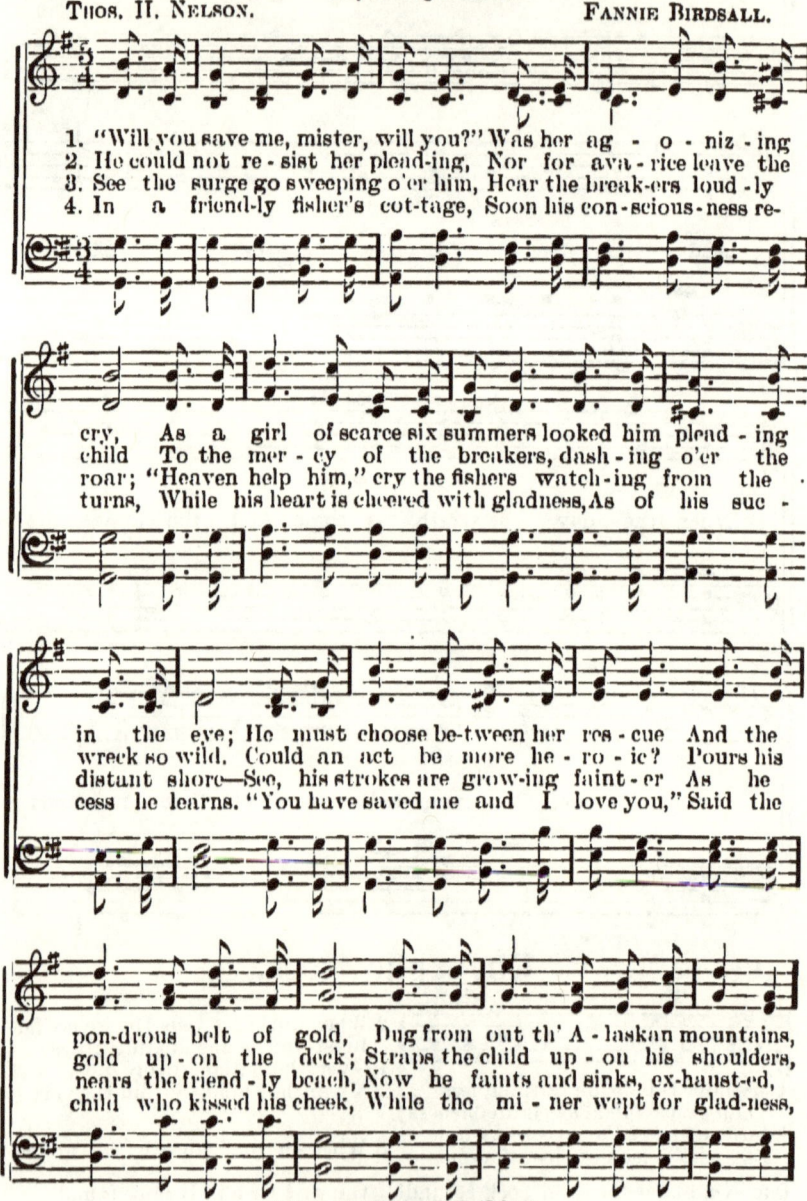

Souls-Or Gold--Concluded.

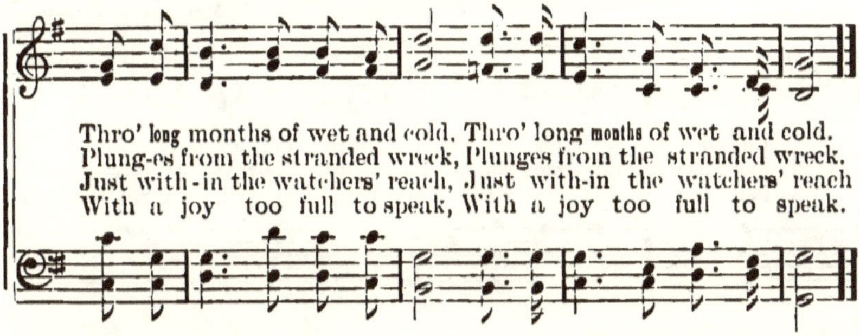

Thro' long months of wet and cold, Thro' long months of wet and cold,
Plung-es from the stranded wreck, Plunges from the stranded wreck,
Just with-in the watchers' reach, Just with-in the watchers' reach
With a joy too full to speak, With a joy too full to speak.

5. Thousands thus today are shipwrecked
On the raging sea of sin,
Sacrifice alone will save them;
Who will toil their souls to win?
Gold and ease must be abandoned,
Even danger be endured,
That their safety from the breakers
Of despair may be secured.

6. We may sink beneath death's billows,
But our eyes will ope' once more
Never more to feel a sorrow
On that blest eternal shore;
When we in that blood-washed circle
Meet the souls our toil has won;
Like the glad Alaskan miner,
We'll be paid for all we've done.

170 There's a Wideness in God's Mercy.

F. W. FABER.   LIZZIE S. TOURGEE.

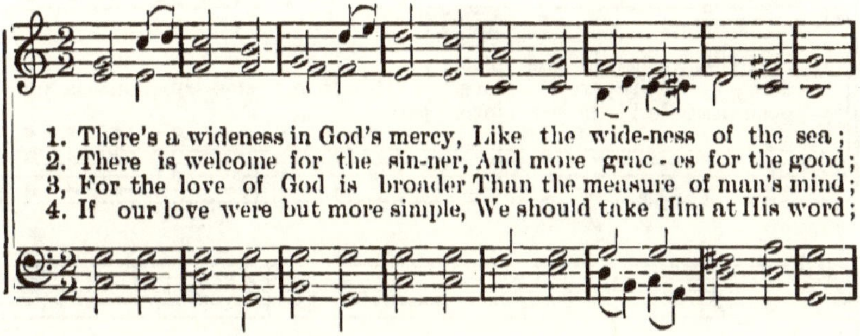

1. There's a wideness in God's mercy, Like the wide-ness of the sea;
2. There is welcome for the sin-ner, And more grac-es for the good;
3. For the love of God is broader Than the measure of man's mind;
4. If our love were but more simple, We should take Him at His word;

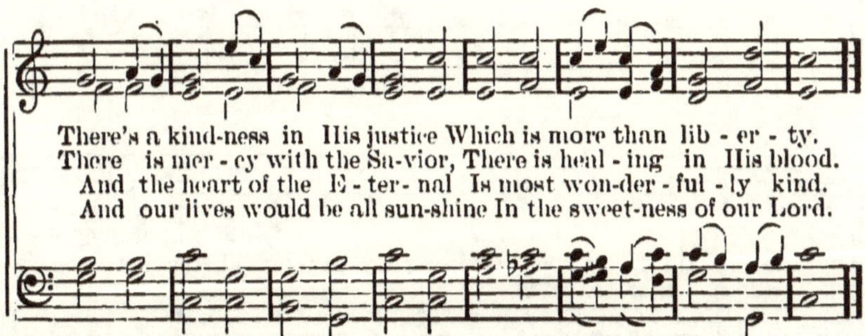

There's a kind-ness in His justice Which is more than lib-er-ty.
There is mer-cy with the Sa-vior, There is heal-ing in His blood.
And the heart of the E-ter-nal Is most won-der-ful-ly kind.
And our lives would be all sun-shine In the sweet-ness of our Lord.

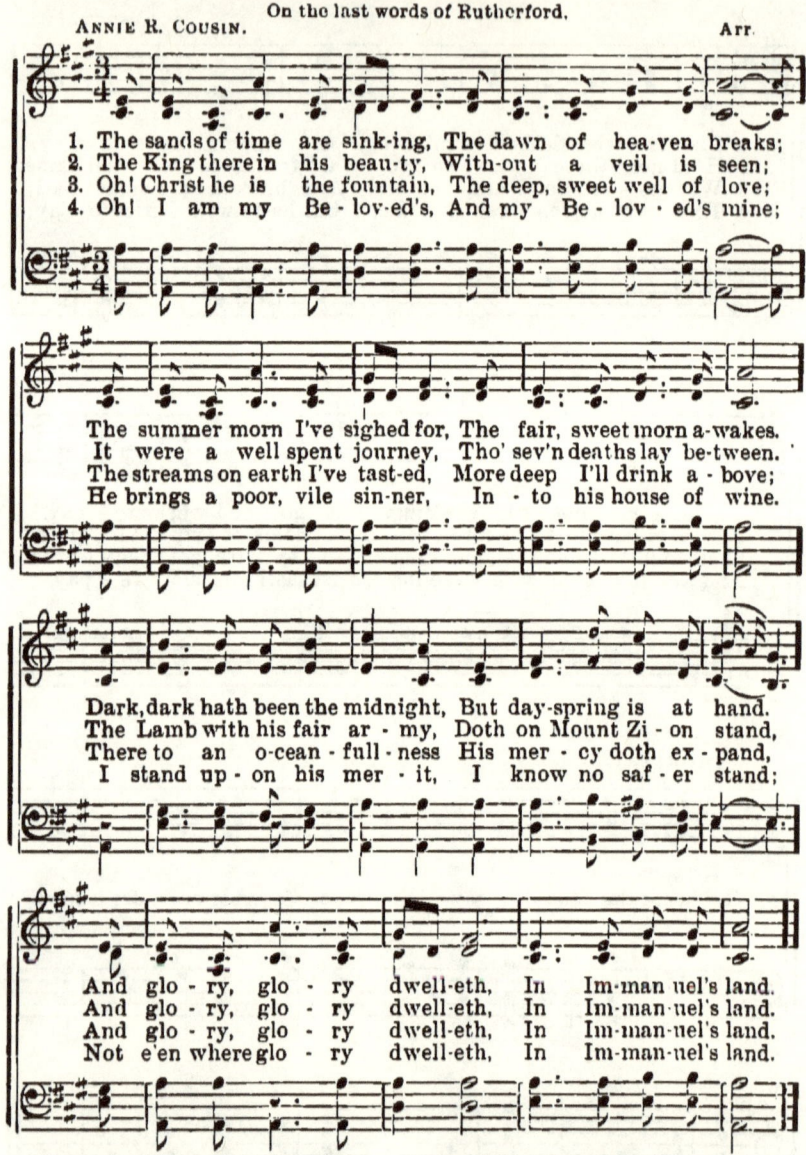

5 I've wrestled on toward heaven,
'Gainst storm and wind and tide;
Now like a weary traveler,
That leaneth on his guide,
Amid the shades of evening
While sinks life's lingering sand,
I hail the glory dawning
In Immanuel's land.

6 Deep waters crossed life's pathway,
The hedge of thorns was sharp,
Now these lie all behind me,
Oh, for a well tuned harp!
Oh, to join the hallelujah!
With yon triumphant band,
Who sing where glory dwelleth
In Immanuel's land.

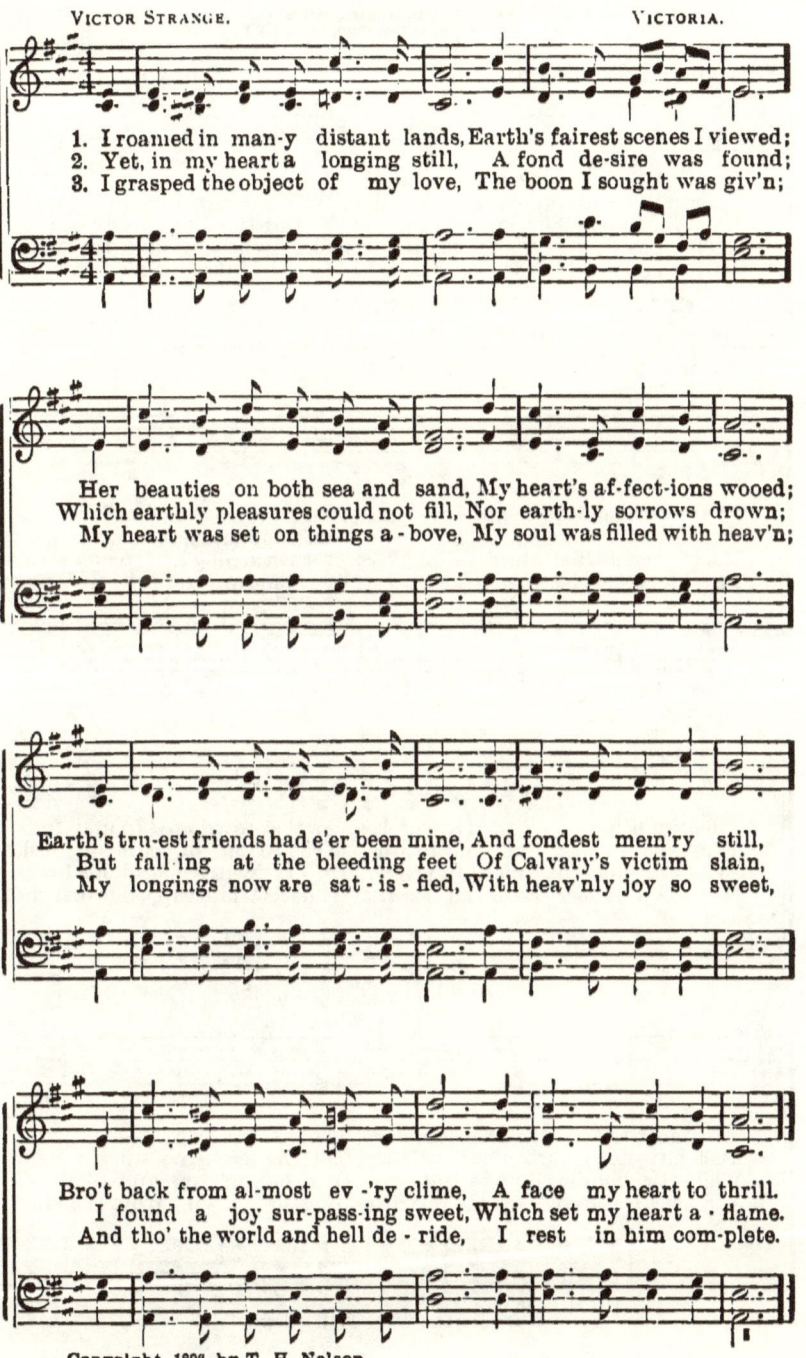

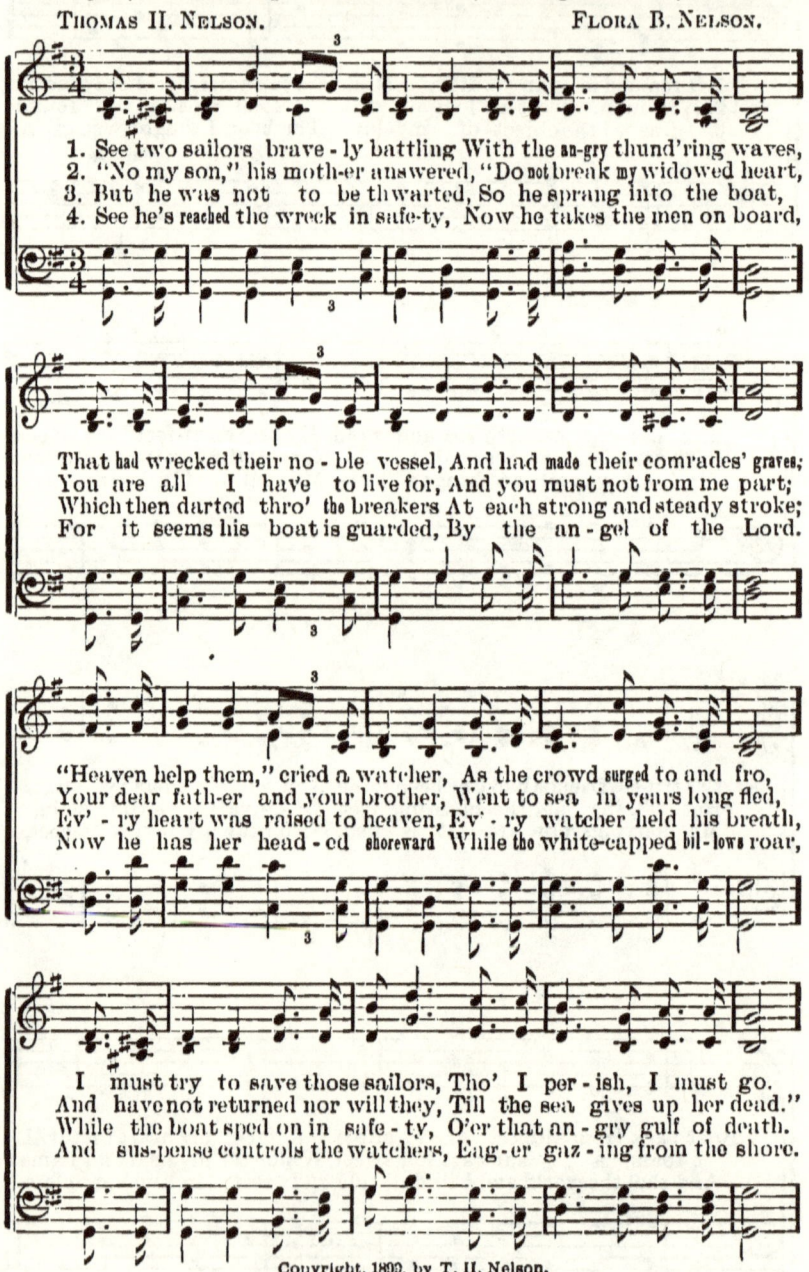

The Rescued Sailors--Concluded.

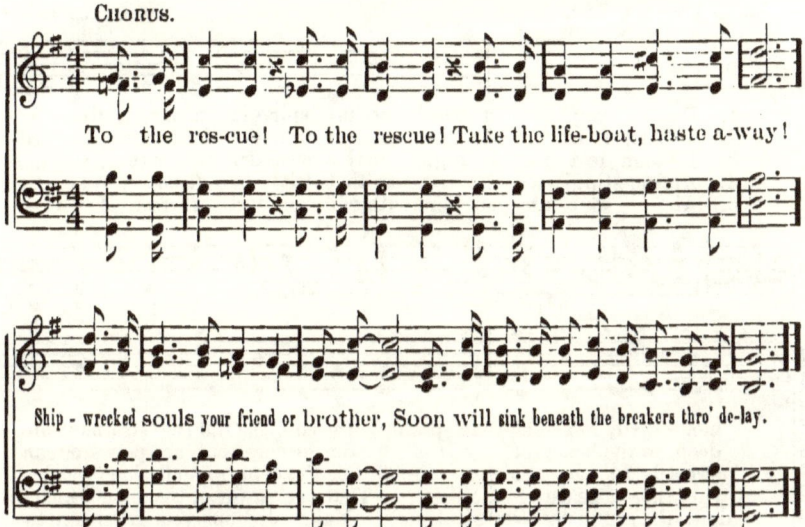

5. Hark! the boy is shouting homeward
In a voice both strong and shrill;
I have saved them, its my father
And my long lost brother Will.
They were just about to perish
And their hopes had well nigh fled,
But the Lord has blest my efforts
And the sea gives up her dead.

6. Thus on sin's most stormy ocean
Where the breakers loudly roar,
There are many ship-wrecked sailors
Drowning full in sight of shore,
Who will volunteer to save them,
They're your brother, father, friend;
God will bless your noble effort
And will crown you in the end.

176. Rock of Ages.

1. Rock of Ages, cleft for me,
Let me hide myself in Thee;
Let the water and the blood,
From Thy wounded side which flow'd
Be of sin the double cure;
Save from wrath, and make me pure.

2. Could my tears forever flow—
Could my zeal no languor know
These for sin could not atone;

Thou must save and thou alone:
In my hand no price I bring;
Simply to the cross I cling.

3. While I draw this fleeting breath,
When my eyes shall close in death,
When I rise to worlds unknown,
And behold Thee on Thy Throne—
Rock of Ages, cleft for me,
Let me hide myself in Thee.

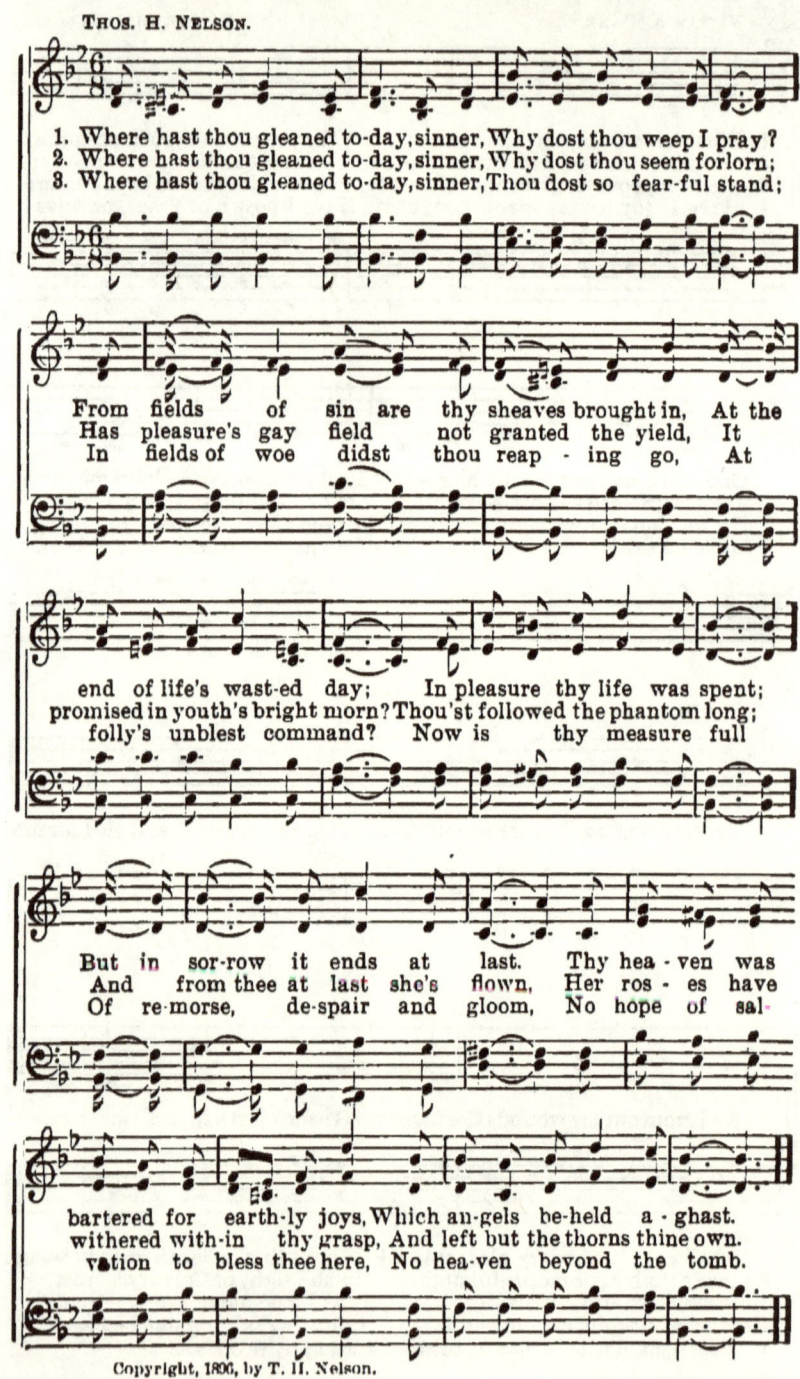

Your Own--Concluded.

Soon will their hopes be flown, Rescue them ere they're gone.
they're gone.

182.   I'm Coming Now to Jesus.

F. B.   Fannie Birdsall.

1. I'm com-ing now to Je-sus, With all my sin and guilt;
2. I've wandered far from Je-sus, And found no rest-ing place;
3. I give up all for Je-sus, I leave the world be-hind;
4. My all I now surrender, No will to have but Thine;

And tho' I am unworthy, For me thy blood was spilt.
I'm com-ing Lord, re-pent-ing, And plead-ing for thy grace.
I'll fol-low where thou leadest, O, Lord I will be thine.
I praise the Lord for-ev-er, The price-less pearl is mine.

CHORUS.

I'm com-ing now to Je-sus, Who can my sins for-give,
I long for Thy sal-va-tion, I shall believe and live.

Copyright, 1899, by T. H. Nelson.

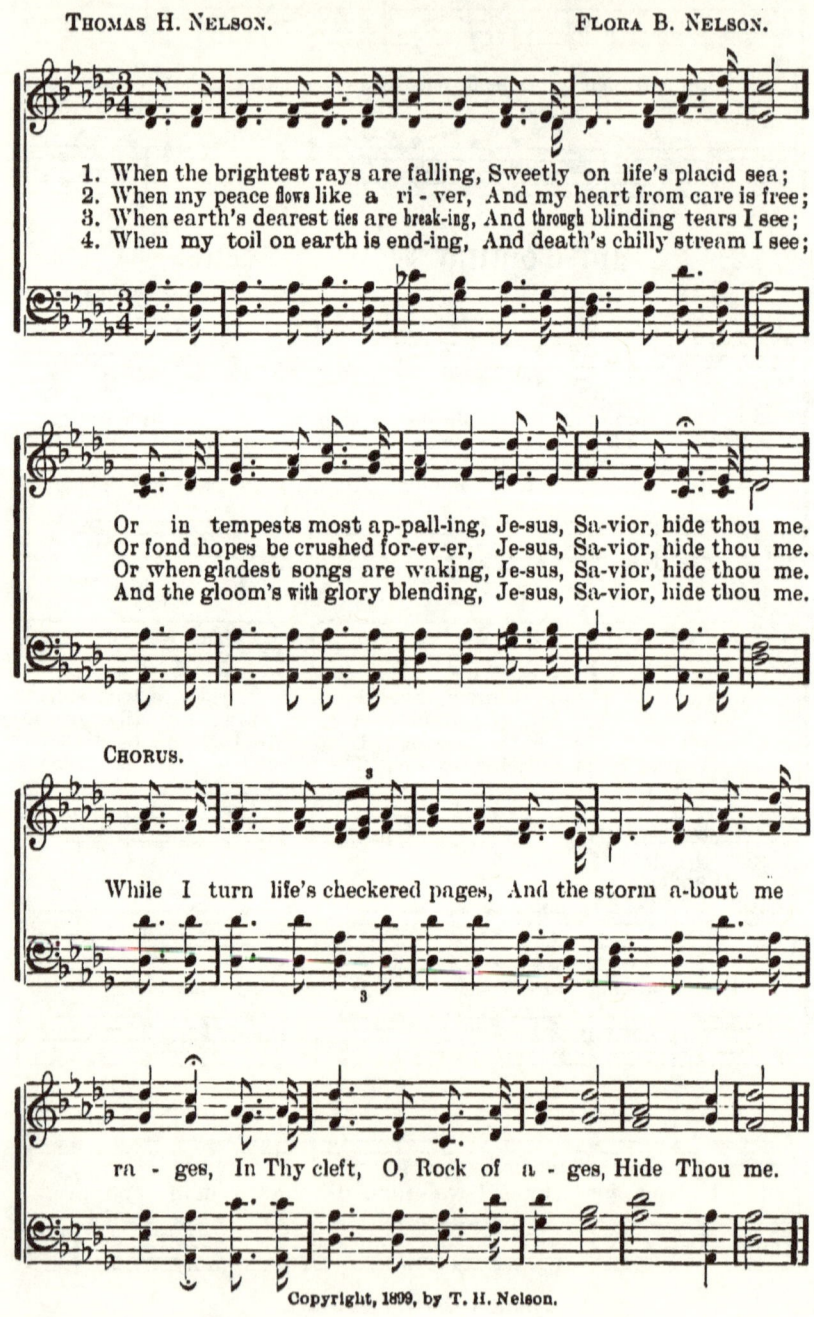

186. Another Year for Jesus.

FRANCIS HAVERGAL.   FANNIE BIRDSALL.

1. An-other year is dawning, Dear Father, let it be;
2. An-other year of mercies, Of faithfulness and grace;
3. An-other year of progress, An-other year of praise;
4. An-other year of service, Of witness for Thy love;
5. An-other year is dawning, Dear Father, let it be;

In working or in waiting, An-other year for Thee.
An-o-ther year of gladness, In the shining of Thy face.
An-o-ther year of proving Thy presence "all the days."
An-o-ther year of training, For holier work a-bove.
On earth, or else in Heaven, An-o-ther year for Thee!

CHORUS.
All my life for Jesus, All my life for Jesus,
Ever, only, all for Him.

187. The Crowning Hour.

1 Servant of God, well done!
  Thy glorious warfare past;
The battle's fought, the race is won,
  And thou art crowned at last.

2 Of all thy heart's desire
  Triumphantly possessed;
Lodged by the ministerial choir
  In my Redeemer's breast.

3 With saints enthroned on high,
  Thou dost thy Lord proclaim,
And still to God salvation cry,
  Salvation to the lamb!

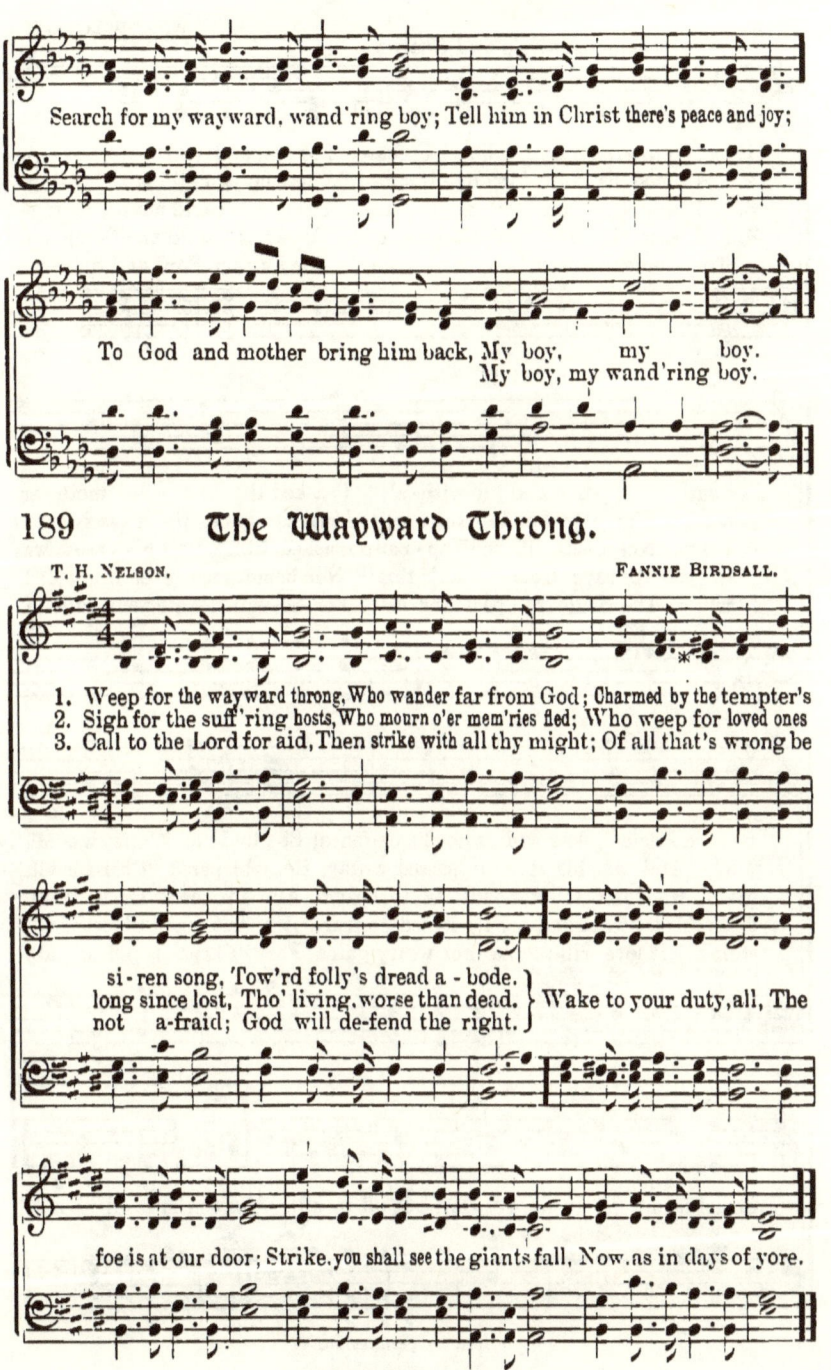

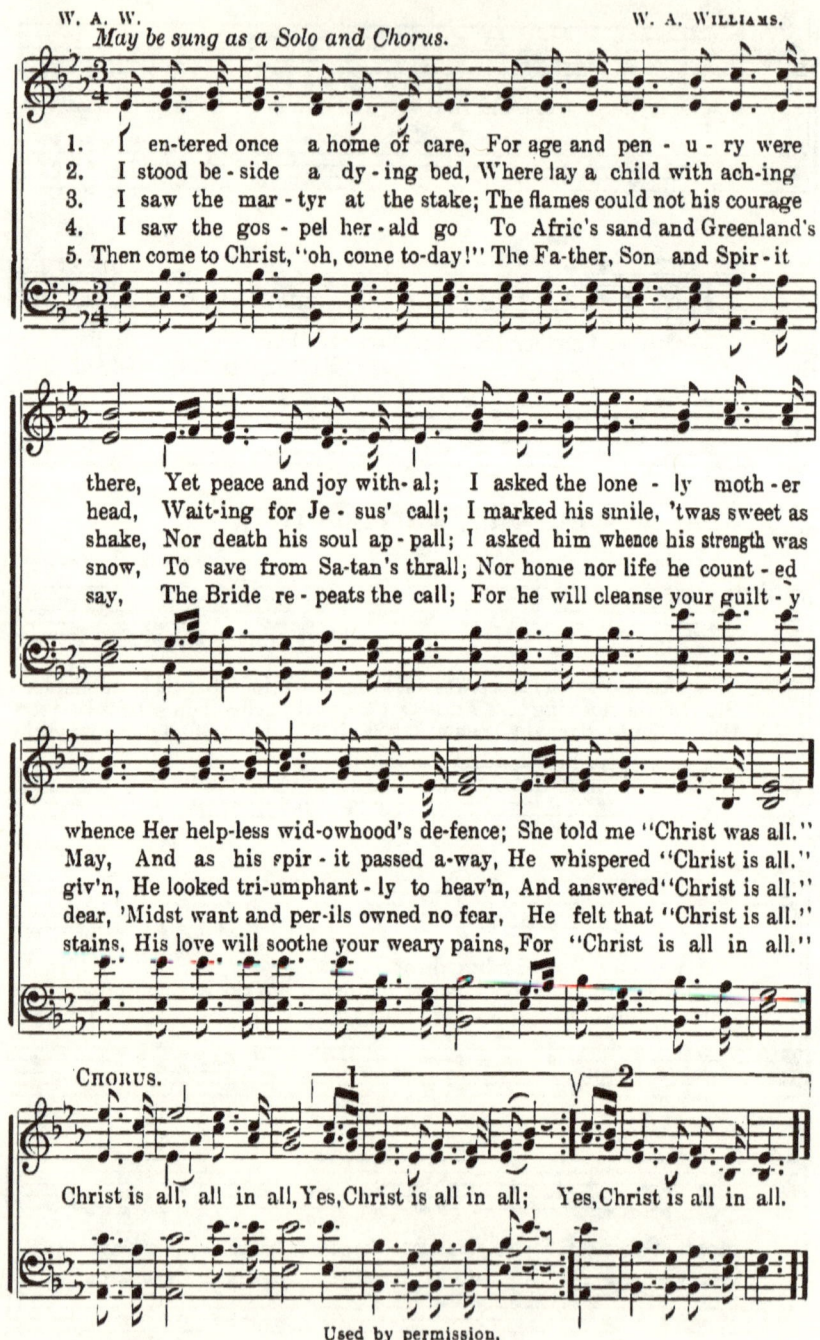

Prophet's Call--Concluded.

CHORUS.

Pow'r to heal the lep-er, Pow'r to raise the dead,
Pow'r to fill the emp-ty pots with oil; Is
waiting for the worker who in Je-sus' steps will tread,
And leave his life of ease for one of toil.

4 See him now—the swelling Jordan, in its onward course is stayed,
And the hardened piece of steel is made to swim;
And the spring of bitter water with a cruse of salt is healed,
And the widow's pots with oil filled to the brim.

5 He, the Shunamite, does raise to life and Naaman's leprous spots,
At his command, the Jordan washes clean;
When at his open sephulcre the funeral march is stopped
His bleaching bones revive the dead again.

6 You, who would have Elisha's power, must take the way he trod.
Sell that thou hast and give it to the poor;
Leave not your treasures in this world to tempt you back from God,
But lay them up on heaven's lasting shore.

The Lost Sheep -- Concluded.

194. Beulah Land.

"Behold, I will send you corn and wine and oil and ye shall be satisfied therewith."—JOEL, 11 : 19.

THOS. H. NELSON.   FLORA BIRDSALL NELSON.

1. There is a land where nature sings The praises of her glorious King;
2. A land where praise employs each tongue, Where harps to heav'nly notes are strung;
3. No al-ien eats her oil or corn, Her children all are native born;
4. A land where milk and honey flow, And all the fruits of Canaan grow;

Where trees in gladness clap their hands, On sunlit slopes of Beulah land.
Where love-lit fires, by seraphs fann'd, Inspire the hearts in Beulah land.
The stirrings of the car-nal man, Are nev-er felt in Beulah land.
Where vines of Eschol shade the strand Of nectar streams in Beulah land.

CHORUS.

My soul enraptured sits and sings, Beneath the shadow of his wing,

And heaven's joy my heart expands, In blissful bow'rs of Beulah land.

5. Then why not emigrate to-day,
From Egypt's swamps of miry clay,
Nor tarry in the desert sand,
But cross the lines to Beulah land.

6. Repent, believe, be born again,
Then let the carnal mind be slain,
Then clean before the King you'll stand,
A native child of Beulah land.

Copyright, 1893, by T. H. Nelson.

195 Rest, Laborer, Rest.

In memory of Rev. V. A. Dake, originator of Pentecost Bands, who died on a return missionary tour from Monrovia, Africa, and was buried in Sierra Leone.

T. H. NELSON. FLORA BIRDSALL NELSON.

With Feeling.

1. Rest, worker, rest, Thy toilsome task is done;
   God deemed it best, 'Neath e-qua-to-rial sun,
   To have thy lonely grave, Kissed by At-lan-tic's wave.

2. Rest, lab'rer, rest, Complete, thy work we find;
   Thou art more blest Than we who're left be-hind,
   Thy task is early done, Rest at God's Harvest Home.

3. Rest, laborer, rest,
   The prize is thine at last,
   On Jesus' breast
   Thou dost forget the past;
   Safe from the strife of tongues,
   Join in the seraphs' songs.

4. Rest, toiler, rest,
   Thy burden's laid aside,
   In white robes dressed
   Beyond death's chilling tide,
   Safe from the darts of hell,
   With all the blood-washed dwell.

5. Rest, reaper, rest,
   The sweat that damped thy brow
   When harvest pressed,
   Is changed to glory now;
   From whitened fields of sin,
   Thy sheaves are coming in.

6. Rest, pilgrim, rest,
   Thy weary march is o'er;
   None may molest
   On that effulgent shore;
   Thy race, at last, is run,
   Thy arduous task is done.

7. Rest, warrior, rest,
   Thine armor thrown aside,
   The victor's crest
   By hands once crucified,
   Is laid upon thy brow—
   No need of armor now.

8. Rest, martyr, rest,
   Where shines eternal day;
   For souls oppressed,
   Thy life was worn away;
   Though some may say 'Twas wrong,'
   The master says: "Well done!"

For funeral occasions first and last stanzas may be omitted.

Copyright, 1896, by T. H. Nelson.

Beautiful Robes--Concluded.

197   Come, Ye Disconsolate.

THOMAS MOORE, alt., and THOMAS HASTINGS.   SAMUEL WEBBE.

1. Come, ye dis-con-so-late, wher-e'er ye lan-guish; Come to the mer-cy-seat, fer-vent-ly kneel; Here bring your wound-ed hearts, here tell your an-guish; Earth has no sor-row that heav'n can-not heal.
2. Joy of the des-o-late, light of the stray-ing, Hope of the pen-i-tent, fade-less and pure. Here speaks the Com-fort-er, ten-der-ly say-ing, "Earth has no sor-row that heav'n can-not cure."
3. Here see the bread of life; see wa-ters flow-ing Forth from the throne of God, pure from a-bove; Come to the feast of love; come, ev-er know-ing Earth has no sor-row but heav'n can re-move.

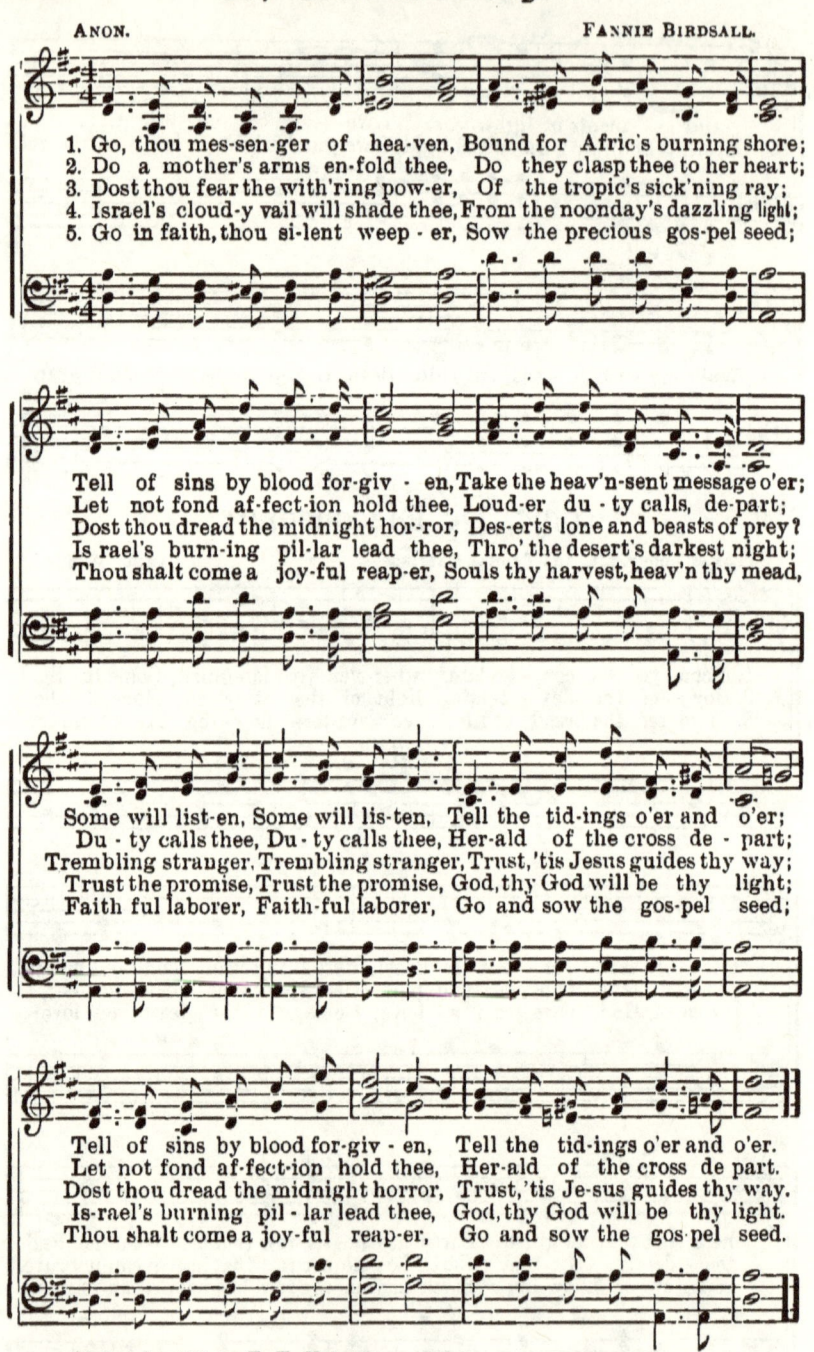

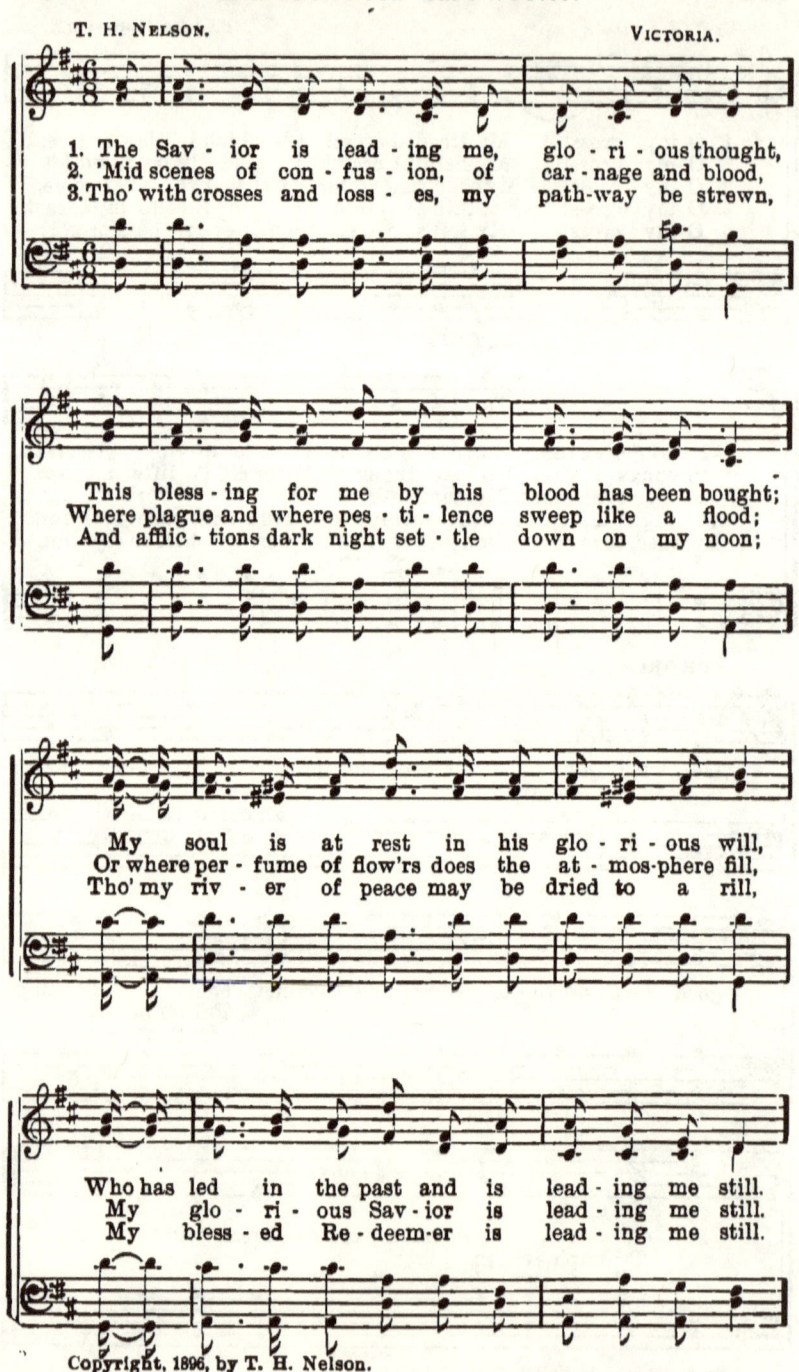

He Leadeth Me Still—Concluded.

4 Though fiercest temptations press hard on my soul,
And bitter afflictions like sea billows roll;
E'en then my poor heart with his love he shall fill,
And my soul shout triumphant, he leadeth me still.

5 And when at the crossing of death's chilly stream,
The earth is receding with time's transient dream;
The joy of the Lord shall my spirit then thrill;
As I shout o'er the billows, he leadeth me still.

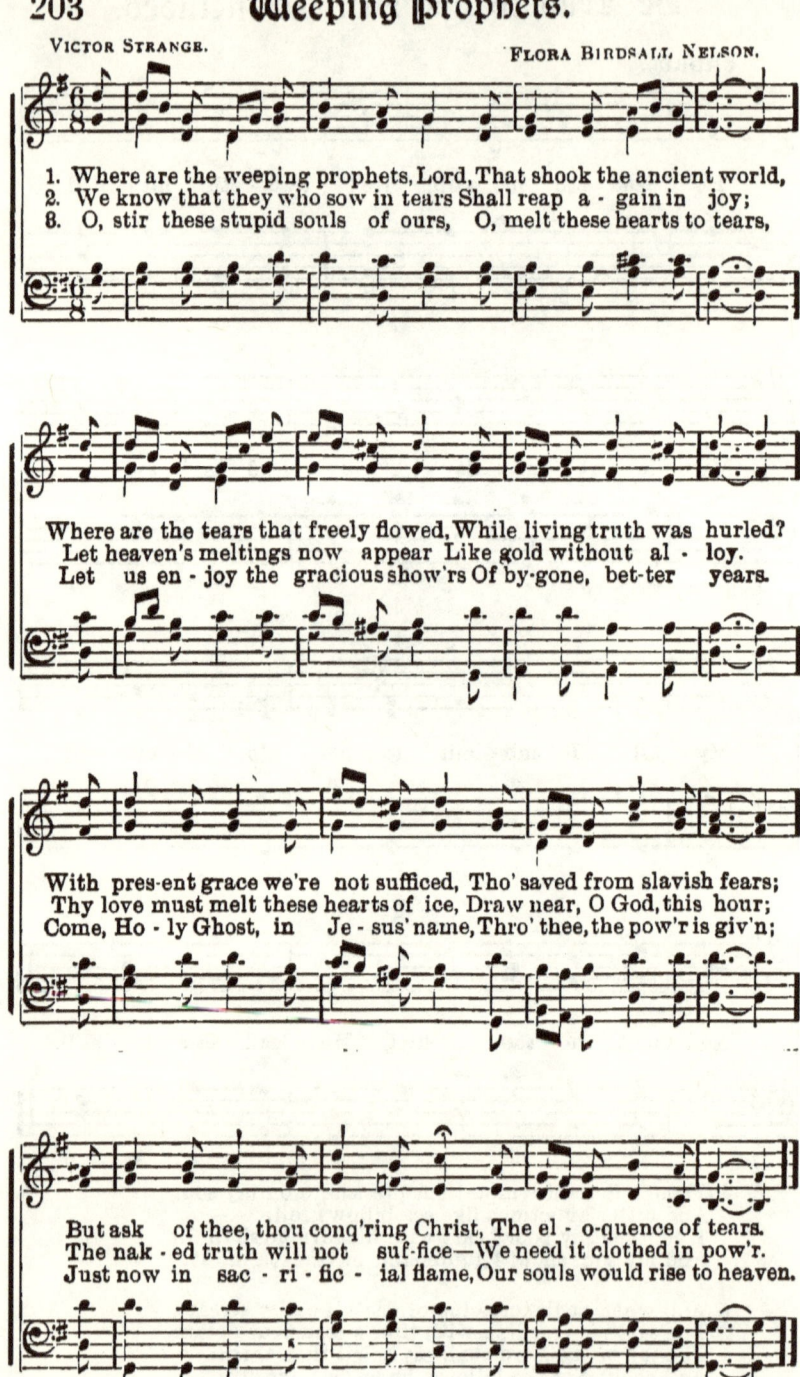

Wondrous Change--Concluded.

dove, Covered with sil - - - ver, yel-low with
the wings of a dove, Covered with sil - ver,

gold, Yet thou shalt be . . . . . . as the wings of a
Yet thou shalt be

Ritard.

dove, Thrilled with a joy . . . that can nev-er be told.
the wings of a dove, Thrilled with a joy

206   **I Am Coming to the Cross.**

Rev. Wm. McDonald.

1 I am coming to the Cross;
  I am poor, and weak, and blind;
  I am counting all but dross,
  I shall full salvation find.

    Chorus.

I am trusting, Lord, in thee,
Blest Lamb of Calvary;
Humbly at thy Cross I bow,
Save me, Jesus, save me now.

3 Here I give my all to thee,
  Friends, and time, and earthly store;
  Soul and body thine to be,—
  Wholly thine forever more.

4 In thy promises I trust,
  Now I feel the blood applied;
  I am prostrate in the dust,
  I with Christ am crucified.

5 Jesus comes! he fills my soul!
  Perfected in him I am;
  I am every whit made whole:
  Glory, glory to the Lamb.

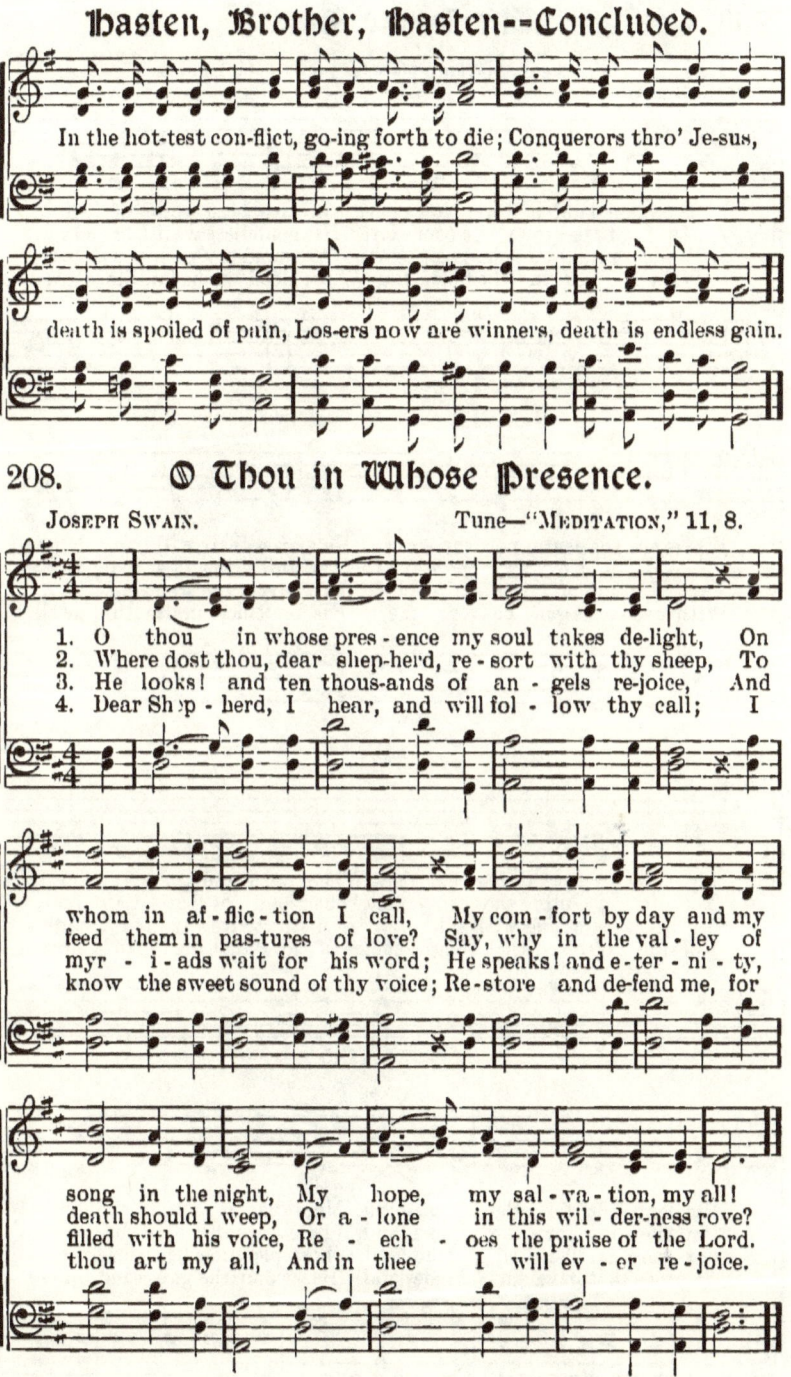

Hasten, Brother, Hasten--Concluded.

In the hot-test con-flict, go-ing forth to die; Conquerors thro' Je-sus, death is spoiled of pain, Los-ers now are winners, death is endless gain.

208. O Thou in Whose Presence.

JOSEPH SWAIN. Tune—"MEDITATION," 11, 8.

1. O thou in whose pres-ence my soul takes de-light, On whom in af-flic-tion I call, My com-fort by day and my song in the night, My hope, my sal-va-tion, my all!
2. Where dost thou, dear shep-herd, re-sort with thy sheep, To feed them in pas-tures of love? Say, why in the val-ley of death should I weep, Or a-lone in this wil-der-ness rove?
3. He looks! and ten thous-ands of an-gels re-joice, And myr-i-ads wait for his word; He speaks! and e-ter-ni-ty, filled with his voice, Re-ech-oes the praise of the Lord.
4. Dear Shep-herd, I hear, and will fol-low thy call; I know the sweet sound of thy voice; Re-store and de-fend me, for thou art my all, And in thee I will ev-er re-joice.

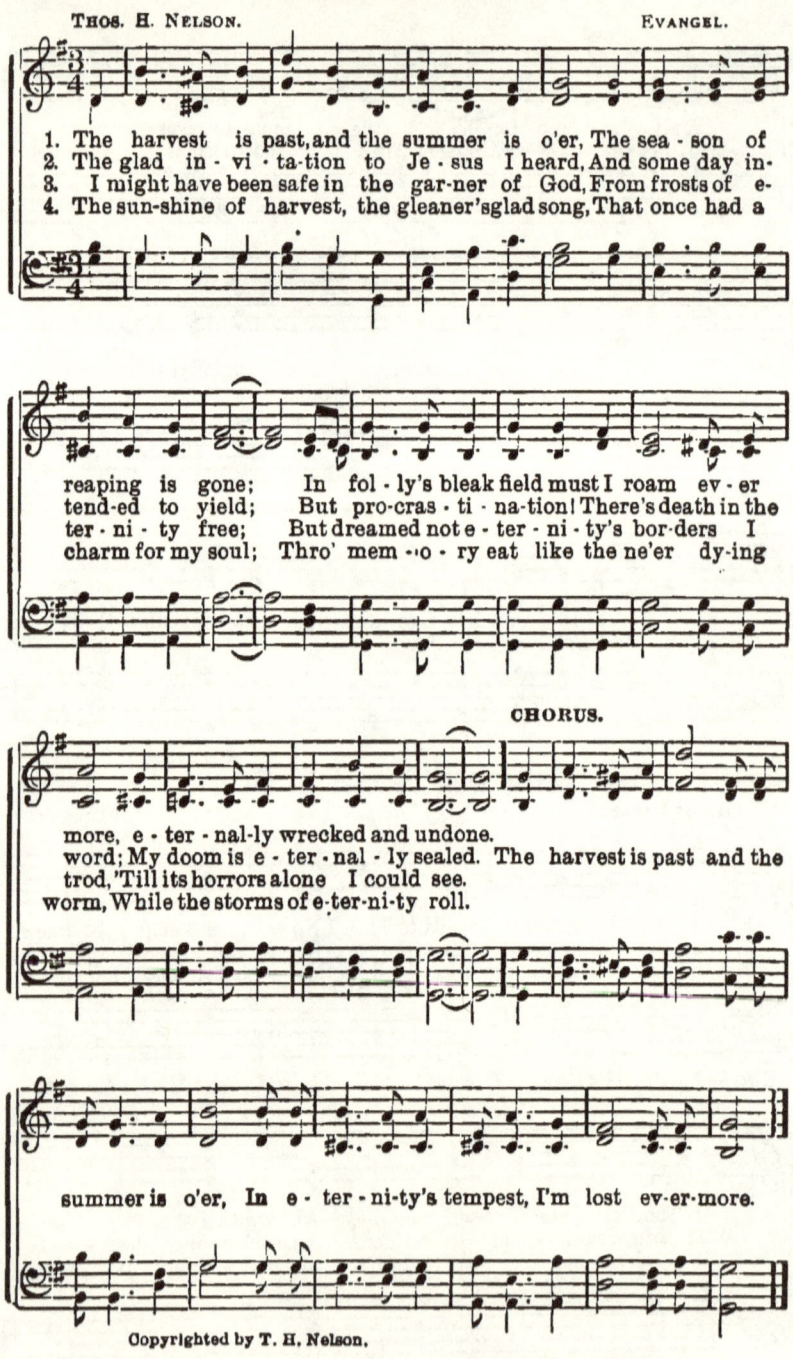

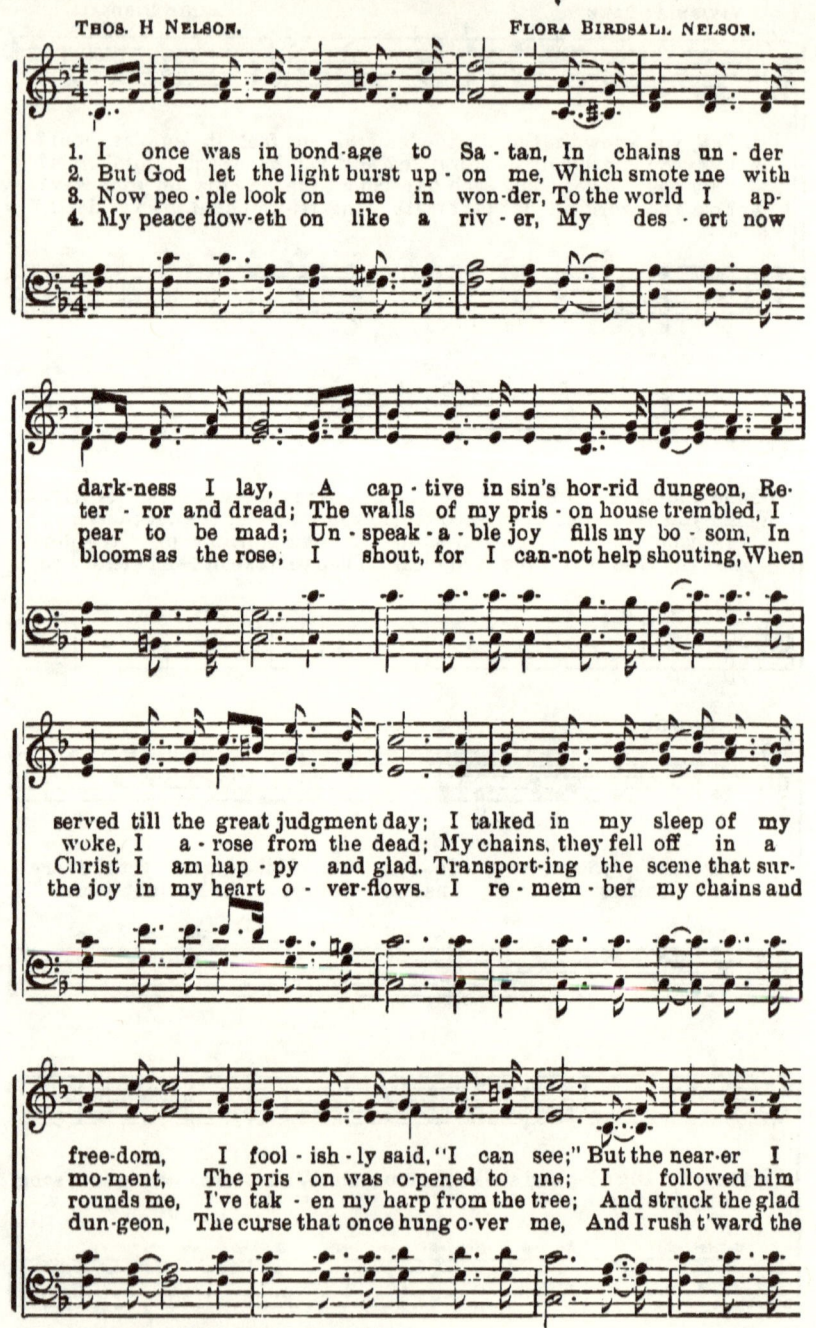

Free Indeed—Concluded.

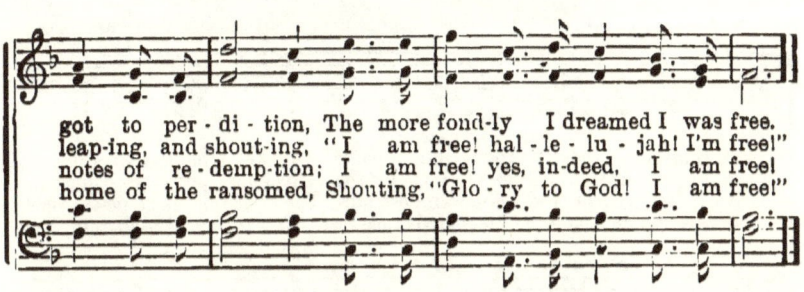

got to per-di-tion, The more fond-ly I dreamed I was free.
leap-ing, and shout-ing, "I am free! hal-le-lu-jah! I'm free!"
notes of re-demp-tion; I am free! yes, in-deed, I am free!
home of the ransomed, Shouting,"Glo-ry to God! I am free!"

214 Lost.

F. A. M.   "The Harvest is past."—BIBLE.   F. A. MILLER.

Slow and with feeling.

1. Lost to the sound of the Spir-it's sweet call, Lost to the
2. Lost a-mid sermons where Sab-bath light gleamed, Lost 'mid the
3. Lost to earth's pleasures that once the soul won. Lost, earth's fond
4. Lost to the home where the ho-ly shall dwell. Lost to the
5. Lost where the bil-lows of tor-ment e'er roll, Lost where God's

gift of God's "Ransom for all," Lost in e-ter-nal gloom
pleadings of God's own re-deemed, Lost while the fam-i-ly
friendship to sor-row a-lone, Lost a-mid ru-ined hopes
songs that the ransomed shall swell, Lost to the cit-y that
wrath-flames en-vel-op the soul. Lost where no gleam of hope

wrought by the fall, Lost! There is par-don no more.
al-tar's light streamed, Lost! The fond plead-ings are o'er.
ev-er un-done, Lost! The en-chant-ment is o'er.
hears no death-knell, Lost! Dear ones beck-on no more.
comes to con-sole, Lost in e-ter-ni-ty's gloom.

REFRAIN.

Lost! Lost! Lost! Lost! There is par-don no more.
Lost! Lost! Lost! Lost! The fond pleadings are o'er.
Lost! Lost! Lost! Lost! The en-chant-ment is o'er.
Lost! Lost! Lost! Lost! Dear ones beck-on no more.
Lost! Lost! Lost! Lost in e-ter-ni-ty's gloom!

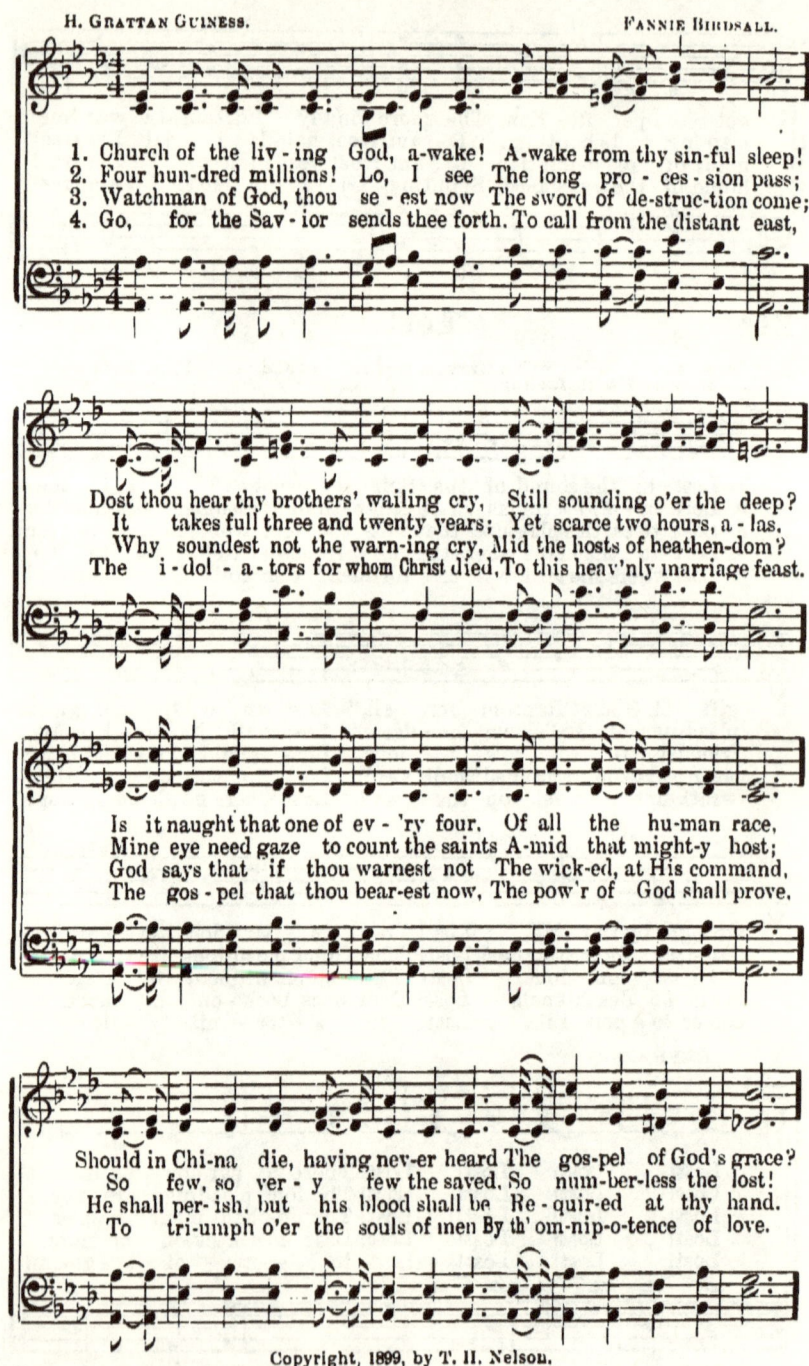

China's Millions—Concluded.

Canst thou shut thine ear to the aw-ful sound—The voice of thy brothers'
The lost! ah, does no righteous voice Ac-cuse us of their
O, cleanse thy hand from mur-der now, The voice of thy broth-ers'
A-wake! for du-ty calls thee forth, The voice of thy broth-ers'

blood?
blood?
blood;
blood;

A mill-ion a month in Chi-na Are dying with-out God.

216 **Happy Day.**

P. DODDRIDGE. English Melody.

1. O hap-py day, that fixed my choice On Thee, my Savior and my God!
Well may this glowing heart rejoice, And tell its raptures all abroad.
Happy day, happy day,
When Jesus washed my sins away!
He taught me how to watch and pray,
And live rejoicing ev'ry day;

2 'Tis done, the great transaction's done!
I am my Lord's, and He is mine:
He drew me, and I followed on,
Charmed to confess that voice divine.

3 Now rest, my long divided heart;
Fixed on this blissful center, rest;

Nor ever from thy Lord depart;
With him of every good possessed.

4 High heav'n that heard the solemn vow,
That vow renewed shall daily hear,
Till in life's latest hour I bow,
And bless in death a bond so dear.

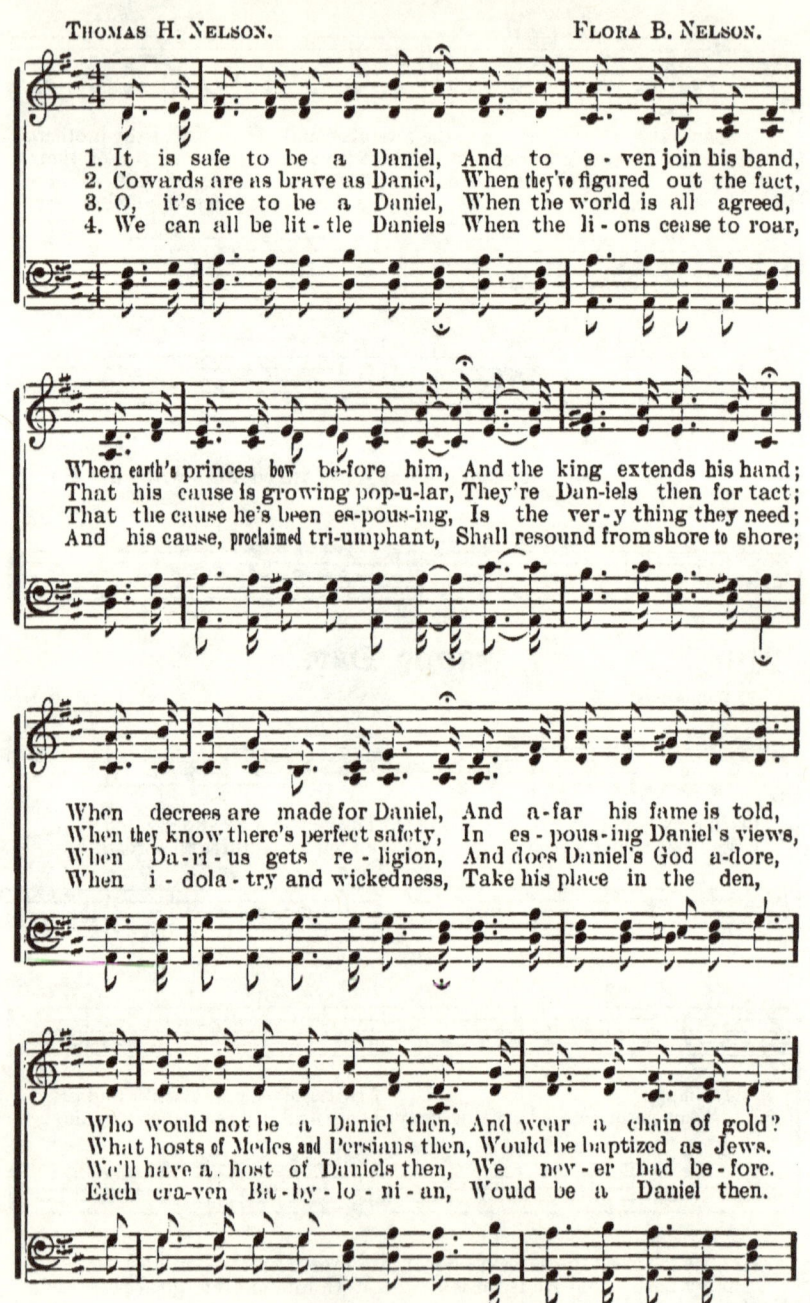

When to be a Daniel—Concluded.

CHORUS.

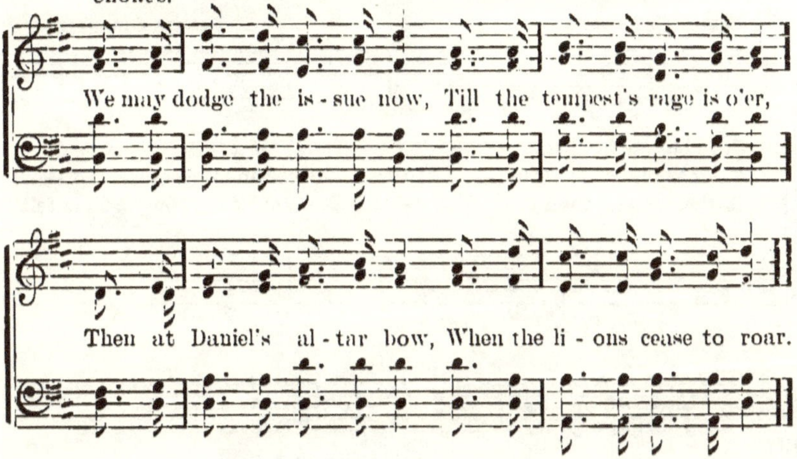

We may dodge the is-sue now, Till the tempest's rage is o'er,
Then at Daniel's al-tar bow, When the li-ons cease to roar.

218 Stand Up for Jesus.

G. DUFFIELD.   G. J. WEBB.

1. Stand up, stand up for Jesus, Ye soldiers of the cross, Lift high His royal
2. Stand up, stand up for Jesus, The trumpet call obey; Forth to the mighty
3. Stand up, stand up for Jesus—Stand in His strength alone; The arm of flesh will

banner; It must not suffer loss; From victory unto victory His army
conflict, In this His glorious day. "Ye that are men now serve Him," Against un-
fail you—Ye dare not trust your own: Put on the gospel armor, And, watching

shall he lead, Till ev'ry foe is vanquished, And Christ is Lord indeed.
numbered foes; Let courage rise with danger, And strength to strength oppose.
un-to prayer, Where duty calls, or danger, Be never wanting there.

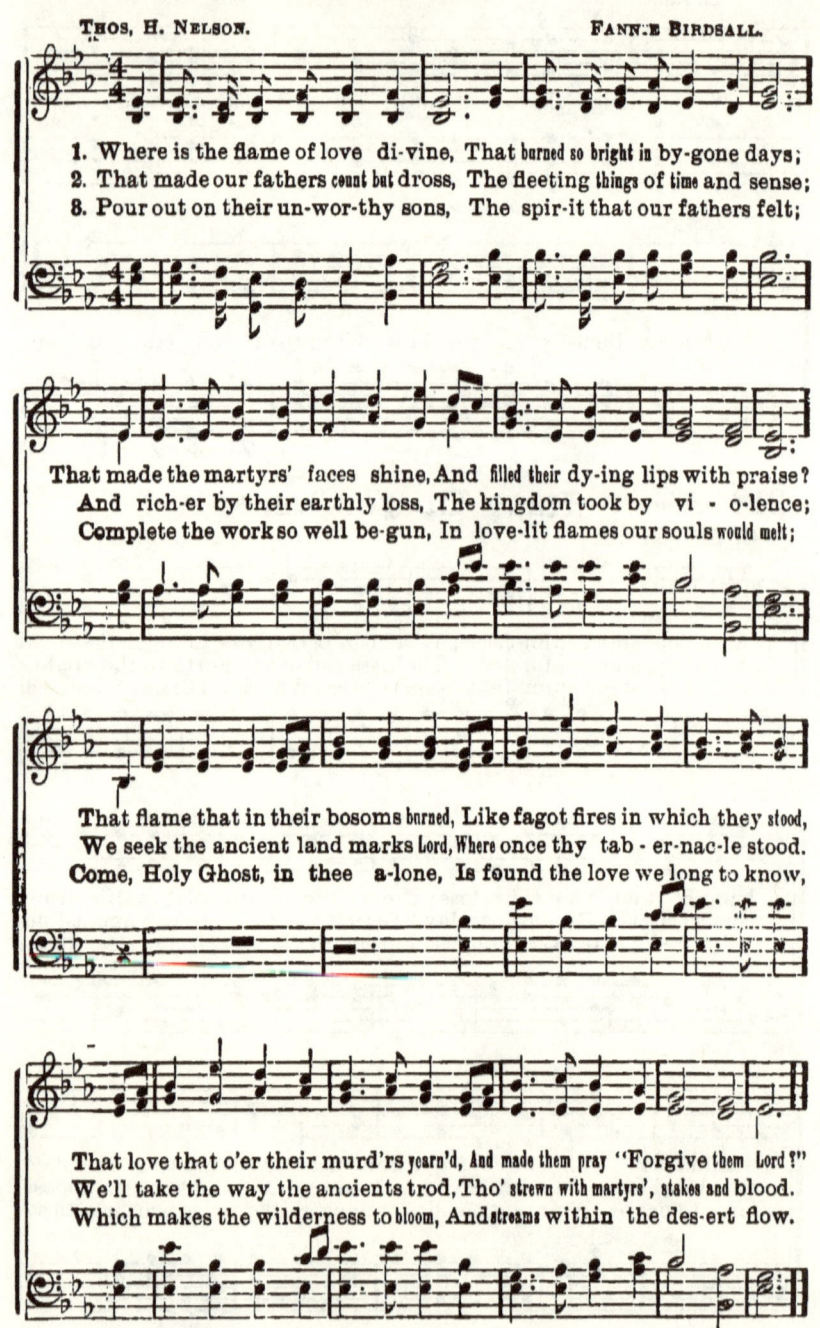

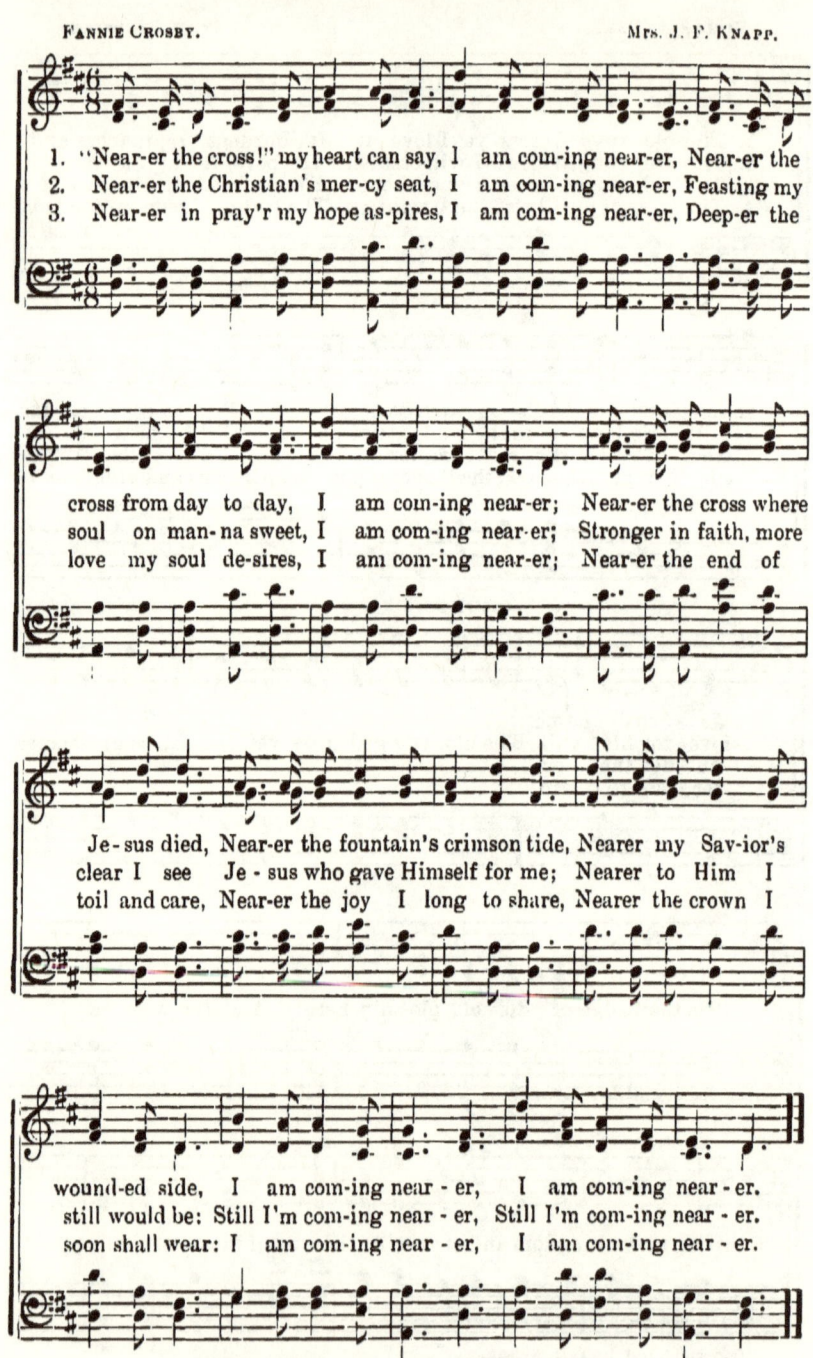

222 Everlasting.

VIVIAN A. DAKE.   FLORA BIRDSALL NELSON.

1. There's a world ev-er-last-ing, Of jas-per and pearl;
2. There's a house ev-er-last-ing, Not build-ed with hands,
3. There's a crown ev-er-last-ing, A crown of pure gold,

And o-nyx and ber-yl! And dia-mond and gold; And
Nor found-ed on sand, But built on the rock, Where
And stars, I am told, If lost ones I bring, To the

glo-ry un-told, And there I shall dwell, ev-er dwell.
com-eth no shock, And there is my home, ne'er to roam.
feet of my King, That crown I shall wear, ev-er wear.

Ev-er dwell, ev-er dwell, And there I shall dwell, ever dwell.
Ne'er to roam, ne'er to roam, And there is my home, ne'er to roam.
Ev-er wear, ev-er wear, That crown I shall wear, ever wear.

Ev-er dwell, ev-er dwell,
Ne'er to roam, ne'er to roam,
Ev-er wear, ev-er wear,

4 There's a hymn everlasting,
The Lamb is the theme,
So strong to redeem,
A hymn never old,
And yet ever told,
That hymn I shall sing, for my King.
REF.—For my King, etc.

5 There's a King everlasting,
He comes on his throne,
His children to own,
They waited full long,
With prayer and with song,
And now he has come, welcome home
REF.—Welcome home, etc.

Copyright by T. H. Nelson.

Saved by Grace--Concluded.

found, And swell the an-them, saved by grace.
where man is found,

226. Step Out on the Promise.

MAGGIE POTTER.   Arr. by E. F. M.   E. F. MILLER.

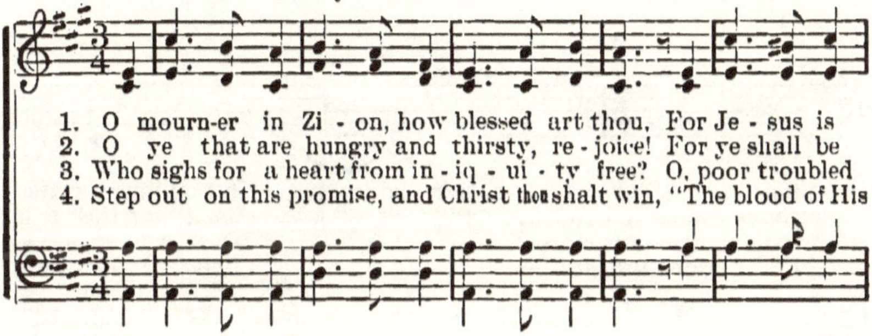

1. O mourn-er in Zi - on, how blessed art thou, For Je - sus is
2. O ye that are hungry and thirsty, re - joice! For ye shall be
3. Who sighs for a heart from in - iq - ui - ty free? O, poor troubled
4. Step out on this promise, and Christ thou shalt win, "The blood of His

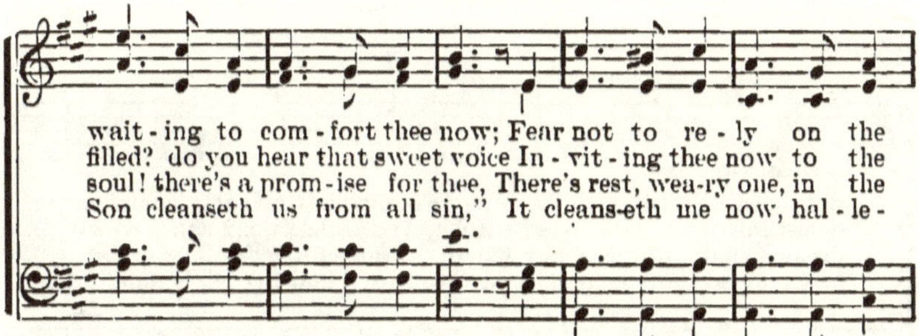

wait - ing to com - fort thee now; Fear not to re - ly on the
filled? do you hear that sweet voice In - vit - ing thee now to the
soul! there's a prom - ise for thee, There's rest, wea - ry one, in the
Son cleanseth us from all sin," It cleans-eth me now, hal - le -

word of thy God;   Step out on the prom-ise,—get un-der the blood.
ban-quet of God;   Step out on the prom-ise,—get un-der the blood.
bo - som of God;   Step out on the prom-ise,—get un-der the blood.
lu - jah to God;   I rest on His prom-ise,—I'm un-der the blood.

Copyright, by E. F. Miller, by per.

Thy Kingdom Come--Concluded.

jus - tice and mer - cy de - scend; Thy com-ing a - lone can true
glo - ry af - ford, and this reign of in - iq - ui - ty end............
this reign of in - iq - ui - ty end.

228 All for Jesus.

MARY D. JAMES. FANNIE BIRDSALL.

1. { All for Je-sus, all for Je-sus! All my being's ransomed pow'rs,
   { All my tho'ts and words and doings, All my days and all my hours.

D. C. *I will fol-low where He lead-eth, I will heed His ev-'ry call.*

CHORUS.

All for Je - sus, all for Je-sus, glad-ly I sur-ren-der all;

2. Let my hands perform His bidding,
   Let my feet run in His ways;
   Let my eyes see Jesus only,
   Let my lips speak forth His praise.

3. Since my eyes were fixed on Jesus,
   I've lost sight of all beside;
   So enchained my spirit's vision,
   Looking at the Crucified.

4. O, what wonder, how amazing!
   Jesus, glorious king of Kings,
   Deigns to call me His beloved,
   Lets me rest beneath His wings.

229. Sweetly Resting.

MARY D. JAMES.
W. WARREN BENTLY.

1. In the rift-ed Rock I'm rest-ing, Safe-ly shel-tered I a-bide;
2. Long pursued by sin and Sa-tan, Wea-ry, sad, I longed for rest;
3. Peace, which passeth under-stand-ing, Joy, the world can nev-er give,
4. In the rift-ed Rock I'll hide me, Till the storms of life are past;

There no foes nor storms mol-est me, While with-in the cleft I hide.
Then I found this heav'nly shel-ter O-pened in my Savior's breast.
Now in Je-sus I am find-ing; In His smiles of love I live.
All se-cure in this blest ref-uge, Heed-ing not the fierc-est blast.

CHORUS.

Now I'm rest-ing, sweet-ly rest-ing, In the cleft once made for me:

Je-sus, bless-ed Rock of A-ges, I will hide my-self in Thee.

Used by permission.

230. Precious Promise.

1 Precious promise God hath given
  To the weary passer by,
On the way from earth to heaven,
  "I will guide thee with mine eye."

CHORUS.—
I will guide thee, I will guide thee,
  I will guide thee with mine eye;
On the way from earth to heaven,
  I will guide thee with mine eye.

2 When temptations almost win thee,
  And thy trusted watchers fly,
Let this promise ring within thee,
  "I will guide thee with mine eye."

3 When thy secret hopes have perished
  In the grave of years gone by,
Let this promise still be cherished,
  "I will guide thee with mine eye."

231 Calvary.

Rev. B. Carradine.   Rev. L. L. Pickett.

1. There's a hill lone and gray In a land far a-way, In a coun-try beyond the blue sea,
2. Oh, so faint on the road,'Neath the world's heavy load,Comes a thorn-crowned Man on the way!
3. Hark, I hear the dull blow Of the hammer swung low, They are nailing my Lord to the tree!
4. How they mock Him in death To His last lab'ring breath,While His friends sadly weep o'er the way!

Where beneath that fair sky,Went a Man forth to die, For the world and for you and for me.
With a cross He is bowed, But still on thro' the crowd He's as-cending that hill lone and gray.
And the cross they upraise While the multitude gaze On the blest Lamb of dark Cal-va-ry!
But tho' lone-ly and faint Still no word of complaint Fell from Him on that hil-lock of gray.

CHORUS.

1–5. Oh, it bows down my heart, And the tear-drops will start,When in mem'ry that gray hill I see;
6. Shout a-loud, then my soul, Let the glad tidings roll From the land to the ends of the sea!

For 'twas there on its side Je-sus suffered and died, To re-deem a poor sin-ner like me.
Je-sus conquered the grave, And has ris-en to save The whole world, and to make us all free.

5 Then the darkness came down,
  And the rocks rent around,
    And a cry pierced the sad laden air!
  'Twas the voice of our King,
  Who received death's dark sting,
    All to save us from endless despair.

6 Let the sun hide its face,
  Let the earth reel apace,   [slain!
    Over men who their Savior have
  But, behold! from the sod
  Comes the bless'd Lamb of God,
    Who was slain, but is risen again.

By permission of L. L. Pickett.

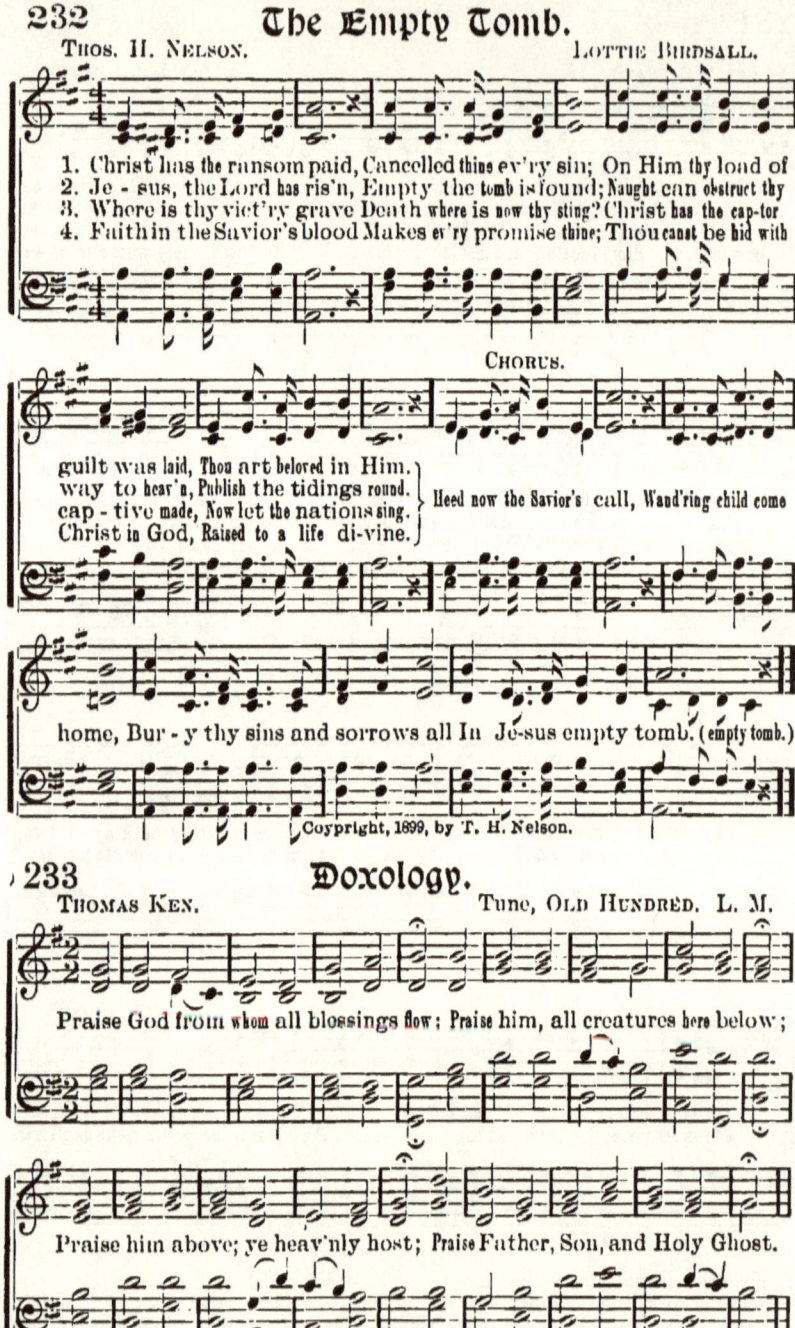

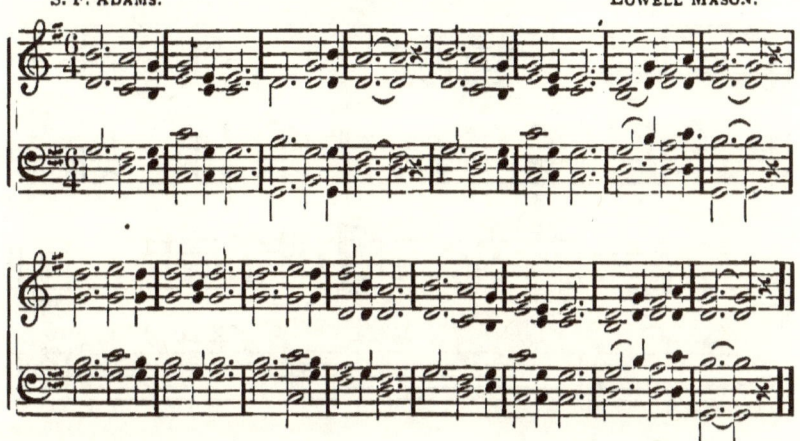

236 Nearer, my God, to Thee.

Nearer, my God, to thee!
  Nearer to thee,
E'en though it be a cross
  That raiseth me;
Still all my song shall be
Nearer, my God, to thee,
  Nearer to thee!

Though like the wanderer,
  Daylight all gone,
Darkness be over me,
  My rest a stone;
Yet in my dreams I'd be
Nearer, my God, to thee,
  Nearer to thee!

Then, with my waking thoughts,
  Bright with thy praise,
Out of my stony griefs
  Bethel I'll raise;
So by my woes to be
Nearer, my God, to thee,
  Nearer to thee!

Or if on joyful wing,
  Cleaving the sky,
Sun, moon and stars forgot,
  Upward I fly;
Still all my song shall be
Nearer, my God, to thee,
  Nearer to thee!

237 Fade, Fade, each Earthly Joy.

Fade, fade, each earthly joy,
  Jesus is mine!
Break, every tender tie!
  Jesus is mine!
Dark is the wilderness;
Earth has no resting-place;
Jesus alone can bless —
  Jesus is mine.

Tempt not my soul away,
  Jesus is mine!
Here would I ever stay,
  Jesus is mine!
Perishing things of clay,
Born but for one brief day,
Pass from my heart away,—
  Jesus is mine.

Farewell, mortality;
  Jesus is mine!
Welcome, eternity;
  Jesus is mine!
Welcome, O loved and blest
Welcome, sweet scenes of rest,
Welcome, my Saviour's breast;
  Jesus is mine!   Mrs. Bonar.

238 More Love to Thee.

More love to thee, O Christ!
  More love to thee;
Hear thou the prayer I make
  On bended knee.
This is my earnest plea,—
More love, O Christ, to thee!
  More love to thee.

Once earthly joy I craved,
  Sought peace and rest;
Now thee alone I seek,
  Give what is best.
This all my prayer shall be,—
More love, O Christ, to thee!
  More love to thee!

Then shall my latest breath
  Whisper thy praise,
This be the parting cry
  My heart shall raise,
This still my prayer shall be,—
More love, O Christ, to thee,
  More love to thee.
        E. P. Prentice.

Dennis. S. M.
Arr. from H. G. Nägell.

239 The Second Death.

O where shall rest be found,—
 Rest for the weary soul?
'Twere vain the ocean's depths to sound,
 Or pierce to either pole.

The world can never give
 The bliss for which we sigh;
'Tis not the whole of life to live,
 Nor all of death to die.

Beyond this vale of tears
 There is a life above,
Unmeasured by the flight of years;
 And all that life is love.

There is a death, whose pang
 Outlasts the fleeting breath:
O what eternal horrors hang
 Around the second death!

Thou God of truth and grace!
 Teach us that death to shun;
Lest we be banished from thy face,
 Forevermore undone. J. Montgomery.

240 The Redeemer's Tears.

Did Christ o'er sinner's weep,
 And shall our cheeks be dry?
Let floods of penitential grief
 Burst forth from every eye.

The Son of God in tears
 The wondering angels see;
Be thou astonished, O my soul!
 He shed those tears for thee.

He wept that we might weep;
 Each sin demands a tear;
In heaven alone no sin is found,
 And there's no weeping there.
  B. Beddome.

241 A Charge to Keep I Have.

A charge to keep I have;
 A God to glorify:
A never-dying soul to save,
 And fit it for the sky.

To serve the present age,
 My calling to fulfill,
O may it all my powers engage,
 To do my Master's will.

Arm me with jealous care,
 As in thy sight to live;
And oh, thy servant, Lord, prepare,
 A strict account to give.

Help me to watch and pray,
 And on thyself rely;
Assured if I my trust betray,
 I shall forever die.

242 And Can I Yet Delay?

And can I yet delay
 My little all to give?
To tear my soul from earth away,
 For Jesus to receive?

Nay, but I yield, I yield!
 I can hold out no more;
I sink, by dying love compell'd,
 And own Thee conqueror!.

Though late, I all forsake,—
 My friends, my all resign:
Gracious Redeemer, take, oh take!
 And seal me ever thine.

Come, and possess me whole,
 Nor hence again remove;
Settle and fix my wavering soul
 With all thy weight of love,

My one desire be this,
 Thy only love to know;
To seek and taste no other bliss,
 No other good below.

My life, my portion thou,
 Thou all—sufficient art;
My hope my heavenly treasure, now
 Enter, and keep my heart.

Duke Street. L. M.

JOHN HATTON.

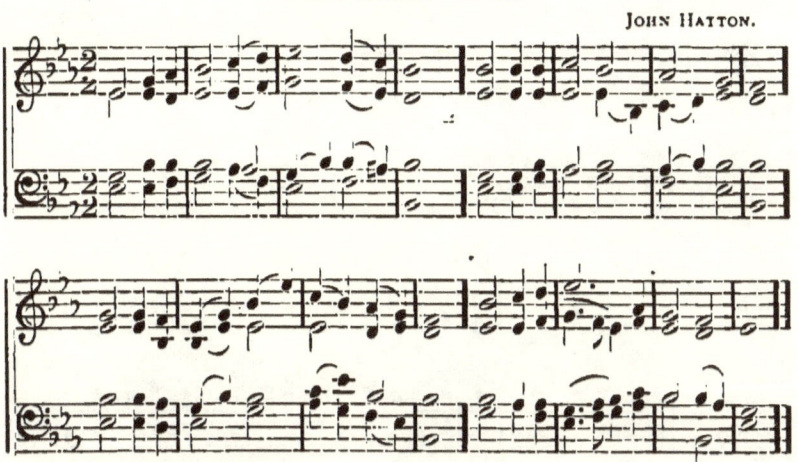

243 The Christian's Prayer.

Saviour of men, thy searching eye
Doth all my inmost thoughts descry:
Doth aught on earth my wishes raise,
Or the world's pleasures, or its praise?

The love of Christ doth me constrain
To seek the wandering souls of men;
With cries, entreaties, tears to save,
To snatch them from the gaping grave.

My life, my blood, I here present,
If for thy truth they may be spent;
Fulfill thy sovereign counsel, Lord;
Thy will be done, thy name adored.

Give me thy strength, O God of power,
Then let winds blow, or thunders roar,
Thy faithful witness will I be:
'Tis fixed; I can do all through thee.
J. J. WINKLER.

244 Thirsting for the Fulness.

I thirst, thou wounded Lamb of God,
To wash me in thy cleansing blood;
To dwell within thy wounds; then pain
Is sweet, and life or death is gain.

Take my poor heart, and let it be
Forever closed to all but thee:
Seal thou my breast, and let me wear
That pledge of love forever there.

How blest are they who still abide
Close sheltered in thy bleed'ng side!
Who thence their life and strength derive,
And by thee move, and in thee live.

Hence our hearts melt, our eyes o'erflow,
Our words are lost, nor will we know,
Nor will we think of aught beside,—
My Lord, my Love, is crucified.
N. I. ZINZENDORF.

245 Glorying in the Cross.

When I survey the wondrous cross,
On which the Prince of Glory died,
My richest gain I count but loss,
And pour contempt on all my pride.

Forbid it, Lord, that I should boast,
Save in the death of Christ, my God;
All the vain things that charm me most,
I sacrifice them to his blood.

See, from his head, his hands, his feet,
Sorrow and love flow mingled down:
Did e'er such love and sorrow meet,
Or thorns compose so rich a crown?

Were the whole realm of nature mine,
That were a present far too small;
Love so amazing, so divine,
Demands my soul, my life, my all.
ISAAC WATTS.

246 Condemned, but Pleading.

Show pity, Lord, O Lord, forgive;
Let a repenting rebel live:
Are not thy mercies large and free?
May not a sinner trust in thee?

My crimes are great, but don't surpass
The power and glory of thy grace;
Great God, thy nature hath no bound,
So let thy pardoning love be found.

O wash my soul from every sin,
And make my guilty conscience clean
Here on my heart the burden lies,
And past offenses pain my eyes.

Yet save a trembling sinner, Lord,
Whose hope, still hovering round thy Word,
Would light on some sweet promise there,
Some sure support against despair.
ISAAC WATTS.

Varina. C. M.
HEINRICH RINK, 1770.

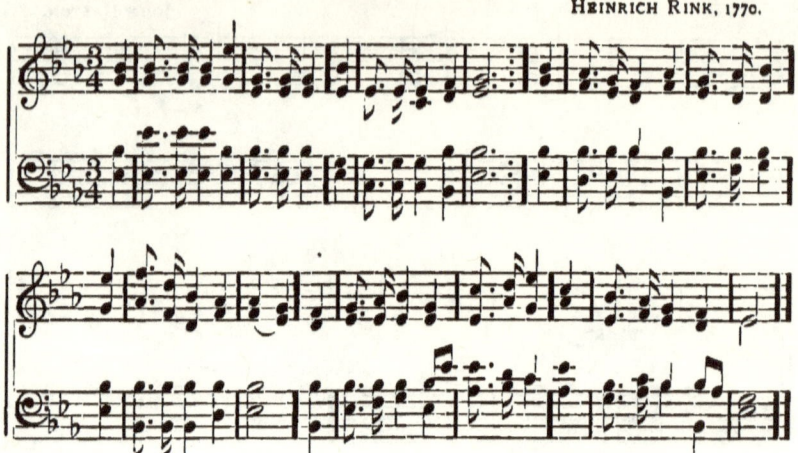

247 A View of Heaven.

On Jordan's stormy banks I stand,
 And cast a wishful eye
To Caanan's fair and happy land,
 Where my possessions lie.

O'er all those wide, extended plains
 Shines one eternal day:
There God, the Son, forever reigns,
 And scatters night away.

No chilling winds or poisonous breath
 Can reach that healthful shore;
Sickness and sorrow, pain and death,
 Are felt and feared no more.

Filled with delight my raptured soul
 Would here no longer stay;
Tho' Jordan's waves around me roll,
 Fearless I'd launch away.
  REV. S. STENNETT.

248 The Wanderer Recalled.

Return, O wanderer, return,
 And seek thy Father's face;
Those new desires which in thee burn,
 Were kindled by his grace.

Return, O wanderer, return;
 He hears thy humble sigh;
He sees thy softened spirit mourn,
 When no one else is nigh.

Return, O wanderer, return,
 And wipe the falling tear;
Thy Father calls, no longer mourn;
 'Tis love invites thee near.

Return, O wanderer, return;
 Begin thy long-sought rest;
The Saviour's melting mercies yearn
 To clasp thee to his breast.
  —W. B. Collyer.

249 Amazing Grace.

Amazing grace! how sweet the sound,
 That saved a wretch like me!
I once was lost, but now am found,
 Was blind, but now I see.

Twas grace that taught my heart to fear,
 And grace my fears relieved;
How precious did that grace appear
 The hour I first believed!

Through many dangers, toils and snares,
 I have already come;
'Tis grace hath brought me safe thus far,
 And grace will lead me home.
The Lord has promised good to me,
 His word my hope secures.
He will my shield and portion be
 As long as life endures.

Yes, when this flesh and heart shall fail,
 And mortal life shall cease,
I shall possess, within the veil,
 A life of joy and peace.
The earth shall soon dissolve like snow,
 The sun forbear to shine;
But God, who called me here below,
 Will be forever mine.   J. NEWTON.

250 Heavenly Canaan.

There is a land of pure delight,
 Where saints immortal reign;
Eternal day excludes the night,
 And pleasures banish pain.

There everlasting spring abides,
 And never-withering flowers;
Death, like a narrow sea, divides
 That heavenly land from ours.

Sweet fields beyond the swelling flood,
 Stand dressed in living green;
So to the Jews old Canaan stood,
 While Jordan rolled between.

Could we but climb where Moses stood,
 And view the landscape o'er,
Not Jordan's stream nor death's cold flood,
 Should fright us from the shore.
  I. WATTS.

St. Martins.   C. M.
Wm. Tansur.

251   Light Shining Out of Darkness.

God moves in a mysterious way,
  His wonders to perform;
He plants his footsteps in the sea,
  And rides upon the storm.

Ye fearful saints, fresh courage take,
  The clouds ye so much dread
Are big with mercy, and shall break
  In blessings on your head.

Judge not the Lord by feeble sense,
  But trust him for his grace;
Behind a frowning providence
  He hides a smiling face.

252   The Name of Jesus.

Jesus, the name high over all,
  In hell, or earth, or sky;
Angels and men before it fall,
  And devils fear and fly.

Jesus, the name to sinners dear,
  The name to sinners given,
It scatters all their guilty fear;
  It turns their hell to heaven.

Jesus the prisoner's fetters breaks,
  And bruises Satan's head;
Power into strengthless souls he speaks,
  And life into the dead.

O that the world might taste and see
  The riches of his grace;
The arms of love that compass me,
  Would all mankind embrace.

253   Praise the Redeemer.

O for a thousand tongues to sing
  My great Redeemer's praise;
The glories of my God and King,
  The triumphs of his grace.

Jesus! the name that charms our fears,
  That bids our sorrows cease;
'Tis music in the sinner's ears,
  'Tis life, and health and peace.

He breaks the power of canceled sin,
  He sets the prisoner free;
His blood can make the foulest clean;
  His blood availed for me.

Hear him, ye deaf; his praise, ye dumb,
  Your loosened tongues employ;
Ye blind, behold your Saviour comes;
  And leap, ye lame, for joy.

254   Victorious Faith.

O, for a faith that will not shrink,
  Though pressed by every foe;
That will not tremble on the brink
  Of any earthly woe.

That will not murmur nor complain
  Beneath the chastening rod,
But, in the hour of grief or pain,
  Will lean upon its God.

A faith that shines more bright and clear
  When tempests rage without;
That when in danger knows no fear,
  In darkness feels no doubt.

That bears, unmoved, the world's dread frown,
  Nor heeds its scornful smile;
That seas of trouble cannot drown,
  Or Satan's arts beguile.

A faith that keeps the narrow way
  Till life's last hour is fled,
And with a pure and heavenly ray
  Illumes the dying bed.

Lord, give us such a faith as this,
  And then, whate'er may come,
We'll taste, e'en here, the hallowed bliss
  Of an eternal home.   W. H. Bathurst.

Zion. 8s, 7s, 4s.

THOMAS HASTINGS.

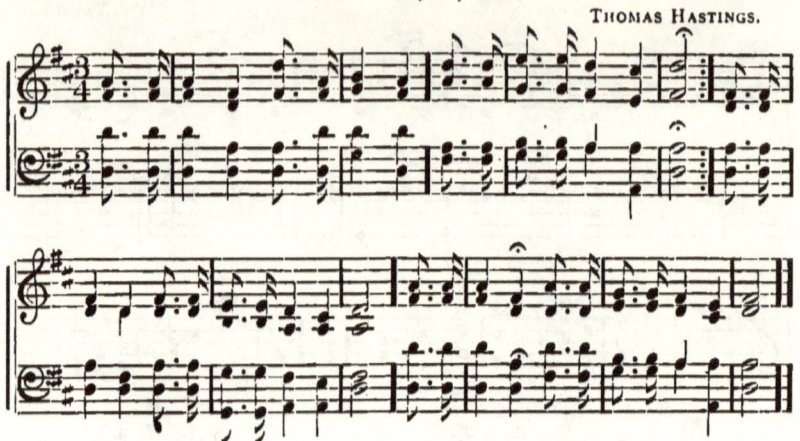

255 The Defence of Zion.

Zion stands with hills surrounded,
  Zion, kept by power divine;
All her foes shall be confounded,
  Though the world in arms combine:
    Happy Zion,
  What a favored lot is thine!

Every human tie may perish;
  Friend to friend unfaithful prove;
Mothers cease their own to cherish;
  Heaven and earth at last remove;
    But no changes
  Can attend Jehovah's love.

In the furnace God may prove thee,
  Thence to bring thee forth more bright,
But can never cease to love thee:
  Thou art precious in His sight,
    God is with thee,
  God, thine everlasting light.
  THOS. KELLEY

256 I Will Praise Thee.

O thou God of my salvation,
  My Redeemer from all sin;
Moved by thy divine compassion,
  Who hast died my heart to win,
    I will praise thee:
  Where shall I thy praise begin?

Though unseen, I love the Saviour;
  He hath brought salvation near;
Manifests his pardoning favor;
  And when Jesus doth appear,
    Soul and body
  Shall his glorious image bear.

While the angel choirs are crying,
  "Glory to the great I AM,"
I with them will still be vying:
  Glory! Glory to the Lamb!
    O how precious
  Is the sound of Jesus' name!

Angels now are hovering round us,
  Unperceived amid the throng;
Wondering at the love that crowned us:
  Glad to join the holy song:
    Hallelujah!
  Love and praise to Christ belong!

257 Guide Me.

Guide me, O thou great Jehovah,
  Pilgrim through this barren land;
I am weak—but thou art mighty;
  Hold me with thy powerful hand:
    Bread of heaven,
  Feed me till I want no more.

Open now the crystal fountain,
  Whence the healing waters flow;
Let the fiery, cloudy pillar,
  Lead me all my journey through:
    Strong Deliv'rer,
  Be thou still my strength and shield!

When I tread the verge of Jordan,
  Bid my anxious fears subside;
Bear me through the swelling current,
  Land me safe on Canaan's side;
    Songs of praises
  I will ever give to Thee.

258. Good News for Zion.

On the mountain top appearing,
  Lo! the sacred herald stands.
Welcome news to Zion bearing,
  Zion, long in hostile hands.
    Mourning captive!
  God himself shall loose thy bands.

Peace and joy shall now attend thee,
  All thy warfare now is past;
God thy Savior will defend thee,
  Victory is thine at last;
    All thy conflicts
  End in everlasting rest.

Arlington. C. M.

Dr. Arne.

259 Soldier of the Cross.

Am I a soldier of the cross,
  A follower of the Lamb;
And shall I fear to own his cause,
  Or blush to speak his name?

Must I be carried to the skies
  On flowery beds of ease;
While others fought to win the prize,
  And sailed through bloody seas?

Sure I must fight if I would reign;
  Increase my courage, Lord;
I'll bear the toil, endure the pain,
  Supported by thy Word.

Thy saints in all this glorious war
  Shall conquer, though they die;
They see the triumph from afar,
  By faith they bring it nigh.

When that illustrious day shall rise,
  And all thine armies shine,
In robes of victory through the skies,
  The glory shall be thine.
Isaac Watts.

260 A Perfect Heart.

O for a heart to praise my God,
  A heart from sin set free;
A heart that always feels thy blood,
  So freely spilt for me.

A heart resigned, submissive, meek,
  My great Redeemer's throne;
Where only Christ is heard to speak,
  Where Jesus reigns alone.

A heart in every thought renewed,
  And full of love divine;
Perfect and right, and pure, and good,
  A copy, Lord, of thine.

Thy nature, gracious Lord, impart;
  Come quickly from above;
Write thy new name upon my heart,
  Thy new, best name of love.

261 Sin Kills Beyond the Tomb.

Vain man, thy fond pursuits forbear;
  Repent, thine end is nigh;
Death, at the farthest, can't be far;
  O think before thou die.

Reflect, thou hast a soul to save;
  Thy sins, how high they mount!
What are thy hopes beyond the grave?
  How stands that dark account?

Death enters, and there's no defence;
  His time there's none can tell;
He'll in a moment call thee hence,
  To heaven, or down to hell.

Thy flesh (perhaps thy greatest care)
  Shall into dust consume;
But, ah! destruction stops not there;
  Sin kills beyond the tomb.
J. Hart.

262 The Dreadful Sentence.

That awful day will surely come;
  The appointed hour makes haste,
When I must stand before my Judge,
  And pass the solemn test.

Jesus, thou source of all my joys,
  Thou ruler of my heart,
How could I bear to hear thy voice
  Pronounce the word, "Depart!"

The thunder of that awful word
  Would so torment my ear,
'Twould tear my soul asunder, Lord,
  With most tormenting fear.

O wretched state of deep despair,
  To see my God remove,
And fix my doleful station where
  I must not taste his love.

Rathbun. 8, 7.
ITHAMAR CONKEY.

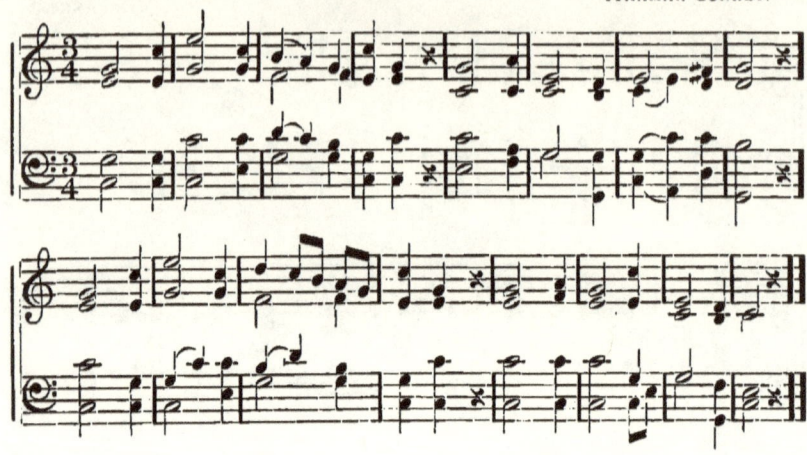

263 Resurrection Song.

Sing with all the sons of glory,—
  Sing the Resurrection song;
Death and sorrow, earth's dark story,
  To the former days belong.

Life eternal! Heaven rejoices;
  Jesus lives, who once was dead;
Join, oh man, the deathless voices,
  Child of God, lift up thy head.

Life eternal! O what wonders
  Crown our faith; what joy unknown,
When amid earth's closing thunders,
  Saints shall stand before the throne.

O to enter that bright portal,
  See that glowing firmament,
Know, with thee, O God immortal,
  "Jesus Christ whom thou hast sent."
  WM. J. IRONS.

264 The Lord Our Helper.

Come, thou Fount of every blessing,
  Tune my heart to sing thy grace;
Streams of mercy, never ceasing,
  Call for songs of loudest praise.
Teach me some melodious sonnet,
  Sung by flaming tongues above:
Praise the mount—I'm fixed upon it,
  Mount of thy redeeming love.

Here I'll raise mine Ebenezer;
  Hither by thy help I'm come;
And I hope, by thy good pleasure,
  Safely to arrive at home.
O to grace how great a debtor
  Daily I'm constrained to be!
Let thy goodness, like a fetter,
  Bind my grateful heart to thee.

Jesus sought me when a stranger,
  Wandering from the fold of God;
He, to rescue me from danger,
  Interposed his precious blood.
On the cross he died to save me,
  Rose to plead my cause above;
Henceforth all my life I give thee,
  Vanquished by such wondrous love.
  R. ROBINSON, alt.

265 The Cross.

In the cross of Christ I glory,
  Towering o'er the wrecks of time;
All the light of sacred story
  Gathers round its head sublime;

When the woes of life o'ertake me,
  Hopes deceive and fears annoy,
Never shall the cross forsake me;
  Lo! it glows with peace and joy.

When the sun of bliss is beaming
  Light and love upon my way,
From the cross the radiance streaming.
  Adds more luster to the day.

Bane and blessing, pain and pleasure,
  By the cross are sanctified;
Peace is there, that knows no measure,
  Joys that through all time abide.
  SIR JOHN BOWRING.

266 The New Creation.

Love divine, all love excelling,
  Joy of heaven to earth come down,
Fix in us thy humble dwelling;
  All thy faithful mercies crown.

Breathe, O breathe thy loving Spirit
  Into every troubled breast;
Let us all in thee inherit;
  Let us find that second rest.

Take away our bent to sinning;
  Alpha and Omega be;
End of faith as its beginning,
  Set our hearts at liberty.

Finish then thy new creation,
  Pure and spotless let us be.
Let us see thy great salvation,
  Perfectly restored in thee.

Changed from glory into glory,
  Till in heaven we take our place,
Till we cast our crowns before thee,
  Lost in wonder, love and praise.
  CHARLES WESLEY.

Hendon. 7.

Moderato. — Cæsar Malan, 1830.

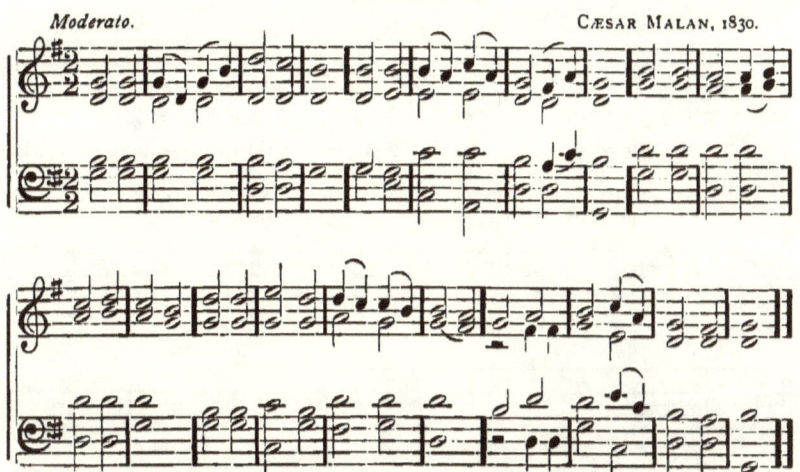

267 Children of The King.

Children of the heavenly King,
As we journey let us sing;
Sing our Saviour's worthy praise,
Glorious in his works and ways.

We are traveling home to God,
In the way our fathers trod:
They are happy now, and we
Soon their happiness shall see.

Fear not, brethren, joyful stand
On the borders of our land:
Jesus Christ, our Father's Son,
Bids us undismayed go on.

Lord, obediently we'll go,
Gladly leaving all below;
Only Thou our Leader be,
And we still will follow Thee.

268 The Danger of Delay.

Hasten, sinner, to be wise!
  Stay not for the morrow's sun:
Wisdom if you still despise,
  Harder is it to be won.

Hasten, mercy to implore!
  Stay not for the morrow's sun,
Lest thy season should be o'er
  Ere this evening's stage be run.

Hasten, sinner, to return!
  Stay not for the morrow's sun,
Lest thy lamp should fail to burn
  Ere salvation's work is done.

Hasten, sinner, to be blest!
  Stay not for the morrow's sun,
Lest perdition thee arrest
  Ere the morrow is begun.

269 Submission to God.

Prince of peace control my will;
Bid this struggling heart be still;
Bid my fears and doubtings cease,
Hush my spirit into peace.

Thou hast bought me with thy blood,
Opened wide the gate to God.
Peace I ask—but peace must be,
Lord, in being one with Thee.

May thy will, not mine, be done;
May thy will and mine be one:
Chase these doubtings from my heart;
Now thy perfect peace impart.

Savior at thy feet I fall;
Thou my life, my God, my all!
Let thy happy servant be
One for evermore with thee.
  MARY A S. BARBER.

270 Encouragement to Pray.

Come, my soul, thy suit prepare;
Jesus loves to answer prayer;
He himself invites thee near,
Bids thee ask him, waits to hear.

While I am a pilgrim here,
Let thy love my spirit cheer;
As my guide, my guard, my friend,
Lead me to my journey's end.

Show me what I have to do;
Every hour my strength renew;
Let me live a life of faith,
Let me die thy people's death.
  J. NEWTON.

271 God's Love.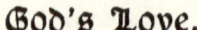

Victor Strange.   Arranged.

1. God's love is as high as the heav-en God's love is as deep as the
   love has my sin all for-giv - en, God's
2. My joy is as deep as the o - cean, My cares are as light as its
   subject of heaven's de-vo - tion, God's

CHORUS.

sea; God's love is sufficient for me. God's love, God's love, God's
foam: A with me wherever I roam.

love is sufficient for me, for me; love is sufficient for me.

3 As rivers in majesty flowing,
   God's goodness and mercy I see;
Like zephyrs from Eden now blowing,
   God's love is extended to me.

4 I'll sing of His Majesty ever,
   His boundless and fathomless love;
And some day, beyond the cold river,
   I'll join in the anthems above.

Copyrighted by T. H. Nelson, 1899.

272 My Beautiful Home.

I've left the land of death and sin,
The road so many travel in;
And if you ask the reason why,
I'm going to seek a home on high,

CHORUS.

My beautiful home, my beautiful home,
In the land where the glorified ever shall roam;

Where angels bright, wear crowns of light,
My home is there, my home is there.

I oftimes weep to see the sin
And wretchedness that men are in;
But my cares all flee, and my tears are dry,
When I look by faith to my home on high.

There are many who would my progress stay,
And beg me not to weep and pray;
But I dare not listen to their cry,
For I seek a glorious home on high.

Say, sinner, will you come with me,
And seek this land of liberty?
Oh, do not stay, but tell me why
You will not seek a home on high.

273 Joy of the Justified.

O how happy are they,
Who the Saviour obey,
And have laid up their treasures above,
Tongue can never express
The sweet comfort and peace
Of a soul in its earliest love.

That sweet comfort was mine,
When the favor divine
I received through the blood of the Lamb;
When my heart first believed
What a joy I received,
What a heaven in Jesus' name!

'Twas a heaven below
My Redeemer to know,
And the angels could do nothing more,
Than to fall at his feet,
And the story repeat,
And the Lover of sinners adore.

O the rapturous height
Of the holy delight
Which I felt in the life-giving blood!
Of my Saviour possessed,
I was perfectly blest,
As if filled with the fulness of God.
CHAS. WESLEY.

275 Come, Almighty King.

Come, thou almighty King,
Help us thy name to sing,
Help us to praise:
Father! all glorious,
O'er all victorious,
Come and reign over us,
Ancient of days!

Come thou incarnate Word,
Gird on thy mighty sword;
Our prayer attend,
Come, and thy people bless
And give thy word success;
Spirit of holiness!
On us descend.

Come, holy Comforter!
Thy sacred witness bear,
In this glad hour:
Thou, who almighty art,
Now rule in every heart.
And ne'er from us depart,
Spirit of power!

To the Great one in three,
The highest praises be,
Hence evermore!
His sovreign majesty
May we in glory see;
And to eternity
Love and adore.

274 The Cry of the Heathen.

From Greenland's icy mountains,
From India's coral strand;
Where Afric's sunny fountains
Roll down their golden sand:
From many an ancient river,
From many a palmy plain,
They call us to deliver
Their land from error's chains.

What though the spicy breezes
Blow soft o'er Ceylon's isle;
Though every prospect pleases,
And only man is vile?
In vain with lavish kindness
The gifts of God are strown;
The heathen in his blindness
Bows down to wood and stone.

Shall we whose souls are lighted
With wisdom from on high,
Shall we to men benighted,
The lamp of life deny?
Salvation!--O salvation!
The joyful sound proclaim,
Till earth's remotest nation
Has learned Messiah's name.

Waft, waft, ye winds his story,
And you, ye waters roll,
Till like a sea of glory,
It spreads from pole to pole:
Till o'er our ransomed nature
The Lamb for sinners slain,
Redeemer, King, Creator,
In bliss returns to reign.
R. HEBER.

276 There is a Spot.

There is a spot to me more dear
Than native vale and mountain;
A spot for which affection's tear
Springs grateful from its fountain.
'Tis not where kindred souls abound,
Though that is almost heaven;
But where I first my Savior found,
And felt my sins forgiven.

Hard was my toil to reach the shore,
Long tossed upon the ocean;
Above me was the thunder's roar,
Beneath, the wave's commotion;
Darkly the pall of night was thrown
Around me, faint with terror:
In that dark hour how did my groan
Ascend for years of error!

Sinking and panting as for breath,
I knew not help was near me;
And cried, "O! save me Lord from death,
Immortal Jesus, hear me."
Then quick as thought I felt him mine,
My Savior stood before me;
I saw his brightness round me shine,
And shouted, "Glory! Glory!"

O sacred hour! O hallowed spot!
Where love divine first found me;
Wherever falls my distant lot,
My heart shall linger round thee;
And when from earth I rise to soar
Up to my home in heaven,
Down will I cast my eyes once more,
Where I was first forgiven.
W. HUNTER.

277 Prodigal's Return.

Oh! I have spent my all in sin,
  My fears begin to rise,
All wretchedness and dark within,
  I dare not lift my eyes.
O my injured Jesus,
  Lamb for sinner's slain,
Though I have wandered from my home,
  I would come back again.

These wretched husks I cannot bear,
  While Father's house is full;
I see my distant home afar,
  But oh! my spirit fails.
Oh! my injured Jesus, etc.

These tattered robes, how bad they look,
  What will my Father say?
Oh! can he take his lost one back?
  Oh! will he hear me pray?
O my injured Jesus!
  Saviour crucified!
All foul and guilty as I am,
  I am coming to thy side.

Yes I will take my journey back,
  Unto my Father's home;
I'll say I've sinned in thy sight,
  And lo! I am undone.
O my injured Jesus,
  Lamb for sinners slain!
I'm on my way to Father's home,
  I am coming back again.

If I could see my Father's face,
  And pledge my humble vows,
I'd only ask a servant's place
  Within my Father's house.
O Hallelujah!
  My Savior's reconciled.
He sees me coming from afar,
  And runs to meet his child.

My Father clasps me to his breast,
  He owns me in my rags;
He kills for me the fatted calf.
  And clothes me with his robe.
O Hallelujah!
  My Father's reconciled!
For me the house will now rejoice,
  My Father owns his child.

278 O Bear me Away.

O bear me away o'er the ocean's tide,
Till I catch the gleam on the farther side;
Where the heathen wait of God to hear,
To learn of his love his rod to fear.

CHORUS.

My heart has gone, I must haste away,
To rescue souls who have gone astray;
In heathen lands they watch and wait,
I long to go ere it be too late.

The harvest is great, the laborers few,
My comrades brave, may he send you?
Alas how few who with willing heart,
From their native land and friends will part.

Shall Jesus come to our earth in vain,
And bear such sorrow, guilt and pain;
Shall we sit content and fold our hands,
Nor tell of his love in heathen lands?

The earth is his with its fullness too,
If he sends you out he will care for you;
May the language then of each heart be.
O what can I do? O Lord, send me.

279 A Great Day Coming.

There's a great day coming, a great day coming,
There's a great day coming by and by,
When the saints and the sinner shall be parted right and left,
Are you ready for that day to come?

CHORUS.

Are you ready? Are you ready?
Are you ready for the judgment day?
Are you ready? are you ready?
For the judgment day?

There's a bright day coming, a bright day coming.
There's a bright day coming by and by,
But its brightness shall only come to them that love the Lord,
Are you ready for that day to come?

There's a sad day coming, a sad day coming,
There's a sad day coming by and by,
When the sinner shall hear his doom, "Depart, I know ye not,"
Are you ready for that day to come?

280 O Day of Rest!

O day of rest and gladness,
  O day of joy and light,
O balm of care and sadness,
  Most beautiful, most bright:
On thee, the high and lowly,
  Through ages joined in tune.
Sing "Holy, holy, holy,"
  To the great God Triune.

Today on weary nations
  The heavenly manna falls;
To holy convocations
  The silver trumpet calls,
Where gospel light is glowing
  With pure and radiant beams,
And living water flowing
  With soul-refreshing streams.

New graces ever gaining
  From this our day of rest,
We reach the rest remaining
  To spirits of the blest;
To Holy Ghost be praises,
  To Father, and to Son;
The church her voice upraises
  To Thee, blest Three in One.

281 The Ninety and Nine.

There were ninety and nine that safely lay,
In the shelter of the fold,
But one was out on the hills away,
Far off from the gates of gold—
Away on the mountains wild and bare,
‖:Away from the tender Shepherd's care,:‖

"Lord thou hast here thy ninety and nine;
Are they not enough for thee?"
But the Shepherd made answer: "This of mine
Has wandered away from me,
And although the road be rough and steep,
‖:I go to the desert to find my sheep.":‖

But none of the ransomed ever knew,
How deep were the waters crossed;
Nor how dark was the night that the Lord passed thro',
Ere he found the sheep that was lost;
Out in the desert he heard its cry—
‖:Sick and helpless and ready to die.;‖

"Lord whence are those blood drops all the way
That mark out the mountain's track?"
"They were shed for one who had gone astray
Ere the Shepherd could bring him back."
"Lord whence are thy hands so rent and torn?"
‖:"They are pierced tonight by many a thorn.":‖

But all through the mountains thunder riven
And up from the rocky steep,
There arose a glad cry to the gate of heav'n,
"Rejoice I have found my sheep!"
And the angels echoed around the throne,
‖:"Rejoice for the Lord brings back His own.":‖

282 Arise My Soul.

Arise, my soul, arise;
Shake off thy guilty fears,
The bleeding Sacrifice
In my behalf appears:
Before the throne my Surety stands,
My name is written on His hands.

He ever lives above,
For me to intercede;
His all-redeeming love,
His precious blood, to plead;
His blood atoned for all our race,
And sprinkles now the throne of grace.

Five bleeding wounds He bears,
Received on Calvary:
They pour effectual prayers,
They strongly plead for me;
"Forgive him, oh, forgive," they cry,
"Nor let that ransomed sinner die."

The Father hears Him pray,
His dear anointed One;
He cannot turn away
The presence of His Son;
His Spirit answers to the blood,
And tells me I am born of God.

My God is reconciled;
His pardoning voice I hear:
He owns me for His child;
I can no longer fear:
With confidence I now draw nigh,
And, "Father, Abba, Father!" cry.

283 There is a Fountain.

There is a fountain filled with blood
Drawn from Immanuel's veins;
And sinners, plunged beneath that flood,
Lose all their guilty stains.

The dying thief rejoiced to see
That fountain in his day;
And there have I, though vile as he,
Washed all my sins away.

Thou dying Lamb! thy precious blood
Shall never lose its power,
Till all the ransomed Church of God
Are saved, to sin no more.

E'er since, by faith, I saw the stream
Thy flowing wounds supply,
Redeeming love has been my theme,
And shall be till I die.

Then in a nobler, sweeter song,
I'll sing thy power to save,
When this poor, lisping, stammering tongue,
Lies silent in the grave.
—W. Cowper.

284 All Victorious Love.

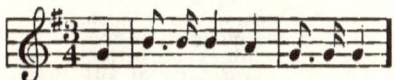

Jesus, thine all-victorious love
Shed in my heart abroad;
Then shall my feet no longer rove,
Rooted and fixed in God.

O that in me the sacred fire
Might now begin to glow:
Burn up the dross of base desire:
And make the mountains flow.

Refining fire, go through my heart;
Illuminate my soul;
Scatter thy life through every part,
And sanctify the whole.

My steadfast soul, from falling free,
Shall then no longer move;
While Christ is all the world to me,
And all my heart is love.
—Charles Wesley.

285 Entire Purification.

Forever here my rest shall be,
　Close to thy bleeding side;
This all my hope, and all my plea,
　For me the Savior died.

My dying Savior, and my God,
　Fountain for guilt and sin,
Sprinkle me ever with thy blood,
　And cleanse and keep me clean.

Wash me, and make me thus thine own;
　Wash me, and mine thou art;
Wash me, but not my feet alone,
　My hands, my head, my heart.

The atonement of thy blood apply,
　Till faith to sight improve;
Till hope in full fruition die,
　And all my soul be love.
　　　　　　　—C. Wesley.

286 Come, Ye Sinners.

Come, ye sinners, poor and needy,
　Weak and wounded, sick and sore;
Jesus ready stands to save you,
　Full of pity, love and power:
　　He is able,
　He is willing: doubt no more.

Let no conscience make you linger,
　Nor of fitness fondly dream;
All the fitness he requireth
　Is to feel your need of him:
　　This he gives you,
　'Tis the Spirit's glimmering beam.

Come, ye weary, heavy-laden,
　Bruised and mangled by the fall;
If you tarry till you're better
　You will never come at all:
　　Not the righteous,
　Sinners Jesus came to call.

Agonizing in the garden,
　Your Redeemer prostrate lies;
On the bloody tree behold him!
　Hear Him cry before He dies,
　　It is finished!
　Sinners, will not this suffice?

287 Retreat.

From every stormy wind that blows,
From every swelling tide of woes,
There is a calm, a sure retreat;
'Tis found beneath the mercy-seat.

There is a place where Jesus sheds
The oil of gladness on our heads;
A place than all besides more sweet;
It is the blood-bought mercy-seat.

Ah! whither could we flee for aid,
When tempted, desolate, dismayed?
Or how the hosts of hell defeat,
Had suffering saints no mercy-seat?

There, there on eagles' wings we soar,
And sin and sense molest no more;
And heaven comes down our souls to greet,
While glory crowns the mercy-seat.
　　　　　　　—H. Stowell.

288 Heart Made Known.

And must I be to judgment brought,
　And answer in that day
For every vain and idle thought,
　And every word I say?

Yes, every secret of my heart
　Shall shortly be made known,
And I receive my just desert
　For all that I have done.

How careful then ought I to live;
　With what religious fear;
Who such a strict account must give
　For my behavior here.

If now thou standest at the door,
　O let me feel thee near;
And make my peace with God, before
　I at thy bar appear.
　　　　　　　—Charles Wesley.

289 Glorying in the Cross.

When I survey the wondrous cross
On which the Prince of glory died,
My richest gain I count but loss,
And pour contempt on all my pride.

Forbid it, Lord, that I should boast,
Save in the death of Christ, my God;
All the vain things that charm me most,
I sacrifice them to His blood.

See, from His head, His hands, His feet,
Sorrow and love flow mingled down;
Did e'er such love and sorrow meet,
Or thorns compose so rich a crown?

Were the whole realm of nature mine,
That were a present far too small;
Love so amazing, so divine,
Demands my soul, my life, my all.
　　　　　　　—Isaac Watts.

290 A Little Talk with Jesus.

While fighting for my Master here,
The devil tries me hard;
He uses all his mighty power
My progress to retard.
He's up to every move,
But yet, through all I prove,
That, a little talk with Jesus makes it right.

||: Oh, a little talk with Jesus makes it right, all right :||
Thro' trials of every kind;
Bless God I always find,
That a little talk with Jesus makes it right.

Tho' dark the night and clouds look black,
And stormy over head,
And trials almost of every kind
Across my path are spread;
How soon I conquer all,
As to the Lord I call,
And a little talk with Jesus makes it right.

Whene'er the fight seems getting dull,
And weariness draws nigh,
And Satan in his craftiness
Whispers, "No longer try,"
I fall upon my knees,
The devil quickly flees,
And a little talk with Jesus makes it right.

And thus by frequent little talks
I gain the victory,
And march right on with cheerful song,
Enjoying liberty;
With Jesus as my friend,
I'll prove until the end,
That a little talk with Jesus makes it right.
—Martin Lock.

291 The Bondage of Love.

O sweet will of God! thou hast girded me round,
Like the deep moving currents that girdle the sea;
With omnipotent love is my poor nature bound,
And this bondage to love sets me perfectly free!

CHORUS:
Hallelujah! hallelujah! my soul is now free!
For the precious blood of Jesus cleanseth even me.

For years my will wrestled with vague discontent,
That like a sad angel o'ershadowed my way;
God's light in my soul with the darkness was blent,
And my heart ever longed for an unclouded day.

My wild will was captured; yet under the yoke
There was pain and not peace at the press of the load,
Till the glorious burden the last fiber broke,
And I melted like wax in the furnace of God.

And now I have flung myself recklessly out,
Like a chip on the stream of the Infinite Will;
I pass the rough rocks with a smile and a shout,
And I just let my God his dear purpose fulfill.

Roll on, checkered seasons; bring smiles or bring tears,
My soul sweetly sails on an infinite tide;
I shall soon touch the shores of eternity's years,
And near the white throne of my Saviour abide.
—George D. Watson.

292 Why Not To-Night?

O do not let the Word depart,
And close thine eyes against the light
Poor sinner, harden not thy heart;
Thou wouldst be saved—why not to-night?

CHORUS:
||: Why not to-night? Why not to-night?
Thou wouldst be saved—why not to-night? :||

To-morrow's sun may never rise,
To bless thy long deluded sight;
This is the time! O then be wise!
Thou wouldst be saved—why not to-night?

The world has nothing left to give—
It has no new, no pure delight;
Oh, try the life which Christians live!
Thou wouldst be saved—why not to-night?

Our blessed Lord refuses none
Who would to Him their souls unite;
Then be the work of grace begun!
Thou wouldst be saved—why not to-night?

293 Shall Life be Wasted?

Shall this life of mine be wasted?
Shall this vineyard lie untilled?
Shall true joys pass by untasted,
And the soul remain unfilled?

CHORUS:
No, no! No, no!
Ever faithful let me be;
And each precious hour redeeming,
Wait for thee, Eternity.

Shall the God-given hours be scattered,
Like the leaves upon the plain?
Shall the blossoms die unwatered,
By the dews of heavenly rain?

Shall I see each fair sun waking,
And not see it wake for me?
Each glad morning brightly breaking,
And not see it break for me?

No, I was not born to trifle
Life away in dreams of sin;
No, I must not, dare not stifle
Longings such as these within.

294 Workers' Warning.
Tune—"Gipsy's Warning."

Precious worker, danger signals
Float around thee; take thou heed,
Bide thee in thy place till Jesus
To another field shall lead;
Siren voices most enticing
Would allure thee from thy trust,
Honeyed words, mere Adam's apples,
'Neath the pressure turn to dust.

Friends will urge, constrain, persuade
you,
Point a better, easier way,
Anything beside, the tempter
Will suggest. Oh, haste away!
Seek another field of labor,
Leave your burdens and your band,
And in other scenes you'll surely
More respect and love command.

Precious jewels thou hast gathered
For thy crowning by and by,
When thy Lord shall call his faithful
To their welcome in the sky;
Wilt thou run the risk of losing
All thy trophies, all thy gain,
Trifle with the souls thy Saviour
Purchased with his blood and pain?

Thou hast felt 'twas God that called
thee,
Has thy God released thee? Hark!
To turn from His will and pleasure
Is to wander in the dark;
Bide thee in thy place, dear worker,
Till thy Lord shall bring release,
Then by Death or Spirit's whisper
It will come on wings of peace.
—Vivian A. Dake.

295 The Mind of Christ.

Jesus, plant and root in me
All the mind that was in thee;
Settled peace I then shall find,
Jesus' is a quiet mind.

Anger I no more shall feel,
Always even, always still;
Meekly on my God reclined;
Jesus' is a gentle mind.

I shall suffer and fulfill
All my Father's gracious will;
Be in all alike resigned;
Jesus' is a patient mind.

I shall triumph evermore;
Gratefully my God adore;
God so good, so true, so kind;
Jesus' is a thankful mind.

Lowly, loving, meek, and pure,
I shall to the end endure;
Be no more to sin inclined;
Jesus' is a constant mind.

I shall fully be restored
To the image of my Lord,
Witnessing to all mankind,
Jesus' is a perfect mind.
—Charles Wesley.

296 The Morning Light.

The morning light is breaking;
The darkness disappears;
The sons of earth are waking
To penitential tears;
Each breeze that sweeps the ocean
Brings tidings from afar,
Of nations in commotion,
Prepared for Zion's war.

See heathen nations bending
Before the God we love,
And thousand hearts ascending
In gratitude above;
While sinners, now confessing,
The Gospel call obey,
And seek the Saviour's blessing,
A nation in a day.

Blest river of salvation,
Pursue thine onward way;
Flow thou to every nation,
Nor in thy richness stay:
Stay not till all the lowly,
Triumphant reach their home;
Stay not till all the holy
Proclaim, "The Lord is come!"
—Samuel F. Smith.

297 Alas! And Did My Savior?

Alas! and did my Saviour bleed?
And did my Sovereign die?
Would he devote that sacred head
For such a worm as I?

CHORUS:
||: O, how I love Jesus, :||
O, how I love Jesus,
Because He first loved me.

Was it for crimes that I have done,
He groaned upon the tree?
Amazing pity! grace unknown!
And love beyond degree!

Well might the sun in darkness hide
And shut his glories in,
When Christ, the mighty Maker, died,
For man, the creature's sin.

Thus might I hide my blushing face
While His dear cross appears;
Dissolve my heart in thankfulness,
And melt mine eyes to tears.

But drops of grief can ne'er repay
The debt of love I owe;
Here, Lord, I give myself away,
'Tis all that I can do.
—Isaac Watts.

298 Sowing the Seed.

Sowing the seed by the daylight fair,
Sowing the seed by the noonday glare,
Sowing the seed by the fading light,
Sowing the seed in the solemn night;
Oh, what shall the harvest be?
Oh, what shall the harvest be?

CHORUS:
Sown in the darkness, or sown in the light,
Sown in our weakness, or sown in our might,
Gathered in time or eternity,
Sure, ah, sure, will the harvest be.

Sowing the seed by the wayside high,
Sowing the seed on the rocks to die,
Sowing the seed where the thorns will spoil,
Sowing the seed in the fertile soil;
Oh, what shall the harvest be?
Oh, what shall the harvest be?

Sowing the seed of a lingering pain,
Sowing the seed of a maddened brain,
Sowing the seed of a tarnished name,
Sowing the seed of eternal shame;
Oh, what shall the harvest be?
Oh, what shall the harvest be?
—Mrs. Emily S. Oakey.

299 Probation Limited.

There is a time we know not when,
A point we know not where,
That marks the destiny of men,
To glorify or despair.

There is a line by us unseen,
That crosses every path;
The hidden boundary between
God's patience and his wrath.

Oh! where is this mysterious bourne
By which our path is crossed,
Beyond which God himself hath sworn
That he who goes is lost?

How far may we go in sin?
How long will God forbear?
Where does hope end? and where begin
The confines of despair?

An answer from the skies is sent:
"Ye that from God depart,
While it is called to-day, repent
And harden not your heart.
—Alexander.

300 Give Us Such a Faith.

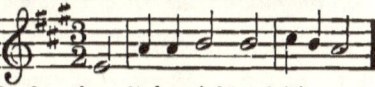

O, for the vital, mighty faith,
To saints of old once given;
The substance of their earthly hope,
The evidence of heaven;
That never feels discouragement,
And never knows defeat,
But in communion with its God
Finds rest and peace complete.

That quenches as in days of old,
"The violence of fire,"
And causes the devouring flame
Of sin to quite expire.
That stops the roaring lion's mouth,
And strength to weakness gives;
Escapes the flaming sword of wrath,
And in God's presence lives.

That brings to life the dead in sin,
And starts the sacred fire,
And puts to flight the alien hosts
Of every base desire.
That sees in the reproach of Christ
Its greatest wealth assured,
And gives the soul a good report
In every test endured.

With powers of darkness we contend,
Till Thou this faith impart,
That stamps the image of his Lord
On each believer's heart,
O, give us this unbounded faith,
Thy work in us complete,
Then we shall cause the darkened hosts
To worship at thy feet.
—T. H. Nelson.

301 Asleep in Jesus.

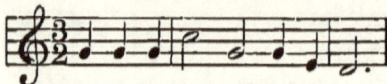

Asleep in Jesus! Blessed sleep,
From which none ever wakes to weep!
A calm and undisturbed repose,
Unbroken by the last of foes.

Asleep in Jesus! O how sweet,
To be for such a slumber meet!
With holy confidence to sing,
That death has lost his venomed sting.

Asleep in Jesus! O for me,
May such a blissful refuge be!
Securely shall my ashes lie,
Waiting the summons from on high.
—Mrs. M. Mackay.

302 Crowning the Savior.

Look, ye saints, the sight is glorious,
  See the Man of Sorrows now;
From the fight returned victorious,
  Every knee to Him shall bow:
    Crown Him, crown Him;
    Crowns become the Victor's brow.

CHORUS:

||: Crown Him, crown Him, angels crown Him;
Crown the Savior, King of Kings. :||

Sinners in derision crowned Him,
  Mocking thus the Saviour's claim;
Saints and angels crowd around Him,
  Own His title, praise His name:
    Crown Him, crown Him;
    Spread abroad the Victor's fame.

Hark, those bursts of acclamation!
  Hark, those loud triumphant chords!
Jesus takes the highest station:
  O what joy the sight affords!
    Crown Him, crown Him;
    King of Kings, and Lord of Lords.
—Thomas Kelly.

303 Following Jesus.

I will follow thee, my Savior,
  Whereso'er my lot may be;
Where thou goest, I will follow,
  Yes, Lord, I'll follow thee.

CHORUS:

Where He leads I will follow,
Where He leads I will follow,
Where He leads I will follow;
  I will follow all the way.

Tho' the road be rough and thorny,
  Trackless as the foaming sea,
Thou hast trod this way before me,
  And I gladly follow thee.

Tho' 'tis lone, and dark, and dreary,
  Cheerless though my path may be,
If thy voice I hear before me,
  Fearlessly I'll follow thee.

Tho' to Jordan's rolling billows,
  Cold and deep, thou lead'st me;
Thou hast cross'd its waves before me,
  And I still will follow thee.

304 My Happy Home.

Jerusalem! my happy home!
  Name ever dear to me!
When shall my labors have an end,
  In joy, and peace in thee?

CHORUS:

||: I will meet you in the city of the New Jerusalem;
I'm washed in the blood of the Lamb. :||

O when, thou city of my God,
  Shall I thy courts ascend,
Where congregations ne'er break up,
  And Sabbath has no end?

Why should I shrink at pain and woe?
  Or feel, at death, dismay?
I've Canaan's goouly land in view,
  And realms of endless day.

Jerusalem! my happy home!
  My soul still pants for thee;
Then shall my labors have an end,
  When I thy joys shall see.
—Unknown.

305 Try us, O, God.

Try us, O God, and search the ground
  Of every sinful heart:
Whate'er of sin in us is found,
  O bid it all depart.

Help us to help each other, Lord,
  Each other's cross to bear;
Let each his friendly aid afford;
  And feel his brother's care.

Up into thee, our living Head,
  Let us in all things grow,
Till thou hast made us free indeed,
  And spotless here below.

Then, when the mighty work is wrought,
  Receive thy ready bride:
Give us in heaven a happy lot
  With all the sanctified.
—Charles Wesley.

306 "For You I am Praying."

I have a Savior, he's pleading in glory,
A dear loving Savior, tho' earth-
 friends be few;
And now he is watching in tenderness
 o'er me,
And oh, that my Savior were your
 Savior too.

CHORUS:
For you I am praying,
For you I am praying,
For you I am praying,
 I am praying for you.

I have a peace: it is calm as a river—
A peace that the friends of this
 world never knew;
My Savior alone is its Author and
 Giver,
And oh, could I know it was given
 to you.

When Jesus has found you, tell others
 the story,
That my loving Savior is your Savior
 too;
Then pray that your Savior may bring
 them to glory,
And the prayer will be answered—
 'twas answered for you!

307 O, For That Flame.

O for that flame of living fire,
Which shone so bright in saints of old;
Which bade their souls to heaven as-
 pire,
 Calm in distress, in danger bold.

Where is that Spirit, Lord, which
 dwelt
In Abram's breast, and sealed him
 thine?
Which made Paul's heart with sorrow
 melt,
And glow with energy divine.

That Spirit, which from age to age,
 Proclaimed thy love, and taught thy
 ways?
Brightened Isaiah's vidid page,
 And breathed in David's hallowed
 lays?

Is not thy grace as might now
 As when Elijah felt its power;
When glory beamed from Moses' brow
 Or Job endured the trying hour?

Remember, Lord, the ancient days;
 Renew thy work; thy grace restore;
And while to thee our hearts we raise,
 On us thy Holy Spirit pour.

308 "None of Self."

Oh! the bitter pain and sorrow
That a time could ever be,
When I proudly said to Jesus,
"All of self and none of thee;"
All of self and none of thee,
All of self and none of thee;
When I proudly said to Jesus,
"All of self and none of thee."

Jesus found me; I beheld Him
Bleeding on th' accursed tree;
And my wistful heart said faintly,
"Some of self, and some of thee;"
Some of self, and some of thee,
Some of self, and some of tnee;
And my broken heart said faintly,
"Some of self, and some of thee."

Day by day His tender mercy,
Healing, helping, full and free,
Bro't me lower, while I whispered,
"Less of self, and more of thee;"
Less of self, and more of thee,
Less of self, and more of thee;
Bro't me lower, while I whispered,
"Less of self, and more of thee."

Higher than the highest heavens,
Deeper than the deepest sea,—
Lord, thy love at last has conquered:
"None of self, and all of thee;"
None of self, and all of thee,
None of self, and all of thee;
Lord, thy love at last has conquered:
"None of self, and all of thee."

309 The Year of Jubilee.

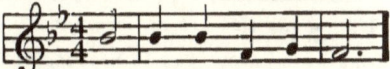

Blow ye the trumpet, blow
 The gladly solemn sound;
Let all the nations know,
 To earth's remotest bound,
The year of jubilee is come;
Return, ye ransom'd sinners, home.

Jesus, our great High Priest,
 Hath full atonement made;
Ye weary spirits, rest;
 Ye mournful souls be glad:
The year of jubilee is come;
Return, ye ransom'd sinners, home.

Ye slaves of sin and hell,
 Your liberty receive,
And safe in Jesus dwell,
 And blest in Jesus live:
The year of jubilee is come;
Return, ye ransom'd sinners, home.

Ye who have sold for naught
 Your heritage above,
Shall have it back unbought,
 The gift of Jesus' love:
The year of jubilee is come;
Return, ye ransom'd sinners, home.
—Charles Wesley.

310. Jewel Gatherer's.

Jewel-gatherers for a crown,
  Know ye not that many a gem,
Now in darkness trampled down
  Might bedeck a diadem?

CHORUS:
Gathering jewels, precious jewels,
  Blood-bought souls we seek to bring.
Gathering jewels, precious jewels,
  For the crown of Christ our King.

Souls for whom the Savior died,
  Souls enwrapped in sinful night,
Go and seek them far and wide;
  They will glitter in His sight.

Gems by cruel hands defaced,
  Pearls in heathen shadows dim,
Brilliants scattered in the waste,
  We must gather up for Him.

With His blood washed bright and pure,
  Graven with His name divine,
These our jewels shall endure,
  When the stars shall cease to shine.

Then our work shall be complete,
  Then we'll lay our jewels down;
Lay them gladly at His feet—
  He will set them in his crown.
    —Miss P. J. Owens.

311. Glory to The Lamb.

I know my sins are all forgiven,
  Glory to the bleeding Lamb,
And I am on my way to heaven,
  Glory to the bleeding Lamb.

CHORUS:
The Lamb, the Lamb, the bleeding Lamb;
  I love the sound of Jesus' name,
  It sets my spirit all aflame;
Glory to the bleeding Lamb.

I plunged beneath the crimson wave, etc.,
  And proved my Lord was strong to save, etc.

The Spirit answers to the blood, etc.,
  And tells me I am born of God, etc.

Oh, wondrous grace so free and full, etc.,
  My crimson stains are now as wool, etc.

I love the Lord, I know I do, etc.;
  The best of all He loves me too, etc.

And this my ceaseless song shall be, etc.,
  That Jesus died to set me free, etc.

312. While God Invites.

While God invites, how blest the day!
  How sweet the Gospel's charming sound!
Come, sinner, haste, O haste away,
  While yet a pardoning God is found.

Soon, borne on time's most rapid wing,
  Shall death command you to the grave,
Before his bar your spirits bring,
  And none be found to hear or save.

In that lone land of deep despair,
  No Sabbath's heavenly light shall rise,
No God regard your bitter prayer,
  No Savior call you to the skies.

Now God invites, how blest the day!
  How sweet the Gospel's charming sound!
Come, sinner, haste, O haste away,
  While yet a pardoning God is found.
    —T. Dwight.

313. The Narrow Way.

I storm the gate of strife,
  I force my passage through,
And all intent on endless life,
  The narrow way pursue.
I leave the world behind,
  After my Lord to go,
Renouncing, with a steadfast mind,
  Its pride, and pomp, and show.

CHORUS:
I take the narrow way,
  I take the narrow way;
With the resolute few, who dare go through,
  I take the narrow way.

No cumbrous garb I wear,
  My progress to impede;
My pilgrim robe, divinely fair,
  Is fashioned all for speed.
I cannot slack my pace
  For earth's fantastic show,
For like a flint I've set my face
  That I'll to Zion go.

I seem to tread in air,
  I seem to walk with wings,
As toward my heavenly mansion fair
  My soul exultant springs.
Right through this world of sin,
  Its frantic cares and strife,
Its Babel roar, and dust and din,
  I rush to endless life.
    —J. McCreery.

314 There's a Highway.

There's a highway for the ransomed,
  where the children of the King,
Upon their pilgrim journey triumphantly may sing,
Of a Savior who redeemed them, and
  delivers from all sin.
His blood now makes me clean.

CHORUS:
  Glory, glory, hallelujah!
  Glory, glory, hallelujah!
  Glory, glory, hallelujah!
  His blood now keeps me clean.

I was pardoned by God's mercy, but
  at heart was evil still,
A carnal mind was in me, which re-
  solves could never kill,
But, blessed be His holy name, He
  changes heart and will!
His blood now makes me clean.

Now, like pebbles in the running brook
  that 'neath the ripples lay,
My heart is sweetly kept from sin
  each moment, night and day;
And as faith the conquest gave me, I
  bid doubts to go their way,
His blood now makes me clean!

On the mountain tops of Beulah, or in
  the vale below,
Where temptations' wildest hurricanes
  their fiercest tempests blow,
In sorrow or in conflict his grace he
  doth bestow,
His blood now makes me clean!

315 The World's Charms Lost.

Let worldly minds the world pursue;
  It has no charms for me:
Once I admired its trifles too,
  But grace hath set me free.

CHORUS:
  At the cross! at the cross!
  Where I first saw the light,
    And the burden of my heart rolled
      away;
  It was there by faith I received my
      sight,
    And now I am happy all the day.

Its pleasures can no longer please,
  Nor happiness afford;
Far from my heart be joys like these,
  Now I have seen the Lord.

As by the light of opening day
  The stars are all concealed,
So earthly pleasures fade away,
  When Jesus is revealed.
            —J. Newton.

316 My Title.

When I can read my title clear
  To mansions in the skies,
I'll bid farewell to every fear,
  And wipe my weeping eyes.

CHORUS:
  || We will stand the storm,
  We will anchor by and by. ||

Should earth against my soul engage,
  And fiery darts be hurl'd,
Then I can smile at Satan's rage,
  And face a frowning world.

Let cares like a wild deluge come,
  Let storms of sorrow fall,—
So I but safely reach my home,
  My God, my heaven, my all.

There I shall bathe my weary soul
  In seas of heavenly rest,
And not a wave of trouble roll
  Across my peaceful breast.
            —Isaac Watts.

317 Alive in Christ.

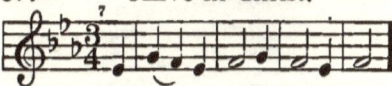

And can it be that I should gain
  An int'rest in the Savior's blood?
Died He for me, who caused His pain?
  For me, who Him to death pursued?
Amazing love! how can it be,
That thou, my Lord, shouldst die for
    me?

'Tis mystery all,—th' Immortal dies!
  Who can explore His strange design?
In vain the first born seraph tries
  To sound the depths of love divine;
'Tis mercy all! let earth adore,
Let angel minds enquire no more.

He left His Father's throne above;
  (So free, so infinite His grace!)
Emptied himself of all but love,
  And bled for Adam's helpless race.
'Tis mercy all, immense and free,
For, O my God, it found out me!

Long my imprison'd spirit lay,
  Fast bound in sin and nature's night;
Thine eye diffused a quick'ning ray;
  I woke; the dungeon flamed with
      light:
My chains fell off, my heart was
      free,—
I rose, went forth, and followed thee.

No condemnation now I dread,—
  Jesus, with all in Him, is mine;
Alive in Him, my living Head,
  And clothed in righteousness divine,
Bold I approach th' eternal throne,
And claim the crown, through Christ
    my own.
            —Charles Wesley.

318. Let Me Die.

O God, my heart doth long for thee;
    Let me die!
Now set my soul at liberty;
    Let me die!
Die to the trifling things of earth,
They're now to me of little worth;
My Savior calls—I'm going forth;
    Let me die!—

Thy slaying power in me display;
    Let me die!
I must be dead from day to day!
    Let me die!
Dead to the world and its applause,
To all the customs, fashions, laws,
Of those who hate the humbling cross,
    Let me die!

O, I must die to scoffs and sneers;
    Let me die!
I must be freed from slavish fears;
    Let me die!
So dead that no desire will rise,
To appear good, or great, or wise,
In any but my Savior's eyes;
    Let me die!

If Christ would live and reign in me,
    I must die;
Like Him I crucified must be;
    I must die.
Lord, drive the nails, nor heed the groans,
My flesh may writhe and make its moans,
But this the way, and this alone—
    I must die.

319. The Old Story.

I love to tell the story
  Of unseen things above,
Of Jesus and His glory,
  Of Jesus and His love;
I love to tell the story,
  Because I know it's true,
It satisfies my longings
As nothing else would do.

CHORUS:

I love to tell the story,
'Twill be my theme in glory
To tell the old, old story,
Of Jesus and His love.

I love to tell the story;
  More wonderful it seems
Than all the golden fancies
  Of all our golden dreams.
I love to tell the story;
  It did so much for me!
And that is just the reason
  I tell it now to thee.

320. Resting at Last.

The conflict is over, the tempest is past,
I'm resting in Jesus, I'm resting at last;
The billows that fill'd my poor soul with alarm,
Are hush'd at his word into stillness and calm.

CHORUS:

Rest, rest, sweet, sweet rest;
I'm resting in Jesus, I'm resting at last.

There's peace in believing, sweet peace to the soul,
To know that he maketh me perfectly whole.
There's joy everlasting to feel his blood flow,
'Tis life from the dead my Redeemer to know.

O hinder me not while His love I proproclaim,
My soul makes her boast of His wonderful name.
I stand with my foot on the neck of my foe,
Then bounding with gladness triumphant I go.

321. Glorious Hope.

O glorious hope of perfect love,
It lifts me up to things above;
  It bears on eagle's wings;
It gives my ravished soul a taste,
And makes me for some moments feast
  With Jesus' priests and kings.

Rejoicing now in earnest hope,
I stand, and from the mountain top
  See all the land below.
Rivers of milk and honey rise,
And all the fruits of paradise
  In endless plenty grow.

A land of corn, and wine, and oil,
Favored with God's peculiar smile,
  With every blessing blest;
There dwells the Lord our righteousness,
And keeps his own in perfect peace,
  And everlasting rest.

Now, O my Joshua, bring me in!
Cast out thy foes; the inbred sin,
  The carnal mind remove;
The purchase of thy death divide!
And O! with all the sanctified
  Give me a lot of love.

—Charles Wesley.

322 Amen to the Truth.

Amen to the truth, even so let it be,
Amen and amen, for the truth maketh free;
Amen and amen, from the pulpit and pen;
||: God's truth, let us have it again and again. :||

Amen to the Word that convinceth of sin,
And tells me I'm vile and polluted within,
And makes me feel wretched, forsaken and lost,
||: And groan for redemption at whatever cost. :||

Amen! let me die and be buried beside
The victim of Calv'ry, the One crucified.
Then seal fast the stone, where nature doth lay,
||: So none but an angel can roll it away. :||

Amen! let me never arise from this death,
Till God breathe within me the life-giving breath;
Till touched by the virtue that only can save,
||: I leave all corruption and rise from the grave. :||

Amen! hallelujah! my soul is now free,
The world, sin and Satan, have no place in me;
I'm dead to the world, but alive unto him,
||: Whose blood now redeems me and keeps me from sin. :||
—W. W. Dixon.

323 The Last Appeal.

Listen, sinner, will you listen,
While I make one more appeal?
Would, with tears, your eyes might glisten,
Would to God, your heart might feel.
You will too, ere long, be dying;
Soon we'll miss you from the earth;
And your cold form will be lying,
'Neath the greensward and the turf.

But the grave is not the ending;
Sin will kill beyond the tomb.
Oh! what awful horrors pending,
In those words, "The sinner's doom."
God has traced it with His finger!
Jesus said it should be so:
He who lives and dies a sinner,
Must endure eternal woe.

You have had the Bible warning,
You have had the Spirit, too,
Ever since life's early morning,
It has striv'n and plead with you:
Many times the teardrop glistened;
Many times your heart did melt;
To the story you have listened,—
Of the pangs your Savior felt.

But the Bible you have slighted,
And the Spirit turned away,
And refused, though oft invited,
To improve the gracious day;
Oh, how hard your heart is getting!
Oh, how sad your state to-day!
Friend, your star of hope is setting;
Haste to Christ without delay.
—Rev. J. E. Gould.

324 The Eden Above.

We're bound for the land of the pure and the holy,
The home of the happy, the kingdom of love,
Ye wanderers from God, in the broad road of folly,
O say, will you go to the Eden above?

CHORUS.
||: Will you go, will you go, :||
O say, will you go to the Eden above?

No poverty there—no, the saints are all wealthy,
The heirs of His glory whose nature is love;
No sickness can reach them, that country is healthy,
O say, will you go to the Eden above?

Each saint has a mansion prepared and all furnished,
Ere from this clay house he is summoned to move;
Its gates and its towers with glory are burnished,
O say, will you go to the Eden above?

March on happy pilgrims, that land is before you,
And soon its ten thousand delights we shall prove;
Yes, soon we shall walk o'er the hills of bright glory,
And drink the pure joys of the Eden above.

And yet, guilty sinner, we would not forsake thee,
We halt yet a moment as onward we move;
O come to thy Lord, in his arms He will take thee,
And bear thee along to the Eden above.

325 My Jesus, I Love Thee.

My Jesus I love Thee, I know thou art mine;
For Thee all the follies of sin I resign;
My blessed Redeemer and Savior art thou;
If ever I loved Thee, my Jesus, 'tis now.

I have loved Thee because Thou hast first loved me,
And purchased my pardon on Calvary's tree.
I love Thee for wearing the thorns on Thy brow,
If ever I loved Thee, my Jesus, 'tis now.

I have loved Thee in life, I will love Thee in death,
And praise Thee as long as Thou lendest me breath,
And say when the death-dew lies cold on my brow,
If ever I loved Thee, my Jesus, 'tis now.

In mansions of glory and endless delight,
I'll ever adore Thee in heaven so bright;
I'll sing, with the glittering crown on my brow,
If ever I loved Thee, my Jesus, 'tis now.

326 Stand up For Jesus.

O who'll stand up for Jesus,
The lowly Nazarene?
And raise the blood-stained banner
Amid the hosts of sin?

CHORUS.
The cross for Christ I'll cherish,
Its crucifixion bear;
All hail! reproach and sorrow,
If Jesus leads me there.

O who will follow Jesus,
Amid reproach and shame?
Where others shrink and falter,
Who'll glory in His name?

Though fierce may rage the battle,
And wild the storms may blow,
Though friends may go forever,
I will with Jesus go.

My all to Christ I've given,
My talents, time, and voice;
Myself, my reputation,
The lone way is my choice.

O Jesus, Jesus, Jesus,
My all-sufficient friend!
Come, fold me to Thy bosom,
E'en to the journey's end.
—L. Hartsough.

327 The Great Judgment Morning.

I dreamed that the great judgment morning
Had dawned, and the trumpet had blown;
I dreamed that the nations had gathered
To judgment before the white throne.
From the throne came a bright shining angel
And stood on the land and the sea,
And swore with his hand raised to heaven,
That time was no longer to be.

CHORUS.
And oh, what a weeping and wailing,
As the lost were told of their fate;
They cried for the rocks and the mountains
They prayed, but their prayer was too late.

The rich man was there, but his money
Had melted and vanished away;
A pauper he stood in the judgment,
His debts were too heavy to pay.
The great man was there, but his greatness
When death came was left far behind;
The angel that opened the records,
Not a trace of his greatness could find.

The widow was there and the orphans
God heard and remembered their cries;
No sorrow in heaven forever,
God wiped all the tears from their eyes.
The gambler was there and the drunkard,
And the man who had sold them the drink,
With the people who gave him the license—
Together in hell they did sink.

The moral man came to the judgment,
But his self-righteous rags would not do;
The men who had crucified Jesus
Had passed off as moral men too.
The souls that had put off salvation—
"Not to-night; I'll get saved by-and-bye,"
No time now to think of religion!"
At last they found time to die.
—War Cry.

328 All Taken Away.

Did you hear what Jesus said to me?
  They're all taken away, away,
Your sins are pardoned and you are free,
  They're all taken away.

CHORUS.

They're all taken away, away,
They're all taken away, away,
My sins are all taken away.

I now believe in Jesus' name,
  They're all taken away;
And now His mighty love I claim,
  They're all taken away;

The spirit answers to the blood,
  They're all taken away;
And tells me I am born of God,
  They're all taken away.

With confidence I now draw nigh,
  They're all taken away;
And father, Abba, father, cry,
  They're all taken away.

The blood of Christ avails for me,
  They're all taken away;
And sets my soul at liberty,
  They're all taken away;

I'll praise Him while He lends me breath,
  They're all taken away;
And sing triumphant over death,
  They're all taken away.

329 Whiter Than Snow.

Lord Jesus, I long to be perfectly whole;
I want Thee forever to live in my soul;
Break down ev'ry idol, cast out ev'ry foe;
Now wash me and I shall be whiter than snow.

CHORUS.

Whiter than snow, yes, whiter than snow;
Now wash me and I shall be whiter snow.

Lord Jesus, look down from Thy throne in the skies,
And help me to make a complete sacrifice;
I give up myself, and whatever I know,
Now wash me and I shall be whiter snow.

Lord Jesus, for this I most humbly entreat,
I wait, blessed Lord, at Thy crucified feet,
By faith, for my cleansing, I see Thy blood flow,
Now wash me and I shall be whiter snow.

Lord Jesus, Thou seest I patiently wait,
Come now, and within me a new heart create;
To those who have sought Thee, Thou never saidst "No,"
Now wash me and I shall be whiter snow.
  —Used by permission of Wm. G. Fischer, owner of copyright.

330 The Lord Will Provide.

Though troubles assail, and dangers affright,
Though friends should all fail, and foes all unite,
Yet one thing secures us, whatever betide,
The promise assures us, "The Lord will provide."

The birds, without barn or storehouse, are fed;
From them let us learn to trust for our bred;
His saints what is fitting shall ne'er be denied,
So long as 'tis written, "The Lord will provide."

When Satan appears to stop up our path,
And fills us with fears, we triumph by faith;
He can not take from us (though oft he has tried)
The heart-cheering promise, "The Lord will provide."

No strength of our own, nor goodness we claim;
Our trust is all thrown on Jesus' name;
In this our strong tower for safety we hide;
The Lord is our power, "The Lord will provide."

When life sinks apace, and death is in view,
The word of his grace shall comfort us through;
Not fearing or doubting, with Christ on our side,
We hope to die shouting, "The Lord will provide."

331 He's Just the Same To-Day.

When Moses and the Israelites
   From Egypt's land did flee,
   Behind them was old Pharo's host—
   In front of them the sea.
God raised the waters like a wall,
   And opened up their way;
||: And the God that lived in Moses'
   time
   Is just the same to-day. :||

When David and Goliath met—
   The wrong against the right—
The giant armed with human power,
   And David with God's might.
God's power with David's sling and
   stone
   The giant low did lay.
||: And the God that lived in David's
   time
   Is just the same to-day. :||

When Daniel faithful to his God
   Would not bow down to men,
And by God's enemies was hurled
   Into the lion's den,
God shut the lion's mouth, we read,
   And robbed them of their prey;
||: And the God that lived in Daniel's
   time
   Is just the same to-day. :||

When Jesus sat upon the Mount
   And taught the gospel plan,
He blessed the meek, the pure in
   heart,
   The persecuted man.
The eager people pressed to hear,
   As He taught them how to pray;
||: And the God that blessed the people
   then,
   Is just the same to-day. :||

When Pentecost was fully come,
   And fire from heaven did fall,
As a mighty wind, the Holy Ghost,
   Baptized them one and all.
Three thousand were converted, and
   Were Christians right away;
||: And the God that lived at Pentecost
   Is just the same to-day. :||
   —Composed and revised by
   A. C. Marshall.

332 Hiding in Thee.

O safe to the Rock that is higher than I,
My soul in its conflicts and sorrows would
   fly;
So sinful, so weary, thine, thine would I be;
Thou blest "Rock of Ages," I'm hiding in
   thee.

CHORUS:

Hiding in thee, hiding in thee;
O, blest Rock of Ages, I'm hiding in thee.

In the calm of the noontide, in sorrow's lone
   hour,
In times when temptation casts o'er me its
   power;
In the tempests of life, on its wide, heaving
   sea,
Thou blest "Rock of Ages," I'm hiding in
   Thee.

How oft in the conflict, when pressed by the
   foe,
I have fled to my Refuge and breathed out my
   woe;
How often when trials like sea-billows roll,
Have I hidden in thee, O thou Rock of my
   soul.
   —Rev. Wm. O. Cushing.

INDEX.

Titles in Capital letters.   First lines in small letters.

—A—

	Page.
ABIDING AND CONFIDING	85
ABIDE WITH ME	109
A CHARGE TO KEEP	211
A child went from his mother	164
ADORATION	117
A friendless prisoner	78
A few days' work in his garden	150
A GREAT DAY COMING	279
ALAS, AND DID MY SAVIOR	83
A LITTLE LONGER	131
A LITTLE TALK WITH JESUS	230
ALL FOR PRECIOUS SOULS	151
ALIVE IN CHRIST	317
ALL MY SPRINGS	152
ALL FOR JESUS	228
All my life long	120
All hail the pow'r of Jesus' name	139
All peace departed	188
ALL TAKEN AWAY	328
ALL VICTORIOUS LOVE	284
ALMOST BUT LOST	156
Almost! Oh, yes, a Savior's loving	156
AMAZING GRACE	249
AMEN TO THE TRUTH	32
Am I a soldier of the cross	259
An alien from God	38
And can it be that I	317
AND CAN I YET DELAY	242
And must I be to judgment	288
ANOTHER YEAR FOR JESUS	186
A NEW HEART HE GAVE ME	204
Another year is dawning	186
ANYWHERE WITH JESUS	122
A PERFECT HEART	260
A resting time is coming	144
ARIEL	75
A rich man was he	140
Arise, my soul	282
ARLINGTON	259
Art thou coming, my beloved	195
ASLEEP IN JESUS	301
A STRANGER TO GOD	18
AT EVENING TIME IT SHALL	123
At home or away	82
A VIEW OF HEAVEN	247
Away in a manger	45
A WHITE ROBE NEEDED	14
A WONDERFUL SAVIOR	191

—B—

BEARING THE CROSS	199
BEAUTIFUL ROBES	196
BEHOLD! A STRANGER	100
Behold the hands	44
BENEDICTION	235
BETHANY	236
BEULAH LAND	194
Be quiet, soul	51
BLESSED ASSURANCE	171
BLIGHTED BOY	22
Blow ye the trumpet	309
BY AND BY	12

—C—

CALLING THE PRODIGAL	80
CALVARY	231
CAST THY BREAD	106
Children of the heavenly	267
CHINA'S MILLIONS	215
CHILDREN OF THE KING	267
CHORUS OF PRAISE	125
CHRIST FOR THE WORLD	121
Christ has atonement for me	63
Christ has the ransom paid	222
CHRIST IS ALL	190
CHRIST IS HERE	1
CHRIST LOVED ME	23
Church of the living God	215
CHURCH MILITANT HYMN	161
CLEANSING IN THE BLOOD	92
CLEANSE ME NOW	130
Come, my soul, they sent	270
Come, thou fount	264
COME, THOU ALMIGHTY KING	275
COME, SINNER, COME	72
COME, YE DISCONSOLATE	197
COME, YE SINNERS	286
COME, YE THAT LOVE	107
COMING BACK AGAIN	127
COMPANIONSHIP WITH JESUS	79
CONDEMNED, BUT PLEADING	246
CONFESS YOUR SINS	212
CONSECRATION	4
CONSIDER HIM	111
CORONATION	139
CROWN HIM	138
CROWNING THE SAVIOR	302

—D—

Dark, dark are the waters	5
Darkness veils the friendly	20
DECIDING TO-NIGHT	116
DENNIS	241
DEVOTION	143
DEPTH OF MERCY	83
Did Christ o'er sinners weep	240
Did you hear what Jesus	328
DOWN IN THE LIC'NCED SAL'N	26
Down in the valley	117
DOXOLOGY	243
DUKE STREET	243

—E—

Earthly friendships all are riven...	151
EARTH'S VANITIES	8
Earth with its dark, etc.	43
ENCOURAGEMENT TO PRAY...	270
ENTIRE PURIFICATION	285
Estranged from God	23
ETERNITY'S BEGGER	140
EVERLASTING	222

—F—

FADE, FADE EACH EARTHLY..	237
Fairest of all the earth	81
Father, I stretch my hands	210
Far away in the depths	177
FIFTY MILLION HEATHEN	10
FOLLOWING JESUS	303
Forever here my rest shall be	285
For of him are all things	125
FOR YOU I AM PRAYING	306
FREE, INDEED	213
From Greenland's icy mountains...	274
From every stormy wind	287

—G—

GIVE US SUCH A FAITH	300
GLORIES OF CHRIST	154
GLORIOUS HOPE	321
GLORYING IN THE CROSS	245
GLORY TO THE LAMB	311
GOD BE WITH YOU	234
GOD CALLS TO-NIGHT	2
GOD IS CALLING	148
God is calling the prodigal	80
God's light has now revealed	92
God's love is as high	271
God moves in a mysterious	251
GOD'S LOVE	271
God speed the day	40
GOING DOWN TO THE GRAVE.	54
GOOD NEWS FOR ZION	258
Go to dark Gethsemane	47
GO, THOU MESSENGER	198
Grace and mercy	235
GUIDE ME	257

—H—

Had I a voice for singing	137
HAPPY DAY	216
Hark! I hear the millions	160
Hark! the herald angel	1
HARVEST IS PAST	211
HASTEN, BROTHER, HASTEN..	207
Hasten, sinner, to be wise	268
HE ANSWERED NEVER A	78
HEART MADE KNOWN	255
HEAR THE CALL	160
Hear the footsteps of Jesus	163
HEAVENLY CANAAN	250
HEAVENLY JOY	174
HEAVEN STILL IS MINE	145
He calms the strife	111
He cometh, he cometh	136
HE HIDETH MY SOUL	191
He is coming, he is coming	48
HE LEADETH ME	7
HE LEADETH ME STILL	202
HE LIVES FOR ME	102
He lives to save from every sin..	102
HE ROLLED THE SEA AWAY...	146
HE'S JUST THE SAME TO-DAY.	331
HIDING, SAFELY HIDING	69
HIDING IN THEE	332
HOLY FLAME	219
HOLY, HOLY, HOLY	21
How many were the years	99

How sweet the joy the Sabbath...	61
How sweet are the tidings	129
HOW VAST THE LOVE OF GOD.	50

—I—

I AM COMING TO THE CROSS...	206
I dreamed that the great	327
I entered once a home	190
I have a Savior	306
I have learned the wondrous secret	85
I have sought pleasure	8
I heard my Savior calling	98
I heard the voice of weeping	96
I know I love thee better	11
I know my sins are all	311
I left my home in heaven	25
I'LL GO EVERY STEP	108
I'LL GO WITH HIM	98
I love to tell the story	319
I'M COMING NOW TO JESUS...	182
I'm lost, O! I'm lost	121
IMMANUEL'S LAND	173
I mourn o'er the years	110
I must have the Savior with me...	3
I MUST TELL JESUS	46
INDIA'S MILLIONS	147
In the cross of Christ	265
In the rifted rock I'm	229
INVITATION	86
I once was in bondage	213
I roamed in many	174
I sat 'mid the tombs	159
I sought for years	225
I storm the gate of strife	313
I think of my Savior	204
I thirst, thou wounded Lamb	244
It is safe to be	217
It may not be on the mountain...	4
It reaches me	158
I turned from all my	223
It was joy to the world	53
It was not nails, but love	143
It was not the din	22
I've found the open fountain	148
I've found the promised fountain...	93
I've left the land of death	272
I'VE MISSED IT AT LAST	36
I've seen the lightning flashing	91
I've no room in my heart	155
I want a principle within	13
I will follow thee, my Savior	303
I WILL GUIDE THEE	230
I WILL PRAISE THEE	256

—J—

Jerusalem, my happy home	304
JESUS CALLS THE CHILDREN.	55
Jesus, I my cross have taken	199
Jesus loves the children	55
JESUS, LOVER OF MY SOUL	19
Jesus, plant and root in me	295
JESUS SAVES	71
JESUS, SAVIOR, PILOT ME	9
Jesus, the name high	252
Jesus, thine all victorious love	284
Jesus, while our hearts	128
JEWEL GATHERERS	310
JOY OF THE JUSTIFIED	273
JOY TO THE WORLD	114
JUST AS I AM	66

—L—

LEANING ON THE EVERL'ST'G	153
LEARN OF HIM	47
LET ME DIE	318
LET ME GO	58
Let worldly minds the	315

Title	Page
LIGHT SHINING OUT	231
Listen, sinner, will you	323
Lo! these years I came	132
Long in far-off countries	17
Look, ye saints, the singht	302
Lord, long have we prayed	227
LOST IN SIGHT OF HOME	17
LOST	214
Lost to the sound	214
Lord Jesus, how long	329
Love divine, all love	266
LOVE FOUND ME	103
LUTHER'S CRADLE HYMN	45

—M—

Title	Page
MAGDALENE	35
MAKE ME LIKE THEE	15
MASTER WANTS WORKERS	84
MEET ME THERE	59
MIGHTY TRUMP	136
MISSIONARY BATTLE SONG	40
MOMENT BY MOMENT	63
MORE LOVE TO THEE	238
MUST JESUS BEAR THE CROSS	49
MY BEAUTIFUL HOME	272
MY BELOVED	135
MY BOY	188
My father is rich	77
MY FAITH LOOKS UP TO THEE	57
MY FRIEND	104
MY HAPPY HOME	304
MY HEAVENLY HOME	64
MY HIDING PLACE	60
My hope is built on	168
MY JESUS, I LOVE THEE	325
MY LIFE FOR THEE	33
MY NEW FRIEND	38
MY REFUGE	67
MY SACRIFICE	113
MY SAVIOR FIRST OF ALL	95
MY SOUL, BE ON THY GUARD	149
MY TITLE	316

—N—

Title	Page
NEARER MY GOD TO THEE	236
NEARER THE CROSS	221
Neath the shadows of the	69
NEEDED—LABORERS	87
Needed—Ten thousand laborers	87
NEVER ALONE	91
NO FACE LIKE THINE	180
NONE OF SELF	308
Now we tell the old, old story	37

—O—

Title	Page
O BEAR ME AWAY	278
O DAY OF REST	280
O do not let the word	292
O for a thousand tongues	253
O for a faith	254
O for a heart	260
O for that flame	307
O for the vital mighty faith	300
O FOR THAT FLAME	307
O glorious hope of	321
O God my heart doth	318
O happy day that	216
Oh, blessed fellowship divine	75
OH, COULD I SPEAK	75
Oh, come to the Savior	112
O how happy are they	273
O how I love the Bible	24
Oh, now I see the crimson	162
Oh, safe to the rock that	332
Oh, this uttermost salvation	158
Oh, to range the sweet plains	157
O I have spent my all	277

Title	Page
O mourner in Zion	226
O MY CROSS	201
Once she was pure	52
Once he was so bright	200
One-tenth of ripened grain	115
ONE-TENTH	115
On Jordan's stormy bank	247
ONLY FOR SOULS	119
On the happy golden shore	59
ON THE VICTORY SIDE	118
On the mountain top	258
ONWARD, CHRIST'N SOLDIERS	32
O sweet will of God	291
O spread the tidings round	34
O the bitter pain and sorrow	308
O thou God of my	246
O THOU IN WHOSE PRESENCE	208
Our souls cry out	118
Out in the darkness	193
Out in the world	62
O valiant hearted soldiers	127
O where is the child	74
O where shall rest be found	239
O who'll stand up for Jesus	325

—P—

Title	Page
PARTING TO MEET AGAIN	27
POWER OF OTHER DAYS	90
Praise God from whom	233
PRECIOUS JESUS	224
PRECIOUS PROMISE	230
PRAISE THE REDEEMER	253
Precious worker, danger signals	294
Prince of Peace	269
PROBATION LIMITED	299
PRODIGAL DAUGHTER	52
PRODIGAL'S RETURN	277
PURITY	13

—R—

Title	Page
REDEEMED	126
Redeemed—how I love	126
RESTING AT LAST	320
RESTING TIME COMING	144
REST, LABORER, REST	195
Rest, worker, rest	195
RESURRECTION SONG	263
RETREAT	287
Return, wanderer, return	248
ROCK OF AGES	176
ROOM IN MY HEART	155

—S—

Title	Page
SALVATION FOR YOU	159
Salvation, O the joyful sound	166
SATISFIED	120
SAVE THE BOY	200
SAVED BY GRACE	295
Savior of men, thy	243
SAVIOR, HIDE THOU ME	183
See two sailors	175
Servant of God, well done	187
SHALL LIFE BE WASTED	293
She a few months ago	35
Shine within me, Holy Spirit	130
Show pity, Lord	246
Sing with all the sons	263
SIN KILLS BEYOND THE TOMB	241
SOFTLY AND TENDERLY	73
SOLDIER OF THE CROSS	250
SOMEBODY'S BOY	62
SOME MOTHER'S CHILD	82
SON, REMEMBER	89
SOULS OR GOLD	169
SOWING THE SEED	298
SPEAK, LORD, TO ME	164
SPEED AWAY	70
STANDING ON THE PROMISES	42
STAND UP FOR JESUS	326

Title	Page
STAND UP FOR JESUS	218
STEP OUT ON THE PROMISE	226
ST. MARTIN'S	256
SUBMISSION	16
SUBMISSION TO GOD	269
SWEET HOUR OF PRAYER	39
SWEETLY RESTING	229

—T—

Title	Page
Take my life	33
Take the world	185
TELL THE WORLD	37
That awful day will	262
THAT DAY OF CALVARY	81
THAT'S ENOUGH FOR ME	223
THE BARREN FIG TREE	132
THE BONDAGE OF LOVE	291
THE CHILD OF A KING	77
THE CHRISTIAN'S PRAYER	243
THE CLEANSING WAVE	162
THE COMING OF THE LORD	101
THE COMFORTER HAS COME	34
The conflict is over	320
THE CROSS IS NOT GREATER	31
The cross that he gave	31
THE CROSS MY BOAST	178
THE CROSS	265
THE CROWNING HOUR	187
THE CRY OF THE HEATHEN	274
THE DANGER OF DELAY	268
THE DEFENSE OF ZION	255
THE DREADFUL SENTENCE	262
THE EDEN ABOVE	324
THE EMPTY TOMB	232
THE FULLNESS	141
THE GREAT JUDGMENT MORN	327
THE GREAT PHYSICIAN	28
THE HARVEST FIELD	172
The harvest is past	211
THE HALF WAS NEVER TOLD	11
THE HOME LAND	209
The infant redeemer	53
THE JOYFUL SOUND	166
THE JUDGMENT	167
THE LAST APPEAL	323
THE LIGHTHOUSE	20
THE LIVING WORD OF GOD	93
THE LORD OUR HELPER	264
THE LORD WILL PROVIDE	330
THE LORD'S GARDEN	150
THE LOST SHEEP	193
The master wants workers	84
THE MIND OF CHRIST	295
THE MERCY SEAT	30
THE MORNING LIGHT	296
THE NAME OF JESUS	252
THE NARROW WAY	313
THE NEW CREATION	276
THE NINETY AND NINE	281
THE OLD RUGGED CROSS	220
THE OLD STORY	319
THE OPEN FOUNTAIN	148
THE PALACE WALLS	43
THE PARADISE OF GOD	137
THE PRECIOUS BIBLE	24
THE PRICE OF A SOUL	121
THE PRODIGAL SON	74
THE PROPHET'S CALL	192
THE REDEEMER'S TEARS	240
THE RESCUED SAILORS	175
THE SABBATH	61
The sands of time have been	56
The sands of time are sinking	173
The Savior is leading me	202
THE SAVIOR WITH ME	3
THE SECOND DEATH	239
THE SOLID ROCK	168
THE SONG OF THE SOUL	137
The sun that rose	123
THE TOILS OF THE ROAD	56
THE VOICE OF WEEPING	96
THE VOICE OF GOD	134
THE WANDERER RECALLED	243
THE WANDERER'S RETURN	99
THE WATERS ARE TROUBLED	94
THE WAYWARD THRONG	189
THE WHOLE WIDE WORLD	65
THE WORLD'S CHARM LOST	315
There are thousands who wander	142
THERE IS A FOUNTAIN	283
There is a land of pure delight	250
There is a land where nature sings	194
There is nothing half so lovely	224
THERE IS A SPOT	210
There is a time	290
There's a great day coming	279
THERE'S A HIGHWAY	314
There's a hill lone and gray	231
There's an awful time of trouble	101
THERE'S A WIDENESS	170
There's a world everlasting	222
There were ninety and nine	281
They hushed their breath that	138
They tell me the path to heaven	104
Thine iniquity swells like the tide	86
THIRST'G FOR THE FULLNESS	244
Thro' God's tender mercy	108
Tho' sumptuous fed	89
Tho' thorns my pathway	60
Tho' troubles assail	330
THOU ART COMING	6
THOUSANDS FOR JESUS	142
Tho' ye have lain	205
Through love for me	113
THY KINGDOM COME	227
THY WILL BE DONE	128
'Tis the Savior's call	10
TO BE LOST IN THE NIGHT	112
Tossed on a troubled stream	145
Traveler, tho' thy feet	131
TRUE TO THE END	41
TRUST AND OBEY	79
TRY US, O GOD	15

—U—

Title	Page
UNANSWERED YET	76

—V—

Title	Page
Vain man, thy fond	261
VALIANT HEARTED SOLDIERS	127
VARINA	247
VICTORIOUS FAITH	254

—W—

Title	Page
WATCH FOR HIS COMING	48
We are living, we are dwelling	161
Weep for the wayward	189
WEEPING PROPHETS	203
We have gathered to hear	27
We have heard the joyful	71
WE'LL GIRDLE THE GLOBE	44
We'll some day know	51
We're bound for the land	324
We shall walk	196
We weep o'er the grave	16
WHAT A FRIEND	105
What a friend we have	105
What a fellowship	153
WHAT A SINNER	165
What have I on earth	178
What if your own	181
When are you coming to Jesus	116
When dead to every other sound	131
When I can read my	316
When I gave all to Jesus	154
When I survey the	245

When Israel out of bondage	146	WHY NOT TO-NIGHT	292
When on wings of faith we rise	12	Will you in the fight be true	41
When out in sin and darkness lost	103	Will you save me	169
When Moses and the Israelites	331	Will you heed the solemn	148
When my life's work is ended	95	WILT THOU BE MADE WHOLE	163
When the brightest rays	183	With empty hands, O heaven	141
When the old prophetic	192	WONDERFUL PEACE	177
When the stars from heaven	167	WONDERFUL STORY OF LOVE	133
WHEN TO BE A DANIEL	217	WONDERFUL CHANGE	2 5
When we walk with the Lord	29	WORKER'S WARNING	294
WHERE AM I DRIFTING	5	WORK FOR THE NIGHT	68
Where are the weeping	203	Wouldst thou ready be	14
WHERE HAST THOU GLEANED	179	Would you know the	212
Where is my wandering boy	26		
Where is the power of other days	90	—Y—	
Where is the flame	219		
While fighting for my	290	YE WOULD NOT	25
WHILE GOD INVITES	312	YOUR OWN	181
While the storms of life	67		
WHITER THAN SNOW	329	—Z—	
WHITER THAN SNOW	110		
WHITHER SHALL I GO	210	ZION	255
WHO IS ON THE LORD'S SIDE,	97	Zion stands with hills	255

www.ingramcontent.com/pod-product-compliance
Lightning Source LLC
Chambersburg PA
CBHW031932230426
43672CB00010B/1895